Ecological Imaginations in
the World Religions

Also available from *Continuum*

The Encyclopedia of Religion and Nature, edited by Bron Taylor

Ecological Imaginations in the World Religions

An Ethnographic Analysis

Tony Watling

continuum

Continuum International Publishing Group

The Tower Building
11 York Road
London SE1 7NX

80 Maiden Lane
Suite 704
New York NY 10038

www.continuumbooks.com

British Library Cataloguing-in-Publication Data
A catalogue record for this book is available from the British Library.

ISBN-10: HB: 1-8470-6428-0
ISBN-13: HB: 978-1-8470-6428-8

Library of Congress Cataloging-in-Publication Data
Watling, Tony.
   Ecological imaginations in the world religions : an ethnographic analysis / Tony Watling.
   p. cm.
 Includes bibliographical references and index.
 ISBN 978-1-8470-6428-8
1. Human ecology–Religious aspects. I. Title.

BL65.E36W38 2009
201'.77–dc22   2008037119

Typeset by Newgen Imaging Systems Pvt Ltd, Chennai, India
Printed and bound in Great Britain by the MPG Books Group

To Mum, Dad, Jenine and Barbara: who would have thought all those years ago at Wyken Grange Road that this would happen.

Contents

Acknowledgements

This book is the result of a Netherlands Organization for Scientific Research (NWO) Fellowship I undertook from 2004–7, in the Faculty of Theology at Leiden University, on the project *Misplaced Vocabularies? Scientific and Religious Notions in Public Discourses on Ecology and Genetics*, part of the larger NWO project *The Future of the Religious Past: Elements and Forms for the Twenty-first Century*. My main stimulus in this was Professor Willem B. Drees. Wim, a specialist in religion and science/technology, and highly perceptive, came up with the original research proposal and oversaw the project and was and is nothing less than encouraging and supportive. Olga Crapels also, working as a doctorate student on the project, provided encouragement and friendship during my time in Leiden, as did Taede Smedes and Rico Sneller. The book also has earlier beginnings from my time in the Department of Anthropology at University College London, both as a student (my B.Sc. and Ph.D. led me into the anthropology/sociology of religion) and a Wellcome Trust Research Fellow (analyzing religious views on genetic engineering). Nanneke Redclift (my Ph.D. supervisor and Welcome Fellowship mentor, a highly formative influence) has always been encouraging and supportive, as has Phil Burnham (not to mention many others). Thanks to Rebecca Vaughan-Williams and Tom Crick at Continuum for their help and to Murali and Newgen Imaging Systems for their editing work. Thanks also to Elisabeth Arweck and the *Journal of Contemporary Religion* for encouragement and support. To all these people and groups I owe my thanks, as I do to Dianne van Oosterhout and her family, Jantien Delwel and Nathan Porath, for their friendship during my stay in Leiden, and to Alison Edwards, John and Julia (and Lee and Louise) Lunetto, Paul and Anne (and Holly) Stafford, and Tony Cooper, for their friendship. Lastly, special thanks to Arona and Cameron Allan and my sisters Jenine (and Rob, Rochelle, Kira and Sian) and Barbara.

Introduction

The modernist vision of technology and progress . . . is most responsible for throwing the life-support systems of the entire planet out of balance . . . Yet, if we Westerners . . . stop shouting our own solutions long enough to hear the many and varied voices that we have these past five centuries been striving to silence, we might be surprised to learn that they are telling us much of value about the world . . . We may even find that the solutions to our problems are already available . . . but the cultural blinders imposed by the dominant ideology have prevented us from seeing them.

(Foltz 2002b:3)

Thou shall inherit the holy earth as a faithful steward, conserving its resources and productivity from generation to generation. Thou shalt safeguard thy fields from soil erosion, thy living waters from drying up, thy forests from desolation, and protect thy hills from over-grazing by thy herds, so that thy descendants may have abundance forever. If any shall fail in this stewardship of the land thy fruitful fields shall become sterile stony ground and wasting gullies, and thy descendants shall decrease and live in poverty or be destroyed from off the face of the earth.

('The Eleventh Commandment', Lowdermilk 2002:12)

The world is faced with an environmental crisis, a degradation of nature of complex, global proportions, what Tucker (2003) sees as biocide and geocide, Gottlieb (1996) as a crisis of our entire civilization, a slow collective suicide, and Gardner (2002) as the defining challenge of our age.[1] Patterns of human production and consumption, industrialization and urbanization, reliance on fossil fuels and nuclear power, industrialized agriculture and fishing, leading to climate change, deforestation and desertification, habitat destruction and species decline, hazardous waste and toxic chemical pollution, threaten the composition of, and life on, earth as we know it. These works of what Loy (2002:73) and Oelschlaeger (1994:95) call '*homo (o)economicus*', Callicott (1997:xiii) '*homo petroleumus*', and Mander (2002:63) 'technological man', where 'progress' and 'well-being' are measured by the industrial production and consumption of energy, food and goods, the acquisition of material objects, and the overreliance on technology, where nature is to be exploited to suit humanity's wants, are seen to threaten the balance, diversity and health, of the earth's ecosystem, creating a situation where humanity's ecological footprint, its use of nature, is outstripping the earth's ecological capacity, a non-benign planetary presence that Mander (2002) sees as a form of obsessive insanity rooted in humanity's failure to grasp or respect the limits of nature (where even the solutions, economic or technological fixes for economic or technological problems, what Dryzek (2005:51) terms a 'Promethean response', perpetuate the process that creates the problem).

The base of this crisis is not seen as being simply economic or technological, however. Rather it is seen as much a moral and spiritual issue at heart, about the *idea* of nature as much as its physical form, a result of a dominant modern Western world-view (what Taylor, C. (2004:1–2) terms the 'modern social imaginary'), a particular anthropocentric and mechanistic imagination devaluing nature and overvaluing humanity, seeing nature as a resource devoid of intrinsic value, subjective meaning or spirit, to be used for the benefit of humanity, leading to destructive rather than protective action towards it (humanity is envisioned as dominant and active, separate from a nature that is subservient and passive – what is seen as the disenchantment of nature, a moral and spiritual emptiness or disorientation, without any guiding environmental ethic, other than an anthropocentric one). Tucker and Grim (1997, 2001), in this sense, see humanity making macro-phase changes to the world with micro-phase wisdom, understanding and altering nature based on a limited set of assumptions about what it (and humanity, and the human–nature relationship) is (or should be):[2] as Gardner (2006:23) also notes 'The world has achieved brilliance without conscience. Ours is a world of nuclear giants and ethical infants.'[3]

Such a way of looking at the world, however, although at present dominant, is only one particular cultural view, among many. What is known as 'nature' is a complex and malleable, socially constructed, concept. Thus there may be other world-views that stress different, less environmentally destructive, views of it. It is argued, therefore, that what is needed is a politicization of nature, creating wider awareness of and diverse access to the construction of reality, recognizing and encouraging counter imaginations of nature: the choice for humanity, for Tucker (2003), is whether to become a healing or deleterious presence on the planet, whether to continue the present environmentally destructive path or to imagine a new environmentally benign one. In this sense, there is seen a need for new, more environmentally friendly imaginations of nature, seeing it as active, meaningful, subjective and spiritual, revaluing it, while devaluing humanity somewhat, recognizing it as part of nature, encouraging caring human action towards it. And, in particular, religion is seen as a possible influential source of such new reimaginations of nature, linking humanity to a wider environmental (and divine) reality, and providing the existential support, moral authority and institutional organization, able to address environmental issues. This book, then, explores such ideas, analysing religious environmentalism, religious response to the modern world-view and the environmental crisis, challenging the anthropocentric modern vision (and its degrading environmental effects), and suggesting alternative eco/theocentric ones (stimulating benign environmental effects). It analyses what could be termed 'religious ecotopias': idealized (utopian) religious imaginations of nature and the human place in it, envisaging a more environmentally oriented humanity in a cooperative, harmonic, interdependent, sacred, relationship with nature.

The concept of 'ecotopia' comes from the novel of the same name by Ernest Callenbach (see Callenbach 2004) imagining the country of Ecotopia, an ecologically sustainable society, distanced from consumerism, industrialization, growth-ism and urbanization, that are seen to form the base for Western society (a dystopia, or imperfect place, in this sense): a more inclusive, spiritual and subjective (not exclusive, rational and objective) mind-set, stressing democratic rather than hierarchical relations and small-scale communal living with minimal consumption and production and renewable energy and materials, limiting exploitation (of humanity and nature). Ecotopia thus imagines a more environmentally friendly, cooperative, humble and spiritual, humanity, in tune with nature, being, for Callenbach (2004:170–2), a 'hopeful' fiction, a positive vision of responsible inhabitation of our planet:

> *Ecotopia* . . . conveys . . . a hopeful sense that there are real alternatives to our present corporatist, militarist, ultra-competitive, oil obsessed course . . . [opening] minds to new possibilities – ripping through the veil of the apparent inevitability of continued environmental degradation, social alienation, community decline, and personal stress . . . *Ecotopia* teaches us . . . that it is okay to dream, to relish turning accepted ideas on their heads, to imagine being happy, to enjoy mutually supportive relations with our fellow sentient beings.

Such ecotopian ideas are also explored by De Geus (1999), analysing and comparing utopian visions of Thomas More, Henry David Thoreau, Peter Kropotkin, William Morris, Ebenezer Howard, Bernard Skinner, Aldous Huxley, Callenbach and Murray Bookchin, seeing in these a social critique and source of ideals for reimagining nature. More (coining the term 'utopia', denoting a perfect place) is seen envisaging the 'sufficient utopia', an ecologically prudent society, overcoming expansionist wants and limiting needs, stressing public ownership of land.[4] Thoreau is seen envisaging the 'utopia of ultimate simplicity' stressing simple, non-materialistic, existence, achieving happiness through appreciating nature (connecting environmental degradation with spiritual poverty).[5] In contrast to these Kropotkin is seen envisaging 'utopia as an ecological community', following natural principles, stressing self-regulating communities of cooperation not competition, sociability not authoritarianism.[6] Morris is seen envisaging the 'utopia of austere beauty', an artistically inclined society of non-authoritarian agrarian communities with modest lifestyle and limited technology, achieving happiness through beauty not consumerism.[7] More recently, Howard is seen envisaging the 'utopia of ecological garden cities' stressing small-scale, sparsely populated, communities, intertwining city and garden, with efficient not unlimited production and consumption.[8] Skinner is seen envisaging the 'utopia of green communities', using psychology to stimulate people to behave responsibly towards nature in small-scale artistic communities with benign technology.[9] Huxley is seen envisaging a 'heavenly utopian island' maintaining ecological balance via a decentralized, tolerant, society of minimal consumption, realizing happiness through artistic and spiritual development.[10] Finally, Callenbach and Bookchin are seen envisaging 'modern ecological utopias', Callenbach stressing a society protecting nature and ensuring physical and spiritual well-being of humanity through self-sufficient communal living and limited consumption/production, Bookchin envisaging the 'utopia of eco-communities' resembling natural eco-systems, with non-hierarchical relations, nature-friendly 'eco-technology', and non-growth production systems (seeing ecological problems as a consequence of distorted capitalist relations).[11]

Such visions of humanity in harmony with nature (which have drawbacks, often being too idealistic, static and unreachable) highlight, for De Geus, the power of images to inspire reflection on present society and suggest alternative ones. In this sense, he argues that there is a need for something more than environmental policies, something which ecotopian visions provide: that is, environmental, personal and social, critique, with alternative visions of the future innovatively addressing environmental issues by reimagining nature and humanity, stimulating new ideologies, moralities and spiritualities. Ecotopian images may thus present modern realities in unusual ways, acting as ecological compasses, influencing and orienting personal and political thought, providing insight into environmental problems by questioning present social developments and providing plausible ideas for their resolution, influential alternative ideological, moral and spiritual, foundations. They may be useful, then, even necessary, for addressing environmental problems, for changing society from an environmentally destructive path to an environmentally benign one, inspiring a new human 'art of living' with nature (e.g. critiquing ideas creating a dominant humanity separate from a subservient nature and stressing ones creating egalitarian interdependence of them).

Human beings possess a unique capacity to imagine the future. Not only can we sense and think about the circumstances of the present, and reflect upon the past, but we can creatively imagine what we and the generations which come after us are to become . . . [This] power of social vision . . . the human ability to imagine constructively – to convert the sensual dream into conscious aspiration . . . at its most radical, invades the prevailing concept of reality, undermines certainties about what humans must always be like, and casts doubt upon the inevitabilities of the relations of everyday life. (De Geus 1999:207)[12]

The appeal and power of ecotopian ideas, for De Geus, is that they question present presuppositions through imagining a future in radically new forms and values, acting as a mirror for present society (highlighting, in particular, its negative aspects) uncovering unnoticed assumptions and developments, highlighting alternative aspects and fostering a heightened sense of reality. They break with the past, encouraging distance from and reflection on every-day life, providing immersion in another one, presenting carefully considered, comprehensive, visions of a reorganized society, a new coherent order and reliable plan that can be compared with other societies. They make (often personalized) statements on truth, happiness and the common good, engaging in a debate on the nature of reality: ironically pricking ideals and experimenting with new environmental, personal and social, forms, going beyond the conventional and escaping dogmatic thinking, confronting the unexpected and investigating alternatives, stimulating an imaginative dream of and intimate connection with another, better, world. They thus have a compelling quality, providing the excitement of looking forward, creating a realization that the precarious uncertainty of life may be an opportunity for change, stimulating people to actively see the future as being in their hands. They are thus an interactive media, encouraging the imaginative formation of opinions, inviting participation. Ecotopian thinking, then, may provide a challenging and instructive approach for solving modern environmental problems, serving as a barrier against despair or defeatism, providing a hopeful source of ideals offering inspiration for change.

That such ecotopian thinking is seen to be needed in the present environmental crisis is because there is seen a need to go beyond the present rational, management, approach to nature that attempts to economically or technologically fix environmental problems, applying different economics or politics or more science and technology to them. Such an approach, based on the dominant modern world-view seeing nature as meaningless, passive material, needing to be managed, is seen to be part of the problem, based on the very construction of nature that causes environmental problems in the first place. Such a management of environmental problems, then, can only occur within the anthropocentric viewpoint of seeing nature as a backdrop, or even hindrance, to human affairs, a problem to be solved, and thus can only ever suggest limited solutions at best while at worst it may actively exacerbate the problem. Modern knowledge, in this sense, objective, reductionist and secular, is not seen as enough to solve environmental problems as it concentrates on the effects not the cause, which is the knowledge itself. Thus, what is seen to be needed is a fundamental reorientation of humanity in nature, a new knowledge, more subjective, holistic and spiritual, beyond limited and destructive modern confines. What is argued for, then, are new imaginations of nature, new ethical and moral codes, to critique, deconstruct and counteract, the dominant and destructive modern vision (not merely fixes of the problems but a fix of the cause of the problems; it is not nature that is the problem, then, but rather the modern human view of it – the environmental crisis is a human crisis).

This approach recognizes that what is known as 'nature' is not static but that it is always a social process, dependent on social constructions in particular contexts, particular times and places, and that the dominant modern form of it is thus but one among many and can be challenged and changed, that nature does not have to be seen as something to be exploited but that it can be seen as integral to humanity's well-being, in a mutually supportive relationship with it. Pre-modern ideas of nature, that the modern world overcame, for example, are seen to have been more animistic, seeing nature as alive and the site of the divine, and different, often non-Western or religious, views that still coexist in the world (including in the West), may see nature in very different, more active, intimate, meaningful, spiritual, possibly more environmentally friendly, ways. Nature is thus always an idea, an imagination, and the way it is imagined leads to the way humanity interacts with it, dominating or liberating, degrading or protecting, it. What is seen as needed, then (and what is and has always occurred, in a sense, although somewhat implicitly and unofficially in modern times), is more diverse imaginations of nature enabling a wider discourse as to what it is or what it should be (and what humanity, or its place in or relationship to nature, is or should be) as well as how it is or should be treated.

There is seen a need to imagine different environmental futures, new visions of progress, to the modern one of ever greater consumption and production and economic and technological expansion. In this book I explore these ideas, analysing environmental reimagination, new visions of nature, humanity and the human–nature relationship. In particular, I concentrate on the religious dimensions of such ecotopian thinking, analysing particular religious ecotopias, reimaginations of nature by religious traditions (both Eastern and Western), or particular environmentally aware members of them. Religion is seen as useful, even essential, in addressing the environmental crisis, able to address its underlying cause, modernity's moral/spiritual malaise, challenging its biophobic values, disenchanting, devaluing and degrading nature, and providing new biophilic ones, re-enchanting, revaluing and revitalizing, it. It is seen as communally, morally and spiritually, oriented, not egoistic or materialist, providing cosmological orientation, critical/prophetic potential, existential support and moral authority, placing humanity in a wider scheme, defining its obligations, combining the ought and the is (tempering anthropo-centrism with eco- or theo-centrism). And as Gottlieb (2006a:13) argues 'the religious vision has always run counter to the "common sense" of its time. Its hallmark is not realism or conformism but a prophetic challenge to con-ventional social standards'. Religion, in this sense, may have always acted as humanity's conscience, being countercultural, highlighting the deficiencies of human thought and action and inspiring new attitudes and actions. It may thus have always expressed utopian visions of nature and humanity (and the divine), better ways of being in the world that humanity should strive towards (although these may have been skewed or ignored). Such visions, then, are seen as needing to be brought to the fore, reinterpreted, and relegitimated.

> Environmental ethicists might do well to consider . . . that any one main-stream religious denomination alone influences the normative choices of more people than all ecophilosophies put together . . . [Furthermore] religion is the institution best suited to deal with the ethical and political questions raised by the eco-crisis, precisely because it empowers citizens to deal with the questions that elude bureaucratic mentality. (Oelschlaeger 1994:42–3)

> Throughout human history, the religions of the world have sought to heal the most profound disorientations of the human heart and mind. It is religious vision that has restored the human condition and guided human effort. All faith traditions envision the universe as revelatory of the sacred . . . All trad-itions of the sacred are channels for humankind to enter into and articulate ecological concern. (Bassett et al. 2000:42)

In line with this thinking religious traditions are being encouraged to engage with environmental issues, to enter what Tucker (2003:9) calls an 'eco-logical phase', re-evaluating themselves in light of environmental issues (posi-tively rethinking their constructions of nature, revaluing it, particularly in light of the fact that many religions, but especially the Judeo-Christian, have been seen as anthropocentric, stressing human dominion over nature, or world-denying, arguing for release from it). This, what Nash (1989) terms the 'greening of religion', has been arising for some time (being linked to the rise of environmentalism), environmentally aware believers, philosophers, theo-logians and religious authorities, encouraging and stimulating traditions to express, or exploring them for, ideas beyond anthropocentrism, expanding their beliefs, ethics, identities, practices and sacredness, beyond humanity to nature as a whole, embracing eco-centric concerns, engaging environmental issues theoretically and practically. In particular, such ideas are being encour-aged, inspired and coordinated, within what Tucker (2003:23) and Taylor, B. (2004:992, 2005c:1377) term a 'field of religion and ecology', an emerging religious/social movement of academics and representatives of various religious traditions (and new religious movements) that analyses and explores and uses, compares and combines, religion in light of environmental issues. This field seeks to develop new religious-ecological thinking with the aim of addressing the environmental crisis and revitalizing religion (either by creating new forms or reinterpreting traditional ones). It is based on a challenge to the ideals and structures of modernity, seeking to provide new ones, re-evaluating and reimagining nature, encouraging a more caring, interdependent, spiritual, human relationship with it.

A main part of the field's development has been the stimulation of religious traditions to think environmentally, to explore and reassess their beliefs, doctrines, ideologies, spiritualities and theologies, for environmental themes. The Harvard series of conferences from 1996–1998 on 'Religions of the World and Ecology', for example, especially addressed such issues, and the Forum on Religion and Ecology, continuing their aims and ideas, still addresses them, analysing and exploring Buddhism, Christianity, Confucianism, Daoism, Hinduism, Indigenous Traditions, Islam, Jainism, Judaism and Shintoism, in this way. A more recent development, the *Encyclopedia of Religion and Nature*, also analyses, explores, highlights and promotes, such issues, serving, along with the Forum, as a baseline for further analysis and exploration (see Taylor and Kaplan 2005). Religious traditions, in this scheme, are seen as legitimate, meaningful and powerful, ways of inculcating environmental consciousness, able to reconceptualize attitudes to nature, existentially engage humanity with it, and socially engage environmental issues and stimulate environmental concern; able to effect the personal and social transformation needed to address the environmental crisis, providing new primary values and sources of social direction. They are thus being encouraged to imagine/explore (reassess/legitimate) environmentally friendly concepts of nature and humanity, providing new ecological metaphors and myths. In particular, the field stresses the need for a diversity of such views, different traditions (and new movements) in communication with one another, used in a self-reflective not a self-promoting way; cross-cultural, mutually enriching, religious reimaginations of nature in dialogue and support, based on the common ground and common good of the earth itself.

My aim is to analyse and explore this religious environmentalism, the encouragement and use of religious traditions to reimagine nature, in particular, ethnographically analysing several religious imaginations – what I term religious ecotopias – stressed in the field, Indian (Hindu and Jain), Chinese (Confucian and Daoist), Buddhist, Jewish, Christian and Islamic. Other traditions could similarly be explored in this way, of course (and are). Indigenous traditions (what are sometimes described as 'primal' or 'tribal' societies or 'first peoples'), for example, are seen as influential sources of environmental ideas, intimate with nature, grateful for its fecundity, stressing kinship with and local knowledge of it, having light ecological footprints, environmental ethics being embedded in their world-views, which demonstrate an interbeing of cosmology and community, an awareness of the integration of spirit and matter.[13] Shintoism, the Baha'i faith, Sikhism and Zoroastrianism have also been explored for environmental themes: the first, seen as a diversity of localized beliefs as well as state practices, entrenched in Japanese folk culture, is seen as stressing kinship and interdependence between deities, nature and humanity, stressing the need for careful actions and rites to balance these;[14] the second is seen as stressing stewardship of the earth, via compassion, justice, moderation and self-sacrifice, seeing nature reflecting the qualities of God and thus needing to be respected and cherished; the third is seen as stressing unity of spirit and matter (nature being a manifestation of God), with the purpose of humanity to achieve a harmonic, mutually cooperative state with nature (via compassion, humility, self-control and a simple life, mastering self not nature); and the fourth, is seen as stressing the role of humanity as being to serve and care for nature (its seven gifts of sky, water, earth, plants, animals, man and fire), re-creating the primeval, unpolluted, perfect unity (via divine attributes of devotion, order, righteousness, right knowledge, truth and wisdom).[15]

New religious movements, such as goddess beliefs and Paganism, have also been explored in connection with the environment, as has, in a similar light, 'Eco-feminism', these seen as stressing holistic visions celebrating the ongoing rhythm of life, death and regeneration, seeing the earth as sacred and alive, stressing a primal perception and earth intimacy, aiming to rethink the dualistic male reality of domination and realize holistic female views of partnership, based on care, compassion and mutuality. And other ideas or movements, not explicitly religious but with spiritual leanings, have also been explored this way. 'Deep ecology', for example, is seen as stressing identification with nature, a wider eco-centric self, intrinsically valuing other life-forms through recognizing human connection to nature, realizing that self equals wholeness not individualism, something seen as awakened through being intuitively open to and aware of the life process (via intimate ritual connection to and discourse with nature, for example, re-earthing). The 'Epic of Evolution', similarly, is seen as a new meaningful transcultural creation myth, stressing the universe as a communion of interdependent subjects (not separate independent objects), based around the sacrifice of relational life (possibly with purpose and design, for example, the anthropic principle) with humanity's natural emergent role being to bring it to self-awareness by engaging it at a primordial level, via intuition. Ideas of 'Gaia' are also influential, these seen as stressing the world as a self-regulating, interdependent, organism, emphasizing identification with a dynamic, sacred nature, stressing an ethical holism where individual interest lies within the whole, the human role being to reciprocally engage and live in harmony with nature through a primal intuitive perception.[16] And what is described as 'post-modern science' is seen stressing imaginative, holistic, organic (possibly teleological) visions, integrating rational empiricism and spiritual awareness, placing humanity within a wider frame of being, highlighting the dynamism, interconnectedness, mutuality and reciprocity, of life.[17]

All these, then, could be said to stress religious-ecotopian imaginations. However, for the sake of analytical coherence and space, I concentrate on the major world religions mentioned. It must be stressed that I am not analysing religious traditions, per se, exploring or mining them for ecological themes, as others attempt to do, but recent environmentally aware interpretations of them within the field of religion and ecology (their use of 'world religions' categories, using the Harvard series as a baseline). I understand that the concepts of 'religion' or 'world religions' are tricky ones, that in their narrow universalizing forms they may be modern Western inventions, imposing on diverse beliefs and practices (especially when dealing with Eastern forms). I understand that religious traditions are diverse and dynamic, not monolithic and static, that there are no core agreed upon Hinduism, Jainism, Confucianism, Daoism, Buddhism, Christianity, Judaism or Islam, nor less any agreed ecological form of them, but rather diverse and contested interpretations.[18] I am thus aware that care needs to be taken when using the concepts: I am not saying that Hinduism, Jainism, Confucianism, Daoism, Buddhism, Judaism, Christianity or Islam, believe, or mean, or say, this or that, but that particular 'ecological' metaphors and myths within them are being highlighted, developed and compared, creating new imaginations of nature which can best be described as ecotopian. It is these new imaginations that I am analysing (and I am aware that I can only give a flavour of them, of their wide dialogues, literatures, texts, themes and traditions, interpreting and collating them via my own academic lens while attempting to convey their important insights). My aim is to analyse new interpretations of religious traditions, new religious inventions, centred upon and coalescing around ecological ideas, and to explore what the resulting religious-ecotopian visions look like, what they might say about nature, about humanity's relationship to and role within it, and about religion in the modern world.[19]

It must also be stressed that I am not an environmentalist, or a theologian, or follower of a particular religion: I am an anthropologist by training and could be best described as an anthropologist/sociologist of religion. I do not aim to provide an environmental or theological analysis, as such, then, or to promote environmentalism (although I think it is a good idea) or religious involvement with environmental issues (although again it seems a good idea). My aim is social scientific – ethnographic and comparative – to qualitatively analyse and highlight new religious forms – religious-ecotopian imaginations – that are developing in the modern world in light of (in response to) environmental issues, creating a new body of religious knowledge and action, both within traditions, stimulating new religious-ecological factions, as well as between them, stimulating a wider religious-ecological movement (which may serve as a neutral, ecumenical, arena for traditions, or environmentally inspired representatives of them, to explore new issues, and either individually or in unison engage modern secular society). Such religious-ecological innovation may not only serve to address environmental issues but may also provide a way for religion to regain (personal, social) relevance, addressing an issue of vital importance in the modern world, as well as challenging the modern values and structures that may have contributed to it (and which may also have contributed to the decline of religion, creating a construction of it limited to the private sphere without public relevance, i.e., secularization).

The structure of the book, then, is based around an analysis of what I see as particular religious-ecotopian visions, Indian, Chinese, Buddhist, Jewish, Christian and Islamic, developing within religious environmentalism and in particular the field of religion and ecology. In the first two chapters I set out the main arguments, theories and themes, providing the background and setting the scene. In Chapter 1, I analyse ideas concerned with the modern world-view, especially its anthropocentric, mechanical, view of nature, stressing humanity as dominant and nature submissive, that has become the dominant social imaginary in the world (causing environmental degradation). Secondly, I analyse the concept of nature, arguing for it as a diverse, fluid, phenomenon, a social practice, thus showing that the modern view of it is but one among many and able to be contested. Thirdly, in this light, I explore an 'ecological model' arising within modern environmentalism, stressing holistic, organic, spiritual, views, seeing nature as meaningful, subjective, and sacred, and humanity as interdependent with it, promoting a new human ecological consciousness based on cooperation not domination. Lastly, I analyse the role of metaphor and myth in the possible construction of new environmentally friendly (religious) world-views, exploring how these are being used to challenge modern views and express a new ecological language, redefining nature and humanity.

In Chapter 2, I analyse the perceived relevance of religion to environmental issues: their moral and spiritual nature, a result of modern values, and the possible ability of religion to respond, through morally and spiritually engaging modernity, being countercultural and prophetic. I also analyse the nature of religion in the modern world, its possible decline or (green) revitalization, analysing theories of secularization and religious responses, exploring the modern construction of religion as a category, as well as challenges to this, exploring the dynamism of religion (as a concept and practice), and examining ideas on new public relevance of religion in confronting the discontents of modernity, such as the environmental crisis, exploring a 'greening' of religion, embracing environmental issues, to this end, highlighting new green religious forms. Thirdly, I analyse the field of religion and ecology, particularly the influential Harvard conferences, Forum on Religion and Ecology and *Encyclopedia of Religion and Nature*. This I approach as a new religious-ecological movement aimed at engaging environmental issues and revitalizing religion, in particular, by encouraging the re-evaluation of religious traditions, their metaphors, and myths, cosmogonies and cosmologies, in ecological terms, essentially encouraging and inspiring the construction, comparison and mutual dialogue, of religious ecotopias.

Chapters 3–8 comprise the main body of ethnographic material, analysing the field's ecological interpretations of religious traditions, different religious-ecotopian imaginations (for clarity ordered historically, in Eastern and Western forms). Chapters 3 to 5 analyse the interpretations of Eastern traditions: Chapter 3 analyses Indian (Hindu and Jain) visions, Chapter 4, Chinese (Confucian and Daoist) visions, and Chapter 5, Buddhist visions. Chapters 6 to 8 analyse the interpretations of Western traditions: Chapter 6 analyses Jewish visions, Chapter 7, Christian visions, and Chapter 8, Islamic visions. Lastly, in Chapter 9, I conclude and sum up the arguments, analysing, comparing and contrasting, the different religious ecotopias, exploring what they might mean for future environmental and religious thinking and action. I draw out the main themes, the particular influential metaphors and myths stressed, from (that form the basis for) each religious ecotopia analysed, summing up what they say about nature and humanity and their relationship. Secondly, with a view to exploring a possible convergence of views I also analyse suggested commonalities in ecological views of religious traditions and draw out from my own analysis some common themes. Lastly, I analyse what such ideas say about religion in the modern world, whether if and how they might be suggesting or creating new religious forms, and what they might contribute to environmental issues.

Notes

1 'Environment' and 'nature' tend to be used interchangeably to denote the non-human world (the latter possibly more encompassing); others terms used include cosmos, creation, earth or world; ecology is increasingly used as it is seen as dynamic and relational, including humanity in the definition (see Tucker and Grim 2001). There may be some overlap in my use of these terms, then, which relects the varying literatures.

2 Referenced to Brian Swimme.

3 Referenced to 'Omar Bradley' from John Bartlett, *Bartlett's Familiar Quotations* (Boston: Little Brown and Company, 1992), p. 685.

4 See More, T. *Utopia* (Harmondsworth: Penguin Books, 1982).

5 See Thoreau, H. D. *Walden and Civil Disobedience* (New York: W. W. Norton & Company, 1966).

6 See Kropoktin, P. *Mutual Aid* (Boston: Porter Sargant Publishers, Inc., 1976).

7 See Morris, W. *News from Nowhere* (London: Routledge & Kegan Paul, 1983).

8 See Howard, E. *Garden Cities of Tomorrow* (Eastbourne: Attic Books, 1985).

9 See Skinner, B. F. *Walden Two* (London: Collier Macmillan Publishers, 1976).

10 See Huxley, A. *Island* (London: Panther Books, 1989).

11 See Bookchin, M. *Toward an Ecological Society* (Montreal: Black Rose Books, 1988).

12 Referenced to Coleman, S., The Use of Utopia: History and Imagination, in *William Morris & News from Nowhere, A Vision for Our Time*, Coleman, S., and O'Sullivan, P., eds (Bideford: Green Books, 1990, p. 9).

13 See Callicott 1997; Foltz 2002b; Gottlieb 1996; Grim 2001; Kinsley 1994; Maguire 2000; Nasr 1996; Rajotte, F. *First Nations and Ecology* (London: Cassell, United Church Publishing House, 1998); Taylor and Kaplan 2005.

14 See Nasr 1996; Palmer and Finlay 2003; Scheid, B. Ecology and Religion: Ecology and Shinto, in *Encyclopedia of Religion*, Jones, L., ed.:2638–41 (Farmington Hills, MI: Thomson Gale, 2005); Taylor and Kaplan 2005; www.environment.harvard.edu/religion/religion/shinto/index.html, 20 Oct. 2008.

15 For analysis of Baha'i, Sikhism and Zoroastrianism, see Bassett et al. 2000; DeWitt 2002; Foltz 2002b; Nasr 1996; Palmer and Finlay 2003; Regenstein 1991; Taylor and Kaplan 2005.

16 Analysis of these movements can be found in Foltz (2002b), Gottlieb (1996), and Taylor and Kaplan (2005). Kassmann (1997) analyses what he sees as 'eutopian' visions in (American) environmentalism: 'Neo-Primitivism', stressing nature's intrinsic value and small-scale societies; 'Mystical Deep Ecology', seeing patriarchy dominating women/nature, stressing female views; and 'Social Ecology', stressing rational moral agents protecting nature.

17 Science (reinterpreted imaginatively/spiritually) is seen as able to provide a cross-cultural environmental ethic, overcoming reductionism and objectivity and embracing holism and subjectivity, something seen developing in cosmology, genetics, neuroscience and physics, and an interdisciplinary 'field of science and religion' stressing consonance, cooperation, interaction or harmonization, between secular reason and spirituality (see Barlow 1997; Brockelman 1999; Callicott 1997; Capra 1982; Metzner 1994; Rue 2000; Taylor 2005a).

18 Chapter 2 analyses these issues theoretically and later chapters have footnotes exploring them in relation to the religious traditions themselves; the field of religion and ecology is aware of the problems of assessing and using traditions this way.

19 Although I aim to be true to context (the field of religion and ecology's interpretations, not traditions per se) inevitably I interpret via my own academic lens covering main themes and meanings that I see coalescing or being formed into new ecotopian accounts (using major English texts, the main language of the field; different interpretations or translations of concepts by different scholars may thus somewhat coalesce in my analysis).

Chapter 1

The Modern World-View, the Ecological Model and the Reimagination of Nature

The modern world-view: Disenchanting, devaluing and degrading, nature

[U]nless we reverse the premises of the type of thought and action productive of our present techno-scientific inferno, we will not escape the disaster towards which it is ineluctably propelling us . . . [this entails] the reversing of a process of ignorance . . . [an] enslavement to an illusory world entirely of our own invention . . . the Cartesian 'Cogito ergo sum' . . . that human thought is the determining factor of all things . . . [assuming] that our senses can perceive things in a kind of objective manner . . . [instead of] by our prior commitments to . . . [a] paradigm to which, whether we are aware of it or not, we give our adherence.

(Sherrard 2002:1–3)

The sad fact is that learned, clever, and powerful though it be, the Cartesian ego . . . can neither find in itself nor create in the larger world lasting peace . . . Having eaten further of the Tree of knowledge, leading to industrialization and the discovery of atomic energy, but not having effectively integrated intelligence with compassion and developed the needed wisdom . . . modern humanity has become a threat to . . . all life on the planet.

(Rockefeller 1992:154–5)

The material effects of the environmental crisis, the physical degradation of nature, are not occurring in a vacuum. Rather they are seen to be a result of a way of conceptualizing the world stimulating destructive action towards it; a particular modern Western world-view which has become dominant, the template for global civilization. Arising in the sixteenth century (influenced by Greek philosophy, Judeo-Christianity and the Renaissance) and progressing via the rise of science in the seventeenth, the Enlightenment in the eighteenth, the Industrial Revolution in the nineteenth, and technological expansion and globalization in the twentieth, this 'modern world-view', what has been called 'modernity' or the 'Enlightenment mentality', has been a dynamic and transformative imagination and ontology (encompassing many social spheres and many cultures, influencing modern global consciousness and identity). Initially a desire to expand human knowledge and liberate individuals from dependence on nature (superstition, the Christian Church) it is seen as developing into a self-centred desire to dominate nature and manipulate it to humanity's needs, an anthropocentric world-view and 'mechanical model' placing priority on reason and economic and technological progress, seeing humanity's destiny in mastering and transcending nature's limitations. In this scheme, humanity and nature, fact and value, mind and body, spirit and matter, subject and object, are separated within atomistic, reductionist, materialism. Nature is reduced to 'material' without life or spirit: previous animistic, medieval or pre-modern, ways of perceiving it, as alive, interdependent and sacred (with purpose, possessing symbolic content more significant than material content), are replaced with a mechanical one, seeing it as a profane repository of resources to be exploited (Berman 1982, 1984; Evernden 1992; Kinsley 1994; McGrath 2003; Nasr 2002; Rockefeller 1992; Sideris 2006; Soule 1995; Weiming 1994).

Such a world-view is seen as based on the ideas of Francis Bacon and Isaac Newton (alongside Copernicus, Descartes and Galileo). Bacon is seen as fashioning a new ethic and philosophy, unifying knowledge and material power, with technology at its source, emphasizing human domination of nature through reason, the objective study and manipulation of it to uncover its truths and further human ends. Progress, in this sense, involves liberation from nature which is identified with the chaotic, passionate female, needing to be rationally bound and ordered by the 'new science' and 'mechanical arts' for the service of man, enlarging the human empire. There is no continuity between humanity and nature here, knowledge is not gained via sympathetic harmony but forced yielding, through artificial means. Alongside these ideas Newton is seen as instigating the mechanical viewpoint, where nature is homogeneous matter, purely physical, working according to one set of predictable laws, without ultimate purpose, a passive machine not an active organism, rationally rather than intuitively understood via parts not wholes. Nature is 'other', lifeless and mindless, denied affinity and spirituality, to be approached instrumentally, to be 'known about' not 'known' (exploring how things are not why they are) by a humanity disembedded from it (e.g. Descartes's 'I think, therefore I am') (Berman 1984; Capra 1982; Kinsley 1994; McGrath 2003; Merchant 2002; Sheldrake 1994; Sideris 2006).

Such anthropocentric ideas sanction humanity's domination and exploitation of nature, avoiding or negating (natural, God-given) limits, following the principle of the will to succeed, 'if it can be done do it' (something also seen as influenced by Darwinian interpretations stressing competitive not cooperative views of nature). This has been described as a 'Faustian' pact, the desire for and 'tragedy' of 'development': longing for and gaining empowerment through separation from and domination of nature via economic and technological development with little thought to or oblivious to consequences or assuming their will be none or that the modern world-view will resolve them. McGrath (2003:83) describes this as 'Prometheus without Pandora': the chance to gain the 'power of the gods' unrestricted by limits, recognizing only possibility not consequence (or conscience; for example, Nietzsche's 'superman', or Frankenstein, the 'modern Prometheus'). Nature, in this scheme, becomes objectified, a commodity, interpreted economically, something to be managed and used, progress equalling economic growth. Consumerism, for Loy (2002) and Maguire (2000), thus becomes dominant, with a religious intensity, a vicious circle of ever-increasing production and consumption pretending to offer secular salvation ('money-theism'), dictating what is valuable: 'instead of economy being embedded in social relations, social relations are embedded in economy'; 'Capital (has) ceased to be a servant and (has) become the master'[1] (see Berman 1982, 1984; McGrath 2003; Mander 2002; Nasr 2002; Sheldrake 1994; Weiming 1994).

The modern world-view, in this sense, is argued as creating a 'disenchantment' of the world, an eclipse of magical or spiritual forces, denying creativity and sacredness to nature (a disbelief of animistic, organic or religious, views, which are deprived of their meaning and power, i.e., secularization).[2] Nature is reduced to profane material without self-determination or final causation, with no internal relations or relations to the divine (no longer a place of prayer or worship but a collection of objects of instrumental value; cosmology becomes reduced to the material sciences and metaphysics to rationalism, i.e., the science/religion divide). Humanity is thus alienated from nature, not intimate with it, disoriented in relation to it, with no sense of place, of wider meaning. It no longer *belongs* in the world; it acts *on* it not *within* it. It no longer has a sense of nature as *creation*. Mander (2002:63) sees this as a 'madness of the astronaut' cut off from the world, a limited self-serving world-view where man is the measure of all things, where ever more complex technological fixes are seen as the only solutions for ever more complex technological problems (Dryzeks's (1995:51) 'Promethean response'), nature being mere resources providing fuel for and receiving the pollution of a biophobic lifestyle. Weiming (1994:19) sees it as the 'crisis of modernity', the inability to experience matter as the embodiment of spirit, leading to the anthropocentric destructiveness of secular humanism, while Loy (2002) sees it as the depletion of moral capital eroding communal, long-term responsibility in favour of individual, short-term benefit. In this scheme, then, nature is measured by 'ecologically illiterate' modern economic and technological standards and degraded as a result (see Berman 1984; Brockelman 1997; Burke 2001; Eder 1996; Kinsley 1994; McGrath 2003; Nasr 2002; Sheldrake 1994; Sideris 2006; Szerszynski 2005; Taylor 2004; Tucker 2002b; Tucker and Grim 1997).

'[Western] Enlightenment is marked by the "disenchantment" of nature, its transformation from something sacred into mere matter available for human

manipulation . . . something to be overcome and mastered for human purposes and not to be imitated, propitiated or religiously celebrated'[3] . . . a
self-centred view of reality that has come into possession of the hardware
[technology] it needs to achieve its goals . . . [encouraging] us to become
enslaved to patterns of consumption and exploitation that can only bode ill
for the environment and for ourselves. (McGrath 2003:54, 67)

Such ideas revolve around the pre-eminence of human creative power, seeing nature as predictable artefact not sacred sign, leading to instrumental
objectivity not subjective communication, knowledge being wrested from
nature not gained by establishing relationship with it. They stress a mathem-
atical reality, quantitative not qualitative understandings, with linear time,
a heliocentric universe (the earth having no special status), and a struggle
for existence, nature being violent not harmonic, needing to be insulated
from or managed via technology (colonizing, taming and utilizing it, to create civilization) (Berman 1984; Capra 1982; Devall and Sessions 1985; Kinsley
1994). From such ideas Devall and Sessions (1985) see arising bureaucrat-
ization, centralized authority/leadership by violence, competition, individualism, narrow definitions of identity (humanity being different from other
species), a materialistic philosophy and a monopoly (not diversity) of secular ideology, while Gardner (2006) sees ecologically problematic elements,
such as, the purpose of life being to generate wealth, to produce/consume
material goods, accepting that waste is inevitable, that nature is valuable for
economic and aesthetic reasons not intrinsically, and that ethics pays a neg-
ligible role in defining progress. In a similar light, for Oelschlaeger (1994),
the modern world-view stresses short-term economic interests not long-term
issues, environmental risks, for example, being acceptable if they are economically beneficial and posing no limits to growth but just requiring engineered
solutions. In this sense, the strategy of managing the earth is seen as feasible
and the politics of interest are seen as sufficient to guarantee that the best
available technology to address environmental problems will be used (and
that it will be sufficient). Within such ideas, humanity is seen as able to control its own destiny, its history being seen as one of progress without limits
where for every problem there is a (human) solution, via economics, politics
or technology (an overriding faith in human civilization and a belief in social
advancement).

This modern world-view influences and is intertwined with virtually all
spheres of modern consciousness and life, civil/military bureaucracies,
democratic polity, education, health, individual rights, industrial capitalism,
law, mass communication, science and technology. It has become taken for
granted, assuming a self-evident reasonableness, becoming, for Oelschlaeger
(1994:54–5), the 'dominant social matrix', and, for Weiming (1994:21, 23),
'the most influential moral discourse in the political culture of the modern

age . . . the unquestioned assumption . . . the common heritage of human-ity'. In this sense, for Evernden (1992) and McGrath (2003), the mechanical *model* of the world has become *reality*, seen as true, the only valid description and explanation of nature, and how to behave towards it, defining shared values for approaching existence (superimposing on previous animistic, organic, religious, ones, a 'colonization' of nature and peoples and ecological and socio-economic impoverishment, with the resulting loss of pre-industrial environmental perceptions and ethics). It thus provides, following Midgley (2005), 'the myths we live by', enabling and dictating a (Western, but increas-ingly globalized and hegemonic) form of what Bourdieu (1977) calls a social/cultural *habitus*, a cluster of implicit, underlying personal and social assump-tions and expectations about nature, humanity and the human–nature rela-tionship, about how to live and relate to each other and the world, how to negotiate ecological, personal and social (and increasingly technological) space, and ecologically, personally and socially, perform based on particular anthropocentric, materialist, mechanical (ecologically destructive), imagery.

In C. Taylor's (2004:1–2) terms, the modern world-view is the dominant 'social imaginary', a modern imagined community and consciousness, a shared conceptual scheme encompassing the modern world. Beginning as a new conception of the moral order of society, occurring in the minds of influential Western thinkers, defining the good, ecologically, individually and socially, it has come to dominate the way humanity imagines the world, shaping larger social strata and becoming self-evident, the natural/normal ways of things, shared by modern humanity, enabling and providing common understandings and action. In a sense, it defines an economic, industrialized, utopia, an ideal order seeing happiness achieved via materialistic lifestyle and technological progress, providing a hermeneutic and an imperative prescrip-tion, being factual and normative, both is and ought (see De Geus 1999): as much as creating disenchantment (of nature) it may be seen as a particular, secular, enchantment (of human powers), a new understanding of existence, situating humanity within an anthropocentric conceptual framework defining a subordinate nature (one without a God, not relating to anything higher than humanity, a horizontal not a vertical social order) that has come to dominate and devalue other forms (see Szerszynski 2005).[4]

Reimagining nature:
Challenging the modern world-view

[P]eople often never learn that [myths] are myths; people become submerged in their viewpoints, prisoners of their own traditions. They readily confuse attitudes toward reality (proclamations of value) with reality itself (statements of fact). Failing to see their own myths as myths, they consider all other myths false . . . Thinking we are

superior to other creatures, for instance, we set ourselves up as such and use them ruthlessly. People that think of themselves as brothers to the beasts live with them in harmony and respect.

(Sproul 1979:3)

The problem, then, is seen as being particular environmentally destructive Western perceptions of nature that have become taken for granted and politically/socially dominant. As Oelschlaeger (1994:3) states 'it is primarily our philosophies, economies, and governments, that motivate and direct the devastating onslaught against the earth'. In this sense, the continuation of modernity is seen as threatening the survival of life on the earth (including humanity's). And environmental solutions based on the modern world-view (Dryzek's (2005:51) 'Promethean response', economic, political, scientific, technological) may never overcome its environmentally degrading effects. Eder (1996), for example, argues that such an environmentalism follows an 'ecological reason' (rather than ecological morality) that rationally aims to reduce the pollution of nature but which is a subordinate aspect of the modern exploitative human interaction with it, judging it by what it can endure, its utilitarian use value, opposing unlimited exploitation but still legitimating some exploitation. Instead of this, then, it is argued that what is needed is to challenge and deconstruct the modern world-view, its construction of nature, and to construct a new (relationship to) nature, a new (environmentally friendly) conception, or conceptions, of reality, of nature, humanity and the human–nature relationship, leading to new patterns of thought and practice (not necessarily denying modern gains but ecologically grounding them). As Berman (1984:10) states '*Some* type of holistic, or participating, consciousness and a corresponding socio-political formation have to emerge if we are to survive as a species'. What is seen as needed is a new social imaginary, or imaginaries, re-enchanting nature or providing different enchantments to modernity: as Szerszynski (2005:124) argues, 'The . . . question is . . . *which* enchantment of nature might offer a genuine alternative to the domination of nature . . . by modern technology' (see Berry 1999; Capra 1982; Gottlieb 1996; McGrath 2003; Nasr 1996; Oelschlaeger 1994; Rasmussen 1994; Rockefeller 1992; Sheldrake 1994; Tucker 2003).

[S]olutions [to the environmental crisis] must involve considerations of ethics and values . . . No political, economic, or technological solutions . . . exist . . . because technological administration and, indeed, science 'left without moral and political guidance', are themselves a part of the etiology of the ecocrisis.[5] (Oeslchlaeger 1994:17–18)

[T]here is a growing recognition that the various sciences, however indispensable they may be in dealing with human despoliation of the earth, are

by themselves incomplete in helping us to behave . . . in a more appropriate
and sustainable manner . . . Increasingly there is a growing recognition that
the value dimension must be an important element in any solution. (Carroll
et al. 1997:3–4)

The modern way of looking at the world, although dominant, is socially constructed. It is a model or paradigm arising within particular conditions and
developments in a particular time and place (albeit now globalized). There are
and have always been other ways of looking at the world, other models and paradigms with other conceptual schemes. In this sense, what is known as 'nature'
(or 'humanity'), in the modern context, is limited, based on particular cultural (Western, economic/technological) assumptions, something Evernden
(1992), in particular, analyses. He sees its objectivity and essentialism, nature
as a whole entity (as well as the possibility of the unnatural), being the product
of Greek (Platonic, Aristotelian) and Christian thought (seeing no concept
of such an entity and no contemplation of action towards it, merely action
towards parts of it, of which humanity is related, before these). This, then, he
sees engendering the dualism of 'nature' and 'non-nature' (this being humanity), leading to abstraction and alienation and subsequent diminishment of the
non-human, through denying it subjectivity and making it devoid of human
participation (and thus other and dangerous). What this shows is that what is
known as nature is a complex and malleable concept, a social practice, developed by particular world-views at particular times and places. It is varied not
singular: there are always diverse contested nature's, including in the West,
despite the hegemony of the modern world-view. This is not to deny its concrete presence but to recognize that this is interpreted by humanity, different
human ideas projected onto it (it has a radical otherness, beyond complete
conceptual grasp, it is neither just 'there' (the essentialist position) nor just
'made-up' (the constructionist position) but a dialectic of real and imagined,
a non-human material reality socially comprehended) (Castree and Braun
1998; Cronon 1996a; Eder 1996; Evernden 1992; Lease 1995; Roeperstorff and
Bubandt 2003; Soule 1995; Szerszynski 2005).

> '[N]ature' is a human idea, with a long and complicated cultural history
> which has led different human beings to conceive of the natural world in
> very different ways . . . creatures and landscapes we label as 'natural' are
> in fact deeply entangled with the words and images and ideas we use to
> describe them . . . we turn them into human symbols, using them as reposi-
> tories for values and meanings which can range from the savage to the
> sacred. (Cronon 1996b:20)

Nature, for Roeperstorff and Bubandt (2003), is thus constantly engaged,
practised, semiotized and reproduced, with powerful emotional, moral and

political, associations. It is, for Evernden (1992), always an ideal (there is a metaphysic behind it). It is historical and social rather than an essential eternal norm (it rests on history not history on it). Cronon (1996a:34–51), in this sense, sees several versions of nature: *naive reality*, one of the oldest meanings, seeing nature as a holistic, uncontested essence, a given; *moral imperative*, grounding moral authority and values in a given nature, basing the ought on the is; *Eden*, seeing nature as a benign, pristine world lost (through human culpability), needing to be regained, based on a moral dualism of good and evil; *artifice/self-conscious social construction*, seeing nature transformed into what it ought to be, a moral ideal, planned and remade to conform to humanity's assumptions (often in response to an Edenic narrative); *virtual reality* seeing nature as an alternative (technological) disembodied cultural space, promising total human control (unreal but possibly becoming conflated with the real – Cronon sees the ozone hole and global warming perceived virtually); *commodity*, seeing nature as a product to be bought and sold (as resources or 'authentic' natural products or settings); *demonic other/avenging angel*, seeing nature as chaotic, dangerous or rebellious (e.g. 'wild' animals, unforeseen events, natural disasters; often seen as moral fables or lessons); and *contested terrain*, seeing different views of nature meeting and conflicting. Similarly, Soule (1995:139–41) stresses different perceptions of nature accumulating like layers (scientific views possibly coexisting with religious ones, possibly within an individual's perception): *Magna Mater*, an animistic sense of divine oneness; *unpredictable/evil bully*, an anarchic, catastrophic force; *aging/reluctant provider*, a supply of resources and services; *wild kingdom*, a place of peace and wonder; *open-air gymnasium*, a place of exercise and accomplishment; *new age temple*, a place of pilgrimage, ritual or healing; *wild other/divine chaos*, where humanity is one species among others; *gaia*, where nature is self-regulating; and *biodiversity*, the Western biologist's view.

For McGrath (2003) there are thus several ways of using the term nature: as a 'realist' concept, referring to the processes and structures in the physical world; as a 'metaphysical' concept, denoting a category that allows humanity to affirm its identity in relation to the non-human; and as a 'surface' concept, referring to ordinary observable features of the world, often contrasted to the urban.[6] The point, McGrath notes, is that humans do not simply see things but see things as something, observing nature through a set of assumptions that condition the seeing. Nature is thus always complex and contested, there are many interpretations and representations of it and there will always be arguments about its meaning. It is argued, therefore, that what is needed is more overt contestation and dialogue about it, a 'politicization of nature' encouraging debate over the construction of reality, critiquing the modern world-view and its construction of nature, and accepting/providing different ones. In this sense, it is the ideal of nature that is at stake (and who or what is allowed to define and dictate it) as much as the physical threat, 'pollution' (or 'cleanliness') being moral as much as physical, imagined as much as real (although the imagined leads to real effects) (see Castree and Braun 1998; Cronon 1996a; Eder 1996; Evernden 1992; Lease 1995; Roeperstorff and Bubandt 2003; Soule 1995).

Reconstructing nature in this way, however, may not be as simple as it seems. There is the danger that such changes may also treat it as an object, similar to but opposing the modern world-view, viewing it romantically (as a pristine 'something' to be preserved) as opposed to instrumentally (seeing it for its use value). And, in this sense, an environmentalism that aims to 'save' nature may be too rigid, dualistic and objectifying. Evernden (1992) sees this when arguing that ecology may function as a 'new oracle' (and authority, beyond the modern), an exemplar of the 'natural', assisting humanity to a healthier relationship to nature by seeking, understanding and revealing, 'natural harmonies' (lessons from nature) essential to happiness and survival (e.g. the myth of the 'balance of nature'). His point is that such a view is still an (essentialist) *idea* of nature, of the proper order and rightness of things, and of proper and right behaviour, just as the modern world-view is, defining, in Mary Douglas's terms, 'purity' (ecological views) and 'danger' (modern views).[7] It is argued, therefore, that environmentalists, as much as anyone, need to be aware that their concepts of nature are culturally determined (while recognizing that nature is not solely cultural, this extreme social constructionist view itself possibly devaluing it), that any static position of what nature is and how it needs to be addressed (used, protected) is limited and can be challenged (being aware that there may be no simple dichotomy of 'modern' versus 'ecological' versions of nature, but rather diverse types coexisting and/or conflicting, and also that environmentalist views can be as much about social control, creating a hegemonic environmental norm, as the modern one) (Castree and Braun 1998; Cronon 1996a; Evernden 1992; Lease 1995; Soule 1995; Szerszynski 2005).

Such awareness is not seen as meaning an abandonment of the possibility of finding more environmentally benign approaches to nature but rather to question certain assumptions about it, about where ideas about it come from and what they are used for, to be self-reflexively vigilant to and take responsibility for the different sorts of natures humanity produces (being culturally and historically minded, recognizing context, diversity and change), accepting that ultimately it is beyond comprehensive conceptual grasp, even while it is within the domain of human responsibility. In this sense, the idea of nature (or any benign reconstruction or re-enchantment of it seeking to protect it, for example, seeing it as active, spiritual, subjective, interconnected with humanity), is seen as needing to be approached within a critical dialogue and action, a common and changeable consensus from differing positions and understandings, without any dominant universalism. For Roeperstorff and Bubandt (2003), the aim should be to pay attention to the way nature is engaged through human imagination and practice, exploring (and comparing) the different ways it is created and experienced. Such is the aim of this book, in a sense, and in the following sections I begin this task through, first, analysing and highlighting new environmental ideas and formations that are arising, coalescing or being constructed – what is seen as an 'ecological model' in response to the modern 'mechanical model' and the environmental crisis, stressing a more intimate and benign human–nature relationship. Secondly, I explore possible means to experience and express such 'ecological' or environmentally friendly views, analysing the role of metaphor and myth in creating an 'ecological reimagination' of nature.

The ecological model: Re-enchanting, revaluing and revitalizing, nature

To respond adequately to the environmental crisis the modern view of nature is seen as needing to be critiqued and contested and new ones (self-reflexively) constructed, the symbolic forms in which it is represented needing to be challenged and reconstructed beyond a utilitarian relationship that has become the modern norm. Such a new attitude to nature, for Eder (1996), builds on contemporary environmentalism that he sees as a turning point in the cultural evolution of modernity providing a new orientation substituting ecology for industrialization and essentially inventing the 'politics of nature'. Seen in its modern form as originating in cyclic waves of protest, with a 'first phase' in the 1960s when the degradation of nature became recognized (and notions of the 'environment' and 'environmental crisis' constructed), and a second 'phase' in the 1980s of regulatory approaches and sustainable development, what Eder sees as the emerging 'third phase' has led to the cultural normalization of environmental concerns and integration with established ideologies (environmentalism as a coherent project) and the crystallization of new cultural patterns.[8] Such patterns have been described as highlighting (coalescing into, creating) an emerging 'ecological' or 'green' consciousness or paradigm, a 'new planetary vision' opposing (or extending) the modern technological age, incorporating a shift from viewing the earth in a (reductionist, static) mechanistic way, as a vast resource, to viewing it in an (holistic, dynamic) organic way, as a living community, and reappraising the human condition within it based on partnership not domination (eco-centrism not anthro/techno-centrism, a paradigm shift that is seen as similar to the change from agrarian to modern views) (Berry 1990; Burke 2001; Callicott 1997; Capra 1982; Dobson 2000; Dryzek 2005; Guha 2000; Hayden 1997; Metzner 1994; Nash 1989; Oelschlaeger 1994; Pepper 1996).

Various changes are thus seen as taking place, or needing to, in this ecological movement within self-perception and social understanding, enabling what Oelschlaeger (1994:56) terms a 'new social matrix', a new ecological way of living: from a conception of God outside nature to seeing it imbued with the divine; from mechanistic to organic views, seeing the earth as an organism and life as autopoietic coevolution, humanity reciprocally intertwined with nature (distrusting objectivity and stressing subjectivity, accepting intuition alongside reason);[9] from an ethic valuing nature for its use to one valuing it intrinsically, recognizing its finite limits but infinite value, stressing eco-centric values preserving biodiversity and ecosystem integrity; from homogenous culture to one embracing diversity, stressing egalitarianism, partnership and spirituality; from a politics for the powerful to citizen democracy, non-violent and environment-focused, attentive to locality while seeking the common good; from an economics based on maximizing profits to one based on sustainability, cooperative and ecology-based, with community and nature-oriented agriculture and renewable technologies (accepting that risk that entails unpredicted or irreversible consequences is unacceptable, no matter how profitable; accepting biophysical limits to growth that no human technology can overcome) (Burke 2001; Hayden 1997; Metzner 1994). Rasmussen (2002:587–8) sees such changes as *economic*, living renewably off nature's income not capital, *social*, equally and sustainably sharing its wealth, *institutional*, creating cooperation not competition, *informational*, deepening and widening education, *demographic*, creating population stability, *technological*, reducing environmental impact, *moral*, widening ethics to all nature, and *religious*, stressing earth-keeping as a vocation, while, for Devall and Sessions (1985), they thrive in a 'minority tradition' of decentralized, non-violent, responsible, simple communities, recognizing organic wholeness and being open to communication with nature.

Such ideas, as these authors note, may be somewhat idealistic, romanticized, simplistic and overly unified (although no less so than the modern world-view). Nevertheless, for them, they offer different ecological, personal and social, possibilities than those presented by the modern world-view, being, for Metzner (1994:170), 'pathways to the ecological age', with humanity needing to muster the personal and political will to walk them. For Berry (1990), they provide a new historical vision of an intimate earth community, a 'dream of the earth', of a more viable existence, seeing human destiny as integral with that of nature, while, for De Geus (1999), they are utopian, imagining a more environmentally friendly humanity, something he argues can be useful in the modern environmentally destructive world. While recognizing that the idea of utopia, the perfect, harmonic society, is open to challenge, often being too abstract, static and unrealistic, De Geus, nevertheless, sees it as the only way to stimulate environmentally responsible behaviour and a sustainable society (still appealing to many people). For him it offers inspiration and new visions, being critical, experimental and prophetic, as well as a source of ideals and optimism, able to challenge present realities, highlight alternative futures, and remind that purposeful choices can be made in creating these. De Geus (1999:255–9) thus sees utopian visions as points of orientation, using the power of imagination to inspire people to make more environmentally friendly choices, acting as a *kaleidoscope*, highlighting alternative images, *coloured glasses*, enabling a viewing of the world through a 'green-tinted' lens, a *mirror*, shedding light on existing frameworks, a *CT-scan*, analysing and deconstructing present society, an *interactive medium*, stimulating reflection on the ultimate goals of society, a *microscope*, magnifying minute or personal effects of wider views, a *telescope*, enabling a comprehensive way of conceiving the distant future, and a *magic lantern*, evoking and inspiring exciting and meaningful images (see Benstein 2002; Carey 1999; Kassman 1997; Levitas 1990, 2000; Marty 2003; Rothstein 2003).

> [T]he green movement is letting an opportunity pass by, by not recognising the true value that lies in [the] utopian tradition . . . utopias [stimulate people] to think actively, thus encouraging reflection. The utopian way of thinking almost inevitably leads the way to taking a stand and critically reconsidering one's own opinions about human happiness, the meaning of life, and the most desirable way in which the economy, society, and state should be organised . . . breaking through fixed patterns of thinking and [testing] unusual combinations of ideas. (De Geus 1999:19, 39)

Callicott (1997), in this sense, sees environmentalism (in its 'radical' rather than 'reform' form[10]) as a visionary mandate to facilitate a new ecological consciousness, challenging modern views and creating new ones. This has been described by Berry (1999) as a 'Great Work', Capra (1982) as a 'Turning Point', and Rockefeller (1992:167) as a 'Great Awakening': imagining and creating a more environmentally friendly society than that of modern industrial civilization (what is seen as the destructive terminal phase of the Cenozoic era); an 'Ecozoic era' of a more benign, mutually beneficial, human mode of presence on the earth as a participating member of the community of nature, moving from a human-centred to an earth-centred norm of reality and value (Berry 1999). The aim, in a sense, is to disenchant the modern world-view, uncovering its taken for granted assumptions, and provide a new ecological enchantment, a new social imaginary (or, recognizing the need for a variety of perspectives in communication, not a hegemonic world-view, imaginaries), stimulating new ecological moralities and lifestyles, re-rooting humanity *within* nature (encouraging subjective engagement *with* it rather than objective action *on* it) evoking wider environmental identity, passion and reverence (creating an 'earth literacy', encouraging the participation of the larger community of life in human decision making). Such ideas, then, involve a critique of existing society and the creation of ideas about what a future society should be like, critiquing modernity's view of nature and imagining new nature's, being not just utopian but 'ecotopian' (stressing, for De Geus (1999), egalitarian attitudes to nature, economic/ecological equilibrium, and simple, sustainable lifestyles, measuring happiness by creativity, relationships and spirituality) (see Berry 1990, 1999; Burke 2001; Metzner 1994; Oelschlaeger 1994; Pepper 1996; Rockefeller 1992; Tucker 2003).[11]

> [W]hat is needed is a commitment, so wholehearted as to be justly termed religious in quality, to a new ecological worldview involving a dramatic transformation of the moral values and basic attitudes that govern life . . . [encouraging] appreciation of the intrinsic value and contribution of all things . . . the way all individuals are reciprocally connected and dependent on the development of the common good. (Rockefeller (1992:141, 165)

Dryzek (2005) sees this as a 'green' consciousness and politics: accepting that natural relationships between humanity and nature have been violated, recognizing the existence and proximity of global limits, accepting that agency can exist in nature, and accepting that humanity can become ecologically aware by using a range of evocative organic metaphors. Sideris (2006) sees such ideas as an 'ecological model' where the well-being of whole is the final goal, interdependence is championed, and relationships between all elements of nature are stressed rather than atomistic isolation. Such a model she sees stressing an ethics built around community and mutuality and care and liberation for nature, a common good for all life-forms (while also celebrating context and difference), being descriptive and prescriptive, seeing intrinsic natural goodness needing to be responded to, humanity needing to learn from nature how to live as a sustaining not destructive presence, replacing competition (a violation of nature's patterns) with cooperation. Berman (1984) sees such a view as 'tomorrow's metaphysics', a new epistemology based on both scientific reason and unconscious knowing, where fact and value, mind and body, subject and object, are united aspects of the same process, where holism, process and relationship, are primary, where beauty, grace and wisdom, are goals, and where quality takes precedence over quantity (logic being both/and, dialectical, rather than modernity's either/or).[12]

For Capra (1982) such ideas stress a new vision of reality, transcending current conceptual boundaries, stressing biological, psychological and social, interdependence of all phenomena. Berry (1990, 1999), in this sense, stresses an 'agenda for the ecological age' of integral human technological relations with earth technologies, creating a sustainable progress for the entire earth community, based around a diverse yet cooperative, bioregional context, providing the setting, and a functional ecological cosmology, providing the 'mystique', the emotional and spiritual influence, able to foster more intimate relations with and a sense of reverence for nature and enhance its properties and spontaneities. Such an agenda, for Berry, is based on a critical and reflective (as much as idealistic) 'reinvention of humanity', the creation of new cultural forms, something he sees as a fundamental aspect of what humanity is and does: a rethinking of humanity not as separate from but integral with nature, enabling ethical relations determined by the well-being of the whole. This, for Berry, involves cosmological-historical considerations, revolving around the origins and evolution of nature and humanity, who we are and what our role is and what nature and its role is. It involves the (reinterpreted) *story* of nature, something he sees communicated and learnt via an 'entrancing' 'shared dream experience', a creative, imaginative process, what he sees as a 'deep cultural therapy', disorienting the modern world-view and reorienting humanity towards communion with nature via imaginative cosmological discourse (replacing the environmentally destructive modern dream with environmentally friendly ecological ones).[13] Dobson (2000) sees this as an 'ecologism' that holds that a sustaining and fulfilling existence presupposes radical change in humanity's relationship with nature and in social life (this going beyond (reform) environmentalism that argues for a managerial approach solving problems without fundamental changes in values or social patterns). Echoing De Geus (1999), he sees this having utopian elements, something he argues all political/social movements require if they are going to be effective, with such ecologism acting as an ideal inspiration for environmental thought and action:[14]

[T]he Utopian vision provides the indispensable fundamentalist well from which green activists . . . need continually to draw. Green reformers need a radically alternative picture of post-industrial society, they need deep-ecological visionaries, they need phantom studies of the sustainable society . . . [reminding] reformists of where they want to go even if they don't really think they can get there. (Dobson 2000:202)

The environmental crisis, in this sense, as Evernden (1992) argues, demands not so much the inventing of 'solutions' but the re-creation of nature (and humanity). As Berry (1999:x, 165) states, 'we must first have a vision of the future sufficiently entrancing that it will sustain us in the transformation of the human project . . . a new revelatory experience . . . [awakening] human consciousness to the grandeur and sacred quality of the Earth'. Nature and humanity thus need to be reinvented. And to do this, for humanity to 'ecologically evolve', to act in a less destructive way, for Evernden (1992:124), involves language, especially metaphor: as he states 'one day the world is re-spoken, and a new being is released'. Similarly, for Berry (1990:42), 'Our challenge is to create a new language . . . a new sense of what it is to be human . . . [bringing] about a completely new sense of reality and of value'. Addressing the environmental crisis, then, in this sense, means challenging the prevailing hegemonic modern language, its anthropocentric metaphors and myths, and providing a new imaginative language, new eco-centric metaphors and myths, in a public discourse about nature, something that, for Berry (1990, 1999), involves a new 'dream of the earth', a mythic vision, or visions, creating an 'ecological trance' instead of, in place of, the modern 'technological trance'.

Metaphors and myths:
The means to reimagine nature

[T]he language that we use to describe our relationship with the land is made concrete in all that we build, in the way that we farm, and in the ways in which we care for the Earth. What we do is a function of what we think, and thought, captured in the beguiling snare of language, defines and can constrain, and even distort our reality. For language, laden as it is with explicit and implicit values, does more than describe, it governs . . . Thus an engineer, a banker and a poet will survey the same landscape and see it quite differently from each other. To one, it is configured according to its geological form; to another it is property and collateral; and to the third it calls forth memory and imagination.

(Cadman 2002:163)

[B]y accentuating certain aspects of existence and leaving others in the background [metaphors] can guide our attention, and influence our perception and thinking . . . 'metaphor implies a way of thinking and a way of seeing *that pervade how we understand our world'.*[15]

(De Geus 1999:230)

Metaphors are recognized as fundamental to the process of reality construction, providing the means to identify similarity and difference and create changes in meaning, enabling the establishing of private and public values and knowledge of and response to the world, stimulating the formation of culture, being a basic pervasive mechanism for understanding experience (most concepts are understood in terms of other concepts). What humans think, feel and do, the way they perceive, draw inferences and act, is a matter of metaphor. Metaphors express fundamental concepts and form coherent systems through which humans conceptualize and organize conventional and new experience. And such metaphoric reality construction works in an indirect way, within the taken for granted, evoking feelings and stimulating meaningful action (although it is not devoid of rationality, rather, for Lakoff and Johnson (1980), it is an imaginative form of it). Metaphors, in this sense, act as tools to comprehend what cannot be totally comprehended, suggesting consideration, sparking the imagination. They are thus heuristic and creative, the cause of the ability to know not merely expressions of knowledge, encouraging imaginative constructions and understandings (e.g. of nature), being a way to say something new (Lakoff and Johnson 1980; McFague 1987; Oelschlaeger 1994).

The metaphorical imagination, then, is seen as crucial in conveying meanings and values (including environmental ones). As Lakoff and Johnson (1980:22) argue 'The most fundamental values in a culture will be coherent with the metaphorical structure of the most fundamental concepts in the culture.' Metaphors are thus essential to the process of environmental seeing, learning and doing, being models of prior thought and ensuing action, not merely a way to view reality but also a licence for changing it. They have the power to stimulate understandings of nature, either in constraining or empowering ways (in an official core ideology or alternative challenging ones). They may, then, be crucial for re-creating the idea of nature and the human place and behaviour within it. New metaphors of nature may alter conceptual systems and perceptions and actions, stimulating the location and cementing of personal and social identities to particular places and practices, inspiring cultural change, re-enchanting and revaluing nature and reintegrating humanity within it. They may be a guide for future environmental action, providing new rationales for environmental behaviour beyond modern efficiency (reminding of old experiences of nature while providing new ones, giving new environmental meaning to lives). The introduction of new metaphors of nature may thus have the power to create new environmental realities (Brockelman 1999; Lakoff and Johnson 1980).

Such metaphoric imaginative power is seen in myth, which, through providing an expression of sacred creativity, provides the basis for human knowledge and action. Myths, authoritative, persuasive dramas or narratives linking immanent and transcendent, known and unknown, revealing in familiar time and place uncommon and universal truths, disclose an ultimate meaning to life, connecting the understanding of it to a wider significant reality. They are metaphoric patterns that evoke and inspire ways of interpreting and acting in the world, being a window through which humanity encounters what is most real and meaningful. They are thus a script for action, inspiring the transformation of life, providing fundamental structures for thought and action, enabling the location of things and decisions about them and the world itself to be made. Mythic imagery thus constitutes a 'mythopoetic system', a symbolic but coherent description of the world, initiating a dynamic, living system of meaning, 'mythopoiesis', stimulating creative imagination and collective consciousness, generating subjective imagery, cultural meanings and moral order (environmentally, personally, socially and spiritually, informed and performed, and thus able to reorient humanity in its environmental, personal, social and spiritual, forms) (Bolle 2005b; Lakoff and Johnson 1980; Laughlin and Throop 2001; Midgley 2005; Sproul 1979).

At the core of every cultural tradition there is a narrative, a myth, which integrates ideas about reality and value ... [providing] a general orientation in nature and in history . . . the most fundamental expression of wisdom in a culture – it tells us what kind of world we live in, what sorts of things are real and unreal, where we came from, what our true nature is, and how we fit into the larger scheme of things. These are all *cosmological* ideas, they inform us about the cosmos and our place in it . . . [and] ideas about *morality* . . . what is good for us and how we should construct ourselves in order to achieve our fulfilment . . . [functioning] as important resources for the construction of personal and social realities. (Rue 2000:23)

Myths are thus etiological, they explain origins or causes establishing and encouraging renewal or reform of reality. Cosmogonies, or creation stories, for example, may legitimate the present (or future) by locating it in sacred time, providing common cognitive legitimacy and meaningfulness, as well as moral values, establishing the structure of all valuation based on a primary reality, linking moral orientations to accounts of sacred origins. Such narratives provide sacred canopies legitimating experience by locating it in a framework of larger significance, providing archetypes of authentic human life in accordance with a universal order, carrying obligations and injunctions for human behaviour. They thus provide the basis for cosmologies that provide human resonance with nature, manifesting the essential structure of reality and the human place in it, providing organizing principles and stimulating the creative activities of cultures, being a charter for conduct, stating paradigmatic truths that define possibilities and limitations, implying and serving to prescribe or influence metaphysical and ethical principles and actions, combing ought and is, giving moral direction to human life (stimulating and justifying the choice of one way of acting over another). Cosmological narratives thus tell humanity where it and the world came from, what they are, and what their roles are, integrating how things are, why they are, and what matters (what is good and bad, how to live in/with nature). They thus provide a compelling (in Berry's (1990, 1999) terms, entrancing) common core of identities and values, manifesting the intrinsic value of the wider environmental (sacred) reality and its dependent parts, being ultimate measures through which environmental, personal and social, identities (progress) are judged (Bolle 2005a; Brockelman 1999; Laughlin and Throop 2001; Long 2005; Lovin and Reynolds 1985; Oelschlaeger 1994; Sproul 1979; Rue 2000; Tucker 2002b).

Humanity has thus been described as a 'mythopoeic' species, *homo narrans*, with a 'mythopoeic drive', dependent on and unable to exist without legitimating narratives through which to understand, engage and order, the world, enabling it to determine what things are, what they mean, how to relate to them, and what to do with them (Barlow 1997; Lakoff and Johnson 1980; Oelschlaeger 1994; Rasmussen 1994; Rue 2000; Sproul 1979). It is through narratives, then, that humanity, personally and socially, perceives and experiences environments and objects, defining reality. Thus language can be a powerful tool for domination or liberation of nature. Different meta-phoric, mythical, cosmogonic and cosmological, views of it have corresponding positive or negative, beneficial or destructive, effects. As Midgley (2005:1–2) argues 'imaginative patterns . . . suggest particular ways of . . . [acting in] the world . . . The way in which we imagine [it] determines what we think important in it'. And, for Barlow (1997), modern society is 'amythic', with a 'diminished' cosmology and 'unattached' morality, individuals being unable to locate meaning in the context of anything greater than themselves or their times. For Berry (1990:205) this is a 'cultural pathology' and for Brockelman (1997:36, 1999:7, 9) a 'cultural illness' or 'myopia', a disorientation or lack of connection to wider being or purpose, an ethical and spiritual empti-ness. In Midgley's (2005) terms this involves patterns of thought from one age or culture (e.g. modern, Western, secular) imposing on and diminishing others (e.g. pre-modern, non-Western, religious) and causing (environmen-tal) problems. For Oelschlaeger (1994) this occurs because modern Western culture has lost faith in its 'metaphorical prime' of Judeo-Christianity and to escape this amythia needs a new viable mythology or legitimating narra-tive, one grounding ethos ecologically in the cosmos. Similarly, Rue (2000) argues that to effectively address the environmental crisis humanity must 'attend to its stories', realigning its narrative and moral compass, reimagin-ing the world and its place in it, creating new ideas of nature (or reinterpret-ations of old ones) beyond the modern one, new environmental insights and truths (see McGrath 2003; Tucker 2002b).

The language humanity uses to describe its relationship to nature, then, is important as it is made concrete in its actions. As Dryzek (2005:10) argues 'the way we construct [and] interpret . . . environmental problems has all kinds of consequences'. Dryzek (2005), in particular, analyses 'environmental discourses', in response to the modern 'industrial discourse', the differing metaphoric languages used to interpret nature and stimulate environmen-tal identities and behaviours, providing basic ideas (e.g. 'web of life') and relationships (e.g. 'cooperation'), what he terms 'promethean', 'survivalism', 'green consciousness' and 'green politics' discourses. The first he sees con-structing ideas of matter, markets and technology, and relationships of com-petition and hierarchy, using mechanistic metaphors. The second he sees constructing the idea of finite resources and relationships of conflict and control, using metaphors of commons, spaceship or virus. The third he sees constructing ideas of global limits and unnatural practices and relationships of (violated) equality, using metaphors of intuition and passion. The fourth he sees constructing ideas of ecosystems and limits and relationships of equal-ity and interconnection, using organic metaphors. Such language, then, for Dryzek, creates different realities, different perceptions of, attachments to and responses to, the world. Similarly Sproul (1979:19) argues that 'words establish realities . . . We create new identities, new things, by giving them new names . . . man, woman, tree, animal . . . terms (which) announce values, functions, and identities'. Providing different environmental discourses (new forms of 'naming') to the modern one, then, is thus seen as a possible way to address and overcome environmental problems through creating different (moral) attachments valuing nature and stimulating care for it. As McFague (1987:3) argues:

> Names matter because what we call something, how we name it, is to a great extent what it is to us. We are pre-eminent creatures of language [which] . . . qualifies [human reality] in profound ways. It follows, then, that naming can be hurtful, and that it can also be healing or helpful. The ways we name ourselves, one another, and the world cannot be taken for granted; we must look at them carefully to see if they heal or hurt.

In line with such ideas McGrath (2003) sees several metaphoric possibilities for a reconstruction of nature, such as seeing it as a book, mirror, theatre or woman arguing, in particular, for 'organismic' views (e.g. romanticism, transcendentalism), stressing nature-affirming metaphors of connectedness, spirituality and wonder. For him, such different concepts may be complementary, helping to illuminate a complex concept, serving as a helpful (or not) lens through which to view nature, allowing it to be read in different (possibly environmentally beneficial) ways. De Geus (1999:231–5), similarly, highlights 'ecological-utopian' metaphoric visions of different human–nature interaction: *artwork*, highlighting beauty, creativity and harmony; *cloister*, highlighting communal instead of private orientations, stressing moderation, self-restraint and spirituality; *garden*, highlighting a designed and tended landscape, inspired by and improving natural forms, suggesting ecologically balanced lifestyle; *natural cycle*, highlighting the prevention and reduction of pollution of ecosystems and the protection of environmental equilibrium; and *wilderness*, highlighting the beauty, harmony and spirituality, of unspoiled nature and thus need for preservation and minimal exploitation of it.

In a similar, but more religious sense, McFague (1987) highlights different 'models of God' that may suggest different relationships to the sacred and subsequent actions towards nature. In this scheme, the classical patriarchal model of God as 'Father', 'King' or 'Lord', envisages God as transcendent, in a dominant hierarchical relationship to nature, with humanity, made in God's image, having a similar relationship to it, leading to exploitation of it. Other imagery, however, may lead to different perceptions and actions. The model of God as 'Mother', for example, suggests ideas of immanence, creativity and interrelatedness, envisaging God loving nature into existence and nourishing it, stressing unselfish sacrificial giving of life not selfish exploitative taking of it, with nature not separate from God or humanity but in

kinship with them. Similarly, the model of God as 'lover' envisages an intimate, mutually supportive relationship between God, humanity and nature,
involving concern, faithfulness and love, a desire for union with a valuable,
responsive nature, taking pleasure in its variety and fulfilment (salvation
being to positively make whole what is valuable not negatively rescue what is
sinful). Lastly, the model of God as 'friend' envisages a committed relationship of affection, respect and trust, between God, humanity and nature, without discrimination, fear or resentment, stressing sustaining companionship,
a mutual responsibility to bear the other (emphasizing humanity as a relational being, denying possession or exploitation). For McFague (1987:122),
then, such different images may:

> sketch the change in attitude, the conversion of consciousness, that could
> come about were we to begin to live inside [them] and allow [them] to
> become a lens through which we looked out on the world. We would no
> longer see a world we named and ruled, or like the artist god, made . . . Our
> positive role [would be] as preservers, those who pass life along and who
> care for all forms of life so they may prosper.

For McGrath (2003) such ideas demonstrate how humanity can *as a result of
its perception of nature* relate to it in a respectful, non-dominant, environmentally
friendly, manner (or a disrespectful, dominant, environmentally unfriendly,
one). Furthermore, his and McFague's (1987) ideas also highlight that, when
considering humanity's relationship to nature and the need for more environmentally friendly images to stimulate new environmentally friendly behaviour,
religion may be an important source.

Conclusions

In this chapter I have analysed what is seen as the underlying cause of the
environmental crisis, the modern, anthropocentric, materialist, imaginary
or world-view (initially Western but now hegemonic and globalized), based
on fact/value, mind/body, spirit/matter, subjective/objective, distinctions, a
'mechanical model' that separates humanity from nature, seeing the former
as active, dominant and purposeful, and the latter as passive matter devoid
of meaning, subjectivity and spirit. This is seen as a moral and spiritual disorientation and disenchantment, where human reason and interest takes
priority and wider identities and interconnections are ignored, this sanction-
ing and stimulating economic and technological progress (at the expense of
moral and spiritual progress), leading to (environmentally destructive) consumerism and industrialization (and a Promethean response to crises, constantly trying to economically or technologically fix them). To address the

crisis, therefore, a new social imaginary, or imaginaries, are seen as needed, eco-centrically based, able to re-enchant and revalue nature (and disenchant humanity and the modern world-view), creating human moral and spiritual reorientation in relation to it, and stimulate new environmentally friendly lifestyles.

In this sense, it is the (hegemony of the) modern concept of nature that is seen as the problem (although this does not deny the material nature of the crisis). Thus it is argued that this needs to be challenged and nature politicized (beginning with the recognition that it is a fluid social practice, a cultural and historical product). New imaginations of nature are seen as needed, ones that give it meaning, subjectivity and sacredness (or present alternative, possibly religious, ones accepted and revitalized, albeit in diverse, dialogic and reflexive, not hegemonic, ways). In line with such ideas, in challenge to the modern 'mechanical model' there has arisen within contemporary environmentalism a coalescing set of ideas that has been described as an 'ecological model' seeing nature holistically and organically, as a dynamic, living, community, of which humanity is an inter-dependent part, stressing a human response to it of reciprocity not domin-ation. Such ideas are seen as reintegrating fact/value, mind/body, spirit/matter, subjective/objective, re-rooting humanity in and revaluing nature, evoking wider environmental identity. They presuppose a radical change in humanity's relationship to nature and provide ideals of interdependence and mutual care to enable it, aiming to evoke or facilitate a new ecological consciousness and age, a transformation of individual and social values (from human-centred to earth-centred).

Such ideas emphasize that what is needed is a new imaginative language, new (utopian/ecotopian) visions of reality, reconnecting humanity and nature, envisioning a peaceful, supportive, interaction between them. The use of metaphor and myth is seen as important to this (humanity being seen as a mythopoeic species), being fundamental and influential means for humanity to re-create conceptions of reality (of nature), stimulating collect-ive understandings, connecting microcosm and macrocosm, able to evoke and inspire an ecological, instead of technological, entrancement. An alter-native ecological language, in this sense, may thus inspire alternative eco-logical thought and action. Ideas of artwork, gardens or organisms, when thinking about nature, may evoke and inspire different attitudes and actions, different relationships, towards it, for example, than that of a machine. In a similar, more religious-oriented vein, imagining God as mother, friend or lover, may evoke and inspire different human attitudes towards nature, more subjective, caring, or relational, ones, than imagining God as a father, King or Lord, stressing objectivity, dominance and exploitation.

Creating a new empowering ecological language and world-view, re-creating nature in environmentally friendly terms, reorienting humanity within it, is thus seen as an imaginative, moral and spiritual, task, and in this light, religion is thought to be useful, even vital, for the purpose. In the next chapter I analyse this in more detail, examining the perceived ecological need for religion, what it may contribute to environmental issues, and how this may affect its role in the modern world, exploring the phenomenon of 'religious environmentalism', most especially a burgeoning 'field of religion and ecology' that encourages and coordinates different religious imaginations of nature challenging the modern world-view and responding to the environmental crisis.

Notes

1   Quotes from Loy (2002:68–9), referenced to Karl Polanyi, *The Great Transformation* (Boston: Beacon Press, 1944, 1957), p. 57, and Tawney, R. H. *Religion and the Rise of Capitalism* (New York: Harcourt, Brace, 1926), p. 86.
2   Berman (1984), Kinsley (1994), McGrath (2003) and Merchant (2002), see a religious genesis to this, Bacon and Newton seeing science glorifying God, influencing secular capitalism (this relating to Weber's ideas (see *The Protestant Ethic and the Spirit of Capitalism*, London: Harper Collins Academic, 1991) and Lynn White's (1967) argument that Judeo-Christianity provided the anthropocentrism necessary to exploit nature).
3   Referenced to Vogel, S., *Against Nature: The Concept of Nature in Critical Theory*, Albany, NY: State University of New York Press, 1996.
4   Szerszynski (2005) sees modern disenchantment as an enchantment building on 'primal', 'archaic', 'monotheistic' and 'protestant' views, and developing into a 'post-modern sacred' of multiple sacred views (older traditions surviving, new ones emerging). Thus there may be no secularization as such but rather a 'secular-sacred' and 're-enchantment' may mean 'disenchantment' of the modern view and revaluing others.
5   Referenced to Maddux, J., National Academy/Royal Society: Warning on Population Growth, *Nature* 355:759, 1992.
6   Referenced to Soper, K., *What is Nature? Culture, Politics, and the Non-Human* (Oxford: Basil Blackwell, 1995).
7   See Douglas, M., *Purity and Danger* (London: Routledge & Kegan Paul, 1966).
8   The environmental movement is traced to the humane movement, pastoralism, the preservationist tradition, romanticism and utopian socialism, with influences including Ralph Waldo Emerson, John Muir, John Ray, John Ruskin, Henry Salt and Henry David Thoreau, and later Edward Abbey, Rachel Carson, Rene Dubos, Dave Foreman, Aldo Leopold and Arne Naess. In its modern form seen as concerned with deforestation, nuclear power, oil crisis, pollution, species loss and tribal land rights, it is seen as including animal welfare, bioregionalism, deep/social ecology, eco-feminism, green politics, process philosophy and wildlife conservation, creating a discourse of 'the environment' and a 'green ideology' of aesthetic appreciation for nature, concern with quality of

life and long-term sustainability, preference for decentralization and simplicity, and stress on intuition, relationship and spirituality (see Dobson 2000; Drysek 2005; Guha 2000; Nash 1989; Oelschlaeger 1994; Pepper 1996; Szerszynski 2005).

[9] Organic, or 'organismic', ideas relate to 'Gaia', initially James Lovelock's hypothesis seeing the earth as a self-regulating interdependent organism but increasingly an ecological world-view incorporating goddess spirituality, seeing the earth as a mother, stressing partnership not hierarchy, eco-feminism, locating environmental degradation in (rational, dominant) male thinking and providing alternative female (intuitive, relational) thinking, autopoietic ethics, seeing individual interest lying within the whole, humanity coevolving with nature (see Lovelock, J. E. *Gaia: A New Look at Life on Earth* (Oxford: Oxford University Press, 1979); Primavesi, A. *Sacred Gaia: Holistic Theology and Earth System Science* (London and New York: Routledge, 2000); Ruether 1992).

[10] A distinction is made between 'radical' and 'reform' environmentalism, the former stressing long-term personal and social change, the latter short-term management of nature. For Taylor (2005b) radical environmentalists (e.g. animal rights, eco-feminism, eco-psychology, Gaia, green anarchy, nature mysticism) critique dominant systems that exploit nature, aiming to care for it. Deep ecology is particularly associated with it, seeing nature as intrinsically valuable, humans embedded in it, stressing wide identification and self-realization, recognizing the whole as greater than the sum of its parts, seeing nature as self (embracing intuition/spirituality) (see Devall and Sessions 1985; Dobson 2000; Drysek 2005; Nash 1989; Pepper 1996; Taylor 1996).

[11] Rockefeller (1992) sees convergence of deep ecology, feminism, holistic philosophies and religious traditions. Capra (1982) stresses Eastern religions, the new physics and systems science. Kinsley (1994) stresses the importance of Henry David Thoreau, John Muir, Murray Bookchin, Wendell Berry, Gary Snyder and Barry Lopez, seeing them as 'eco-visionaries'. Berry (1999:176–93) sees a fourfold 'wisdom': *indigenous*, intimate participation with nature; *women*, unity and maternal nourishing; *classical traditions*, revelatory experience of natural spirituality; and *science*, self-sustaining universe. Aldo Leopold's 'land ethic' is also seen as influential, stressing a weblike living earth and humanity needing to 'think like a mountain', from nature's point of view (see Dobson 2000; Foltz 2002b; Gottlieb 1996; Kinsley 1994; Nash 1989; Rockefeller 1992).

[12] Berman call this a 'Batesonian holism' world-view, following the ideas of anthropologist Gregory Bateson (see *Steps to an Ecology of the Mind*, London: Paladin, 1973).

[13] Berry (with Brian Swimme) envisions the 'universe story' of evolution evoking belonging and shared perception, stressing the universe as multiform yet interconnected (possibly with purpose, for example, anthropic principle), based on sacrificial creation, reality being creative mutuality, humanity's natural emergent role being to intuitively bring the universe to self-awareness (see Swimme, B., and Berry, T. *The Universe Story: From the Primordial Flaring Forth to the Ecozoic Era. A Celebration of the Unfolding of the Universe*, New York: HarperSan Francisco, 1992).

14 Ecologism is seen as radical environmentalism with a spiritual component. Dobson (2000) sees roots in ecological sentiments of the Palaeolithic/Neolithic, nineteenth-century scientific rationalism and romantic arcadianism, and the 1960s/70s ecology movement, as well as the organic holism of deep ecology, Gaia, and the new physics (see Kassmann 1997; Pepper 1996).

15 Referenced to Morgan, G., *Images of Organization* (London: Sage Publications, pp. 13, 336).

Chapter 2

Religious Environmentalism: Reimagining and Revitalizing Nature and Religion

An environmental need for religion

[T]he environmental crisis . . . has a spiritual and religious dimension and is the result of the forgetting of certain perennial truths which . . . traditional humanity always had . . . looking at the world of nature as a sacred presence . . . Without resuscitation of this religious and metaphysical view of nature, everything else we say about the environmental crisis is just cosmetics and politics. We have to experience the profound rebirth of our conception of the world as temenos, *a sacred precinct.*

(Nasr 2002:118–19, 135)

[T]he ecological crisis is pre-eminently a spiritual crisis of the greatest magnitude. Its resolution depends on a . . . profound reshaping of how we think and live so that we may deepen our kinship with all life, create a new vision of human presence within the Earth community, and craft new patterns of ecological wholeness and human justice . . . understanding the spiritual dimension of the environmental crisis [is] a matter of great urgency.

(Hull 1993:7–8)

The environmental crisis is seen as a moral and spiritual issue, a result of (modern) meanings and values, as much as (forming the basis for) economic or technological actions. As Northcott (2000:168) argues 'worship . . . is at the heart of [the] crisis . . . the modern devotion to the cult of consumerism . . . is driving [it]' while, for DeWitt (2002:45), '[the] crisis is an outward manifestation of a crisis of mind and spirit . . . concerned with the kind of creatures we are and what we must become in order to survive'.[1] Thus what is seen as needed is moral and spiritual reorientation, counterbalancing modern moral and spiritual disorientation. As Brockelman (1997:39–40) puts it, seeing environmental problems resulting from a modern 'spiritual world-view', 'spiritual fire must be fought with spiritual fire' with an alternative spiritual vision needing to be constructed as a base for new environmental ethics. Thus, for Rockefeller

(1992:147), the 'spiritual quest of our time' is to critique and transform modern egocentric attitudes of greed and domination and create community with nature, what Gardner (2006) sees as redefining progress from material gain to harmony with nature and Gottlieb (2006a) as spiritual goals replacing material goals. Thus, for Carroll et al. (1997:4):

> Environmental issues demand both spiritual and moral consideration . . . We need to get our bearings again: ecologically, ethically, and spiritually . . . we will be safer and better served if instead of ecological anxiety we advocate a positive position of moral responsibility founded on a spiritual sense of our role and place within the deeper and encompassing reality of nature. We need an ecology of wonder and enchantment, a spiritual awareness of the intrinsic value or epiphany that nature manifests and the proper sense of gratitude, humility and awe that goes with it.

In this sense, it has been argued that religion, with its diversity of world-views, its recognition of and encounter with the moral and spiritual nature of the world, interrelating God, humans and nature, can be useful in addressing environmental issues and stimulating a new environmental consciousness.[2] As Gardner (2006:6) argues 'we need a transformation of mind and heart, desire and intention . . . a sense of mystery and humility, gratitude and celebration. We need what some might call healthy religious wisdom.'[3] And, for Palmer and Finlay (2003:xv), 'We see, do, and are what we think, and what we think is shaped by our cultures, faiths and beliefs . . . [thus if] environmentalists [need] a framework of values and beliefs . . . where better to turn . . . than . . . the original multinationals . . . the major religions of the world?' Religion, then, is seen as able to challenge modern views and provide new or (reinterpreted) traditional ones, transforming human consciousness, stimulating the embracing and protecting, not rejecting and degrading, of nature.

> Where are we to find people who love life in all its forms enough not only to sound warnings but also to heed them and to turn the ship toward safe waters? Where might we find those with the sensitivity toward nature in all its miraculous forms, a reverence and concern for all of creation deep and broad enough to overcome its casual destruction for abysmally self-centred and limited human concerns? Where else, indeed, might we find such people but in our churches, synagogues, mosques, and ashrams where creation is thought to be holy . . . Without the passion and discipline of religious life, it may be impossible actually to alter our behavior toward the environment. (Carroll et al. 1997:2)

> [T]he spiritual dimension of life provides a relatively untapped reservoir of wisdom, imagination and strength for meeting the challenge of a damaged

Earth and for calling humanity into a new relationship with the natural order . . . [offering] the depth needed to understand the crisis, the courage to confront destructive patterns, the commitment and staying power to engage the crisis over the long haul, and a hopeful spirit from which a new and sustainable culture may be born . . . [a] depth of insight into what has gone wrong, and a greater wisdom as how now to act . . . a way of seeing and knowing [surpassing] conventional understanding. (Hull 1993:7–8)

Religion – beliefs, communities, ethics, institutions, myths, rituals, symbols, texts, traditions – is seen to offer reservoirs of commitment, imagination and wisdom, applicable to environmental issues. Religious traditions are seen as having large bases of adherents and organizational resources (most people in the world still living their lives within religious world-views) as well as histories of ethical and social reflection (often forcing humanity to face up to its moral failings), stimulating empowerment, justice and social action (many revolutionary movements growing from religious circles). They are seen as providing linguistic, ritual and symbolic, frameworks, collective visions and legitimating narratives, grounding people within nature, creating knowledge about its and humanity's purpose and role. They are thus seen as having the charismatic power and moral authority and critical and prophetic potential to challenge destructive lifestyles, offer alternative visions, and stimulate change (alerting people to the ethical implications of environmental behaviour, providing celebration and worship at nature, as well as ideals and hope, overcoming apathy and despair). Religion, then, is seen as able to provide powerful, personal and social, metaphorical and practical, resources (which are seen as dynamic and open to change) for environmental engagement (Foltz 2002b; Gardner 2002, 2006; Gottlieb 1996, 2006a, 2006b; Hull 1993; Maguire 2000; Nasr 2002; Oelschlaeger 1994; Palmer and Finlay 2003; Rockefeller 1992, 1997; Taylor and Kaplan 2005; Tucker 2003, 2006; Tucker and Grim 2005).

In particular, it is stressed that religions are oriented to something other than egoism and materialism, seeing a point to life beyond accumulation, stressing the interdependence and spirituality of nature. For Maguire (2000) all religions have the same common starting point, an experience of wonder and reverence for the sanctity of life, stressing owing as much as owning, obligations as much as rights, a sense of the common good, stressing a communal 'we-self' rather than individualistic 'I-self'. Similarly, Rockefeller (1992, 1997) sees a religious quest to expand the self highlighting the Buddhist, Hindu and Jain, concept of *ahimsa* or not harming, Christianity emphasizing *agape* or love, Daoism connecting spirit and matter via a life-force, *qi*, Hinduism teaching that humanity and nature are interdependent parts of undifferentiated divine *Brahman*, Islam stressing a sacramental view of the world, emphasizing purity of heart, Jainism widening morality to include all life, and Judaism stressing the land as a divine gift and not destroying it. In this sense, religions are seen as stressing self-sacrificial virtues (e.g. asceticism, compassion, duty), encouraging cooperation not competition, having, for Gardner (2006), an influential power, one based on love, from the heart not the head, embracing deeper, emotional, experiential, imaginative, meaningful, knowledge, beyond rational ego (see DeWitt 2002b; Gardner 2002; Gottlieb 2006a, 2006b; Nasr 1996, 2002; Oelschlaeger 1994).

> It is the limitations and promptings of the heart that remind human beings of a better way, of ideal possibilities . . . It is through imaginative vision and the power of faith that people let go their egoism, overcome their fears, and commit themselves to the ideal . . . Faith has the power to take the self beyond itself to a new self . . . a change of heart . . . awakening to the needs and capacities of human nature for growth and for cooperating, sharing, loving, and creating. (Rockefeller 1992:168)

Religions are thus seen as providing what Gardner (2006:155) and Rue (2000:xiv) call 'wisdom traditions', comprehensive understandings of what nature (and humanity) is, what is/should be of value, what does/does not matter, exploring and answering questions that relate to the nature, purposes and possibilities, of life: Who are we? Why are we here? What are we doing? What is the world? What is our relation to the world? What are our powers or limits of our powers? They are seen to stress the order of nature, providing holistic awareness of the web of life (dependent on/in union with the divine), embedding humanity in a wider world of meaning and responsibility (translating nature's patterns into interpretative meanings, via ritual and symbol, providing orientation to life's continuity and change), defining nature, humanity and the human–nature relationship (as well as the divine, divine–nature, divine–human and divine–nature–human relationships) (Gardner 2002; Gottlieb 1996, 2006a, 2006b; Nasr 1996, 2002; Oelschlaeger 1994; Palmer and Finlay 2003; Parks 1993; Rockefeller 1992; Tucker 2006; Tucker and Grim 2005). As Brockelman argues (1999:20) 'the great spiritual traditions urge us to see a more ultimate and meaningful reality beyond the individual . . . Brahman, the Tao, the Dharmakaya . . . the Trinity'. For Tucker (2002b:73–4), religion is thus a means of cosmological orientation and ethical relationship, revealing (the human place in) the patterning of life:

> This patterning is called by many names . . . In Hinduism and Buddhism, it is *Dharma*, or law; in Confucianism, it is *Li*, or principle; in Taoism, it is the *Tao*, or the way . . . Religions thus mediate between the patterns of nature and those of the individual by creating stories of our origins, rituals to ensure continuity through the various stages of life from birth to death, and codes of behaviour that aim to maximise harmonious relations and thus

survival itself . . . connecting self, society, nature, and the larger field of being in which they exist.

For Oelschlaeger (1994), religion is the only widely available (influential) discourse able to challenge the modern world-view. Whereas the latter (what he sees as a rational-based consensus, including the official definition of environmentalism), expresses a final vocabulary that closes rather than opens discourse about caring for creation, the common good being individual and consumerist, biased towards physical problems with human ramifications, religious discourse is seen as expressing a vocabulary (seen as able to adapt to change yet remain consistent with tradition) that opens discourse about caring for creation, the common good being about person-in-community, quality not quantity of life. Similarly, for Nasr (1996:272–3), only religion can challenge what he sees as the 'misdirecting of the yearning of the soul', the decentring of humanity in modernity (its alienation from nature). Such a yearning, for the absolute and infinite, he sees at the core of humanity and when denied to the divine (as in modernity) becomes absolutized in humanity itself (man the measure of all things), seeking the infinite in the finite, changing the direction of progress away from the soul journeying to God to materialism. Satisfying spiritual creativity, in this scheme, thus becomes unsatisfying invention, a need for material accumulation and transformation. Only religion, for Nasr, can redirect humanity away from this and back towards the former, creating a (spiritually) humble rather than (anthropocentrically) hubristic attitude: 'Only religion can discipline the soul to live more ascetically, to accept the virtue of simple living and frugality . . . [revealing] the relativity of man'.

Religions are thus seen as able to provide resources to conceptualize environmental issues and deal with them, opening up a critical personal and social space to discuss nature and humanity's place and role within it (asking 'what' or 'why' questions – what is progress, why is it as it is – rather than 'how' questions – how can something be achieved). In particular, they are seen as able to provide a new evocative and influential religious-ecological (ecotopian) language, able to 'reimagine' nature and humanity and their relationship, creating epiphanies of a larger reality and deepening the moral sensitivity to nature that is seen as needed to change human thought and behaviour and overcome environmental problems. As Palmer and Finlay (2003:51) argue 'it is by telling . . . stories that religions are . . . most persuasive and positive in protecting the environment, both by reminding people of the right way of doing things and by promoting a greater sense of responsibility for natural resources'. Thus, for Tucker (2003:35:108–9):

[R]eligions can play a vital [ecological] role . . . providing both spiritual resources and . . . culturally particular but globally comprehensive environmental ethics. Of particular relevance here are the common concerns of *reverence* for the Earth, *respect* for other species, *responsibility* to the welfare of future generations, *restraint* in the consumption of resources, and *redistribution* of goods and services more equitably . . . religious traditions can help to unlock [a] language of dialogue with the Earth and for the Earth. For buried deep within [their] symbol systems and ritual practices . . . is a language of connection to the spiritual dimensions of nature . . . with [their] help . . . a new kind of listening to the Earth is at hand . . . [enabling] humans to join the great community of life . . . [responding with] gratitude for the gift of life.

Religion in the modern world: Decline or (green) revitalization

For Tucker (2002b:65), then, 'the moral force of religion may be instrumental in alerting people to the . . . implications of what we are doing to the planet, by unbridled industrialisation'. This – what Kalland (2005) sees as the 'religious environmentalist paradigm',[4] the appeal to religion to engage and solve environmental problems – may be so but there may inherent difficulties in this project. Religion may no longer have the moral or social capital to effect such change. It is seen as challenged and in decline in the modern world, its meanings subsumed and no longer relevant within the modern world-view and its institutions losing control of social life to modern bodies. This, the so-called secularization debate, ideology, myth, paradigm or thesis (in its basic, strongest, form) sees religion as formerly central in peoples lives, a sacred canopy providing private and public meaning and influence, until, with the advent of the Reformation, Enlightenment, Scientific Revolution and Industrialization (modernity essentially), it became challenged (seen as false, irrational, undemocratic or dangerous) and replaced with secular beliefs and practices. Religious institutions thus are said to have lost and are still losing their followers, their doctrines, rituals and symbols, losing prestige and significance, at most demoted to the private sphere with no social significance (see Beyer 1994; Bruce 1996; Casanova 1994; Davie 2000; Hamilton 1995; McGuire 1997; Norris and Ingelhart 2004; Woodhead and Heelas 2000).

Such a challenge to religion is seen in terms of several interconnected areas: *differentiation* sees modern society having specialized spheres and religion rather than being encompassing is separated from medicine, politics or science, with limited influence, no longer a taken for granted authority but having to compete for it (voluntarily chosen or rejected); *rationalization* sees increasing emphasis on functional means–ends rationality and weakening of religion's plausibility (no place for mystery, the supernatural, i.e., the disenchanted iron cage of economic rationalism); *privatization* sees differentiated spheres relegated to private space, losing public influence, religion being merely a form of self-expression (believing but not belonging). Such ideas, however, may not be so simple or clear-cut. There is no doubt that major religious changes have been and are occurring. Religion (especially in the West) is different than formerly. It has been challenged by new personal and social ideas and its linkages to personal and social life are changing (it has lost some significance, in differing contextual ways). However, this does not necessarily mean a linear progression of a monolithic 'secularization' replacing a monolithic 'religion'. Many theories now recognize that secularization is a more complex, and not inevitable or irreversible, process, part of religious change. Some reject the term altogether because of this. Similarly, some critique the concept of religion (hence 'spirituality' is often evoked as a more usable, broad, dynamic, concept). A golden age of religion may never have existed and neither is modernity necessarily a secular golden age. The concepts, as well as the actualities, are more complex and dynamic. Religion and secularization may thus be, and may have always been, part of a *process* of official and unofficial, private and public, actions at particular times in particular places (Bruce 1996; Casanova 1994; Hamilton 1995; McGuire 1997; Norris and Ingelhart 2004; Woodhead and Heelas 2000).

What is known as 'religion' (or the 'secular'), as a coherent encompassing project, is an invention, its genealogy being, for Asad (1993), a Western political mythology, part of Enlightenment classification, paralleling the invention of liberal European identity aiming to create a universalized means of comparing systems of beliefs independent of context and which became the dominant definition via European expansion, subsuming non-Western, views (emerging in the fifteenth century as a universal impulse (*religio*, opposed to communities of believers) and developing, via the 'wars of religion' in the sixteenth and seventeenth centuries, into ideas of formalized beliefs separated from the state, to allow freedom and avoid violence; thus political religion was/is seen as intolerant). In this sense, also, non-Western religions may be seen as Western inventions: 'Buddhism', 'Confucianism', 'Daoism' or 'Hinduism', for example, may be imposed concepts, universalizing diverse, fluid, phenomena: Masuwaza (2005) sees the genealogy of global religion involving orientalist Enlightenment knowledge categorizing peoples into Christians, Jews, Mohammedans and Heathens, or Western (reason) and Eastern (tradition), great tradition (major religions) and little tradition (indigenous traditions), forms or, latterly, 'world religion' forms of Buddhism, Christianity, Confucianism, Daoism, Hinduism, Indigenous Traditions, Islam, Jainism, Judaism, Shinto, Sikhism and Zoroastrianism. Non-Western societies, of course, may not have experienced this religious history and may not see religion in this way (being more practically/politically inclined in their beliefs) and thus may challenge the Western model. Thus what may be needed are more open-ended, fluid concepts and stress on the contextual dynamics of religious change, where it is waxing and where waning, where influential and where not, and why. This does not mean that the concepts of 'religion', 'secularization' or 'world religions', may not still be useful analytical categories and meaningful social forms, they may be, but that they need to be used carefully and reflexively, with awareness of their biases and limitations as well as their creative and transformational abilities and lived experience (see Bowen 1998; Bruce 1996; Casanova 1994; Clarke and Byrne 1998; Connolly 1999; McGuire 1997; Thomas 2005).[5]

The religious and the secular, then, are context dependent concepts, part and parcel of the modern world-view (similar to the Western idea of nature) and are increasingly being reassessed (in a fragmenting 'post-modern' world challenging meta-narratives and highlighting creativity). In this sense, some arguments stress that 'desecularization' may be occurring, religion challenging secular developments or existing alongside them in a bricolage of socio-cultural forms. Woodhead and Heelas (2000), for example, see *secularization*, religious disappearance and/or privatization, and *detraditionalization*, internalization of authority/faith, occurring alongside *universalization*, an ecumenical, inclusive, quest for the sameness, recognizing the common value of religions, and *sacralization*, a revitalization of religion and re-enchanted conversion of the secular realm, dependent on circumstances. They thus see coexisting religious forms: *religions of difference*, distinguishing between divine, humanity and nature, tradition-based, stressing this-worldly asceticism, prescribed worship and political mobilization (e.g. charismatic, fundamentalist); *religions of humanity*, balancing divine, humanity and nature, tolerant and universalizing, stressing individual experience and critique of authority (e.g. liberal denominationalism); and *spiritualities of life*, asserting identity between divine, humanity and nature, stressing natural/spiritual order and transformative experience (e.g. New Age). Similarly, Beyer (2003:54–8) sees: *organized religion*, stressing rules and structures, articulating a clear purpose (e.g. Catholicism, Sufi brotherhoods); *politicized religion*, using the state to enforce religious precepts and practices, making it central in life (e.g. Israel, Muslim countries); *social movement religion*, amorphous, episodic, non-authoritarian, challenging existing social arrangements (e.g. New Age); and *communitarian/individualistic religion*, contextual, implicit, forms, without clear organization (e.g. indigenous, secular). There may be a lot of ferment here then, then, with no monolithic understanding or practise of religion, this providing a context where diverse religious forms can thrive (or be recognized) (see Beyer 1994; Casanova 1994, Hamilton 1995; Hervieu-Leger 2000; Norris and Ingelhart 2004; Szerszynski 2005).

Religion, then, may still survive, inspiring personal and social beliefs and identities (or in Davie's (2000) and Hervieu-Leger's (2000) terms 'memories'[6]), albeit in more diverse and dynamic forms than previously thought. What is seen as a 'worldwide resurgence' or restructuring of religion's role in modern global society may be particularly occurring as modernity may have deleterious personal and social (environmental) effects evoking and requiring moral response while isolating individuals from the moral resources needed to achieve this (inhibiting other moral viewpoints, for example, religious ones). For example, ideas of 'ethical religion' or 'world theology' posit that religion might coalesce around and provide answers to global ethical issues, such as environmental degradation (or injustice, poverty), that modernity might create or fail to adequately deal with. Such ideas see religions undertaking a transsocial role defining and maintaining the global common good, becoming resources for re-creating private beliefs (e.g. existentially reconnecting individuals to nature) and publicly addressing issues (e.g. environmental degradation). In this scheme, then, religions may critique, negotiate or reject the legitimacy of modern ideals and structures and provide alternative ones in a moral and political contestation (capitalizing on a loss of faith in modern reason-based structures), gaining legitimacy and influence via a discursive space of public interaction, forcing modern society to reflect on itself. Hence, they may play an important role in the ongoing construction of the world, enabling its discontents to be addressed, providing alternatives that ethically unite humanity (possibly as a defence of traditional identities against market or state penetration or by maintaining the principle of the common good against individualism) (Beyer 1994; Casanova 1994; Davie 2000; Haynes 1998; Hervieu-Leger 2000; Thomas 2000, 2005; Woodhead and Heelas 2000). As Thomas argues:

> Religion and spirituality rather than becoming marginal and vestigial are moving to the centre of our cultural preoccupations because of the social and political crisis in the secular liberal state, disillusionment with a world based on science, technology and bureaucratic rationality . . . [This] is part of a broader shift towards a 'post-materialistic' politics, often expressed by the new social movements, including religious ones, and a new 'politics of meaning' that has tried to link religious and spiritual concerns with social and economic ones (2000:48) . . . What is called political religion or politicized religion emerges out of a perceived failure of secular, state-run, nationalism to produce democracy, and the failure of the neo-liberal prescription of free markets and open economies, which produced more inequality than development . . . It marks the end of a certain kind of modern faith in the idea of progress, and an optimism about the ability of science and technology to solve the problems created by the modern world. (2005:41–2)

For Beyer (1990, 1994), such religious action allows religion to move out of its privatized sphere by providing an indispensable service to the whole of society. That this can occur is because, for Beyer, religion, despite being a differentiated subsystem in modernity, is potentially applicable to everything, being holistic rather than specialist. So although without direct influence, being generally relevant to all situations but specifically relevant to few, it is able to influence society indirectly, prophetically and reflexively addressing holistic matters that are excluded by other subsystems, problems they create without solving, ones which are not inherently religious but require religious thought and action (environmental, personal or social, discontents). For Beyer, this links religious function (private belief) and performance (public practice) by tying global public issues to deeper religious values and meanings, providing a service that is necessary for everyone but which is also essentially religious. Hervieu-Leger (2000) sees such modern discontents enabling religion the space to revitalize itself as 'utopian spaces', moral and spiritual spaces for meaning created by modernity's corrosion of the traditional religious base, that modernity itself, concerned only with rational, economic or technological, progress, is unable to fill. Such utopian spaces, then, are where the limits of modernity's vision lie, where it is unable to provide meaningful guidance (at least morally/spiritually) but where religion (in new reassessed forms) concerned with meaning, morals and spirituality, can. The crises, dislocation and uncertainties, the unfulfilled desires, created by modernity thus invoke appeals to utopian imagination, a rethinking of humanity's place and purpose, which religion is able to provide (see Davie 2000; Levitas 1990).[7]

For Beyer (1990, 1992, 1994), environmentalism is one such way – one utopian space – where religion can influence the modern world and become revitalized. Environmental issues, for Beyer, provide an arena for religious expression through being not only matters of public concern but also indicators of deeper malaise, modernity's moral/spiritual vacuum, concretizing its problematic effects as not just specific destructive activities but a consequence of all human activity, something that religion, concerned with meaningful, holistic, cosmic order and root indeterminacy of human activity and its consequences, is used to addressing (giving meaning to and promising the power to overcome problems through circumventing the everyday and indicating the transcendent which is not subject to indeterminacy). Thus religion may be able to place environmental issues in a wider frame of reference, linking them to the production of values, and provide a basis to resolve them. Assuming a priestly and prophetic role it may be able to present them as the results of disordered or unjust human relations and provide the ideological and organizational resources to conceptualize and deal with them, providing a viable self-conception of global society (in relation to the transcendent and cosmic order). In this way, for Beyer, religion may (once again) become a source of collective obligation and regain moral and social capital such that deviation from its norms will bring negative (environmental and by association human) consequences (for religious and non-religious alike) while action in accordance with them will be positive and legitimate (essential for the environment and human society).

[E]nvironmental problems present a clear performance possibility for religion and religious professionals in particular: threats to the ozone layer or to species habitats are results of the operation of the more dominant global instrumental systems. Religion, it would seem, might be able to provide a message that addresses the root causes of these problems. Ecological crisis . . . may be that which brings even the non-believers to hear the new religious message or the revitalized old one . . . [and] it might be argued that the purely . . . functionally religious, is a necessary component for solving the problems . . . the production and elaboration of ethical principles necessary for meeting the problem of environmental degradation may be accomplished via the complex of beliefs, practice, social networks, and organizations that historically constitute differentiated and institutionalized religion. (Beyer 1994:220, 222)

To adequately achieve this religious traditions are seen as needing to reinterpet themselves in more environmentally consciousness ways, to enter what Tucker (2003:9) calls an 'ecological phase', expanding concern from God–human and human–human relations to human–nature (and God–human–nature) ones. Judeo-Christianity, for example, or one Western interpretation of it (following Genesis (1.26–8), where humanity is to 'have dominion' and 'subdue' nature), most influentially for Lynn White (1967), has been seen as anti-environmentalist through anthropocentric views, promoting what Callicott (1997:15) terms a 'mastery' or 'despotic' interpretation where humanity, made in God's image, is encouraged to see itself as above nature and allowed or expected to dominate and exploit it. It is thus thought to have established the hierarchical dualism of humanity and nature, humanity's home being with God in Heaven not with the rest of creation, celebrating difference and superiority not similarity and equality, seeing salvation for humanity alone, setting the metaphysical foundations for environmentally destructive behaviour (this leading to much environmentalism seeing religion as part of the problem and shunning its ideas).

These may be biased or limited interpretations based on a few lines of Scripture, ignoring interpretations stressing God sustaining nature, human responsibility for it, or the need to overcome sinful humanity (e.g. Genesis 2, stressing humanity is from the earth, to care for it in a stewardship; or injunctions not to destroy or waste it). A different or more complete reading may thus produce more nuanced understandings. White (1967) himself sees religion as part of the solution to the environmental crisis (his desire being to reform not destroy it), arguing for alternative Christian interpretations, in particular, stressing the compassion and respect for nature of St Francis of Assisi, proposing him as a patron saint of ecologists.[8] Nevertheless, it may be that religion, if not a direct cause of environmental problems, may have been an implicit influence on the modern world-view (and part of its Western universalist conceptions, excluding much unofficial 'nature religion') and may also have concentrated on human issues to the exclusion of nature, been a conservative societal force, protective of power and prestige, or been late in engaging environmental issues (not adequately wearing its critical countercultural mantle of the prophet). It has been argued, then, that it may need to embrace nature and environmentalism more directly (Berry 2000; Callicott 1997; Gardner 2002,

2006; Gottlieb 2006a; Kinsley 1994; Nash 1989; Oelschlaeger 1994; Sideris 2006; Tucker 2003, 2006; Tucker and Grim 2005; Whitney 2005).

Such religious environmental awareness (i.e. 'eco-theology') has been growing during a period Nash (1989) terms the 'greening' of religion. He traces this to (Christian) recognition of stewardship, the idea that humanity is given responsibility to care for creation, to St Benedict of Nursia, practising an ethical attitude to nature, to St Francis, seeing life-forms as siblings, glorifying God, including them in spiritual fellowship, to John Ray and Alexander Pope, in the seventeenth century, and Henry David Thoreau, John Muir, Edward Evans and Liberty Hyde Bailey, in the nineteenth and twentieth centuries, critiquing anthropocentrism, seeing humanity accountable to God for its treatment of creation, and to Walter Lowdermilk, in the 1930s, using stewardship to rationalize the conservation movement, making it a moral matter, seeing religion central to environmental ethics (adding an 'Eleventh Commandment' stressing human responsibility for nature). More recent influences, for Nash, include Joseph Sittler, in the 1950s, proposing a 'Theology for Earth', seeing nature created by and with potential for God's grace, Richard Baer, in the 1960s, stressing prophetic challenge to nature's exploitation, seeing it belonging to God not humanity, and the US Council of Churches, Faith-Man-Nature Group, analysing humanity's relationship to nature in light of religion, promoting ethical imperatives for conservation, especially Paul Santmire's idea of the Kingdom of God supporting ethical extension, God as ruler being interested in the care of His natural subjects, an expanded morality also seen in John Cobb Jr and Charles Birch's ideas, influenced by Alfred North Whitehead and Pierre Teilhard de Chardin's process philosophy, seeing nature as dynamic, God infused interactions, not inert matter. Alongside these developments, Nash sees recognition of wider, possibly greener, religious viewpoints (Eastern, indigenous):[9] for example, Buddhist, Daoist, Hindu and Jain, rejection of anthropocentrism and dualism and stress on holistic existence, self realized in the whole, with nature significant, imbued with spirit; Gary Snyder's combined Buddhist/Native American ethic and poetic advocacy of nature's rights, including it in a moral community/social contract, stressing intimacy with it, seeing plants and animals as 'people' to be accorded a voice, limiting egoism, stressing custodianship (see Nasr 1996).[10]

In line with such ideas Taylor (2001a, 2001b, 2004, 2005a, 2006), and Taylor and Kaplan (2005) highlight the growth of 'nature religion' or nature-based spiritualities, what Taylor (2004:991) sees as 'nature-related religious production': (diverse, often contested) religious perceptions and practices characterized by a reverence for or worship of nature, taking it as a symbolic centre and/ or considering it sacred. These are traced to romanticism, the early conservation movement, early anthropology, process philosophy, and the 'greening' of the 1960s/70s (when the term 'nature religion' began to be employed), being seen as either primitive or dangerous (experiential/oriental/polytheistic

not rational/occidental/monotheistic) or spiritually authentic and ecologically beneficent (an antidote to modernity's moral/spiritual malaise, stressing
ethical obligations towards nature)). More recent developments are seen in
a proliferation of 'pagan environmentalism', a bricolage of countercultural,
earth-based, spirituality movements sharing a sense of connection to nature
and of ultimate meaning and transformative power in it (influenced by
ancient primal religion based on personal experiences fostering bonding with
it). Taylor (2004:992–1005, 2006:597–604) sees such 'green religion' split into
three areas: *environmentally concerned world religions* aiming to identify environmental obstacles or resources in religious traditions and promote their environmentally friendly behaviour, either by defending them as providing green
alternatives or acknowledging their environmental culpability and advancing
ideas for green reform of them; *'nature-as-sacred' religions*, covering paganism, indigenous traditions and New Age spirituality, seeing a sacred earth,
worthy of care and reverence, stressing consciousness change and ecological
resistance movements; and post- or non-supernaturalistic *'spiritualities of connection' to nature*, based on evolutionary science (that erodes supernaturalistic
beliefs), stressing a plausible cosmology evoking awe and belonging in relation
to nature.

In this sense, then, Taylor (2004) posits a possible green future for religion
with religious traditions becoming more environmentally friendly and possibly a civic planetary 'earth religion' developing. In particular, to consolidate
and further this 'religious greening' or 'religious-ecological phase' there has
arisen what has been described as a 'field of religion and ecology', an academic, religious and social, movement that seeks to enable the exploration
and promotion of eco-religious ideas to be located and carried out, spiritual
awareness of nature deepened, and religious-ecological activism encouraged
(something covering all of the nature religions mentioned above but perhaps
most (or initially) concerned with environmentally concerned world religions)
(see Gottlieb 2006b; Taylor 2005a, 2005c; Taylor and Kaplan 2005b; Tucker
2003; Tucker and Grim 1997, 2001, 2005).

The field of religion and ecology: Exploring and encouraging eco-religious views and actions

The field of religion and ecology is a range of ideas and initiatives, incorporating religious traditions, new religious movements and environmental
movements, that is coalescing (or being created) into a recognized religious
and social form, a religious-ecological movement (what Gottlieb (2006a:113,
117) sees as 'religious environmentalism': a 'worldwide movement of political,
social, ecological, and cultural action'), aimed at nurturing (spiritually) ecological humans, preventing harmful ecological practices and effecting new

ones. To name but a few major recent influences on and actions within it (see Bassett et al. 2000; Berry 2000; Gardner 2002, 2006; Gottlieb 2006a; Taylor 2005a, 2005c; Tucker 2003, 2006; Tucker and Grim 1997, 2001, 2005):

- Activities since the 1970s by the World Council of Churches: for example, the 1975 call to establish a just, participatory and sustainable, society; the 1979 conference on faith, science and the future, calling for new biblical interpretations of nature and human dominion; the 1983 assembly on justice, peace and the integrity of creation; the 1991 conference on the Holy Spirit renewing creation; the 1992 call for eco-justice; the 2000 World Peace Summit of Religious and Spiritual Leaders, calling for an ethic of global stewardship.
- Activities by the United Nations Environment Programme; for example, the Environmental Sabbath initiative, from 1984, aiming to create a renewing rest day for the earth; the Interfaith Partnership for the Environment, from 1986, a global network of faith traditions working to bring together the forces of religion and ecology; the International Seminar on Religion, Culture, and Environment, in 2001, elucidating interdenominational aspects of religion and ecology.
- World Wildlife Fund sponsored meetings in Assisi, in 1986, resulting in the Assisi Declarations, statements by religious traditions outlining their distinctive approaches to (care of) nature, stressing interconnectedness of religion and environmental concerns, seeing religious traditions stressing the dignity of nature and the duty to live harmoniously within it (and thus their value in re-establishing ecological harmony; see WWF 1986).
- Global Forums of Spiritual and Parliamentary Leaders, from 1988 to 1993, especially the 1990 statement 'Preserving and Cherishing the Earth: An Appeal for Joint Commitment in Science and Religion' stressing that environmental problems demand a broad religious as well as scientific perspective: 'As scientists [we] have had profound experiences of awe and reverence before the universe. We understand that what is regarded as sacred is more likely to be treated with care and respect' (Tucker and Grim 2005:2612).
- The 1991 'Joint Appeal in Religion and Science: Statement by Religious Leaders at the summit on the Environment' aiming to enhance collaborative religious and scientific environmental participation, seeing a prophetic responsibility to communicate stewardship; the 1992 'World Scientists Warning to Humanity' also called for environmental cooperation of business, science and religion, stressing the need for an earth-ethic.
- Activities, since 1991, by the Religion and Ecology Group of the American Academy of Religion, both academic analysis and normative ethics, reconfiguring religions to promote sustainable lifestyles (stressing preservation of nature as a sacred duty), revitalizing 'eco-friendly' indigenous religions, and stimulating new religious-ecological movements.

- Activities by the Islamic Foundation for Ecology and Environmental Sciences, the US National Religious Partnership for the Environment (Coalition on the Environment and Jewish life, Evangelical Environmental Network, National Council of Churches Eco-Justice Working Group, US Conference of Catholic Bishops) and the Parliament of World Religions (statement of Global Ethics of Cooperation of Religions on Human and Environmental Issues).
- The 1994 Evangelical Declaration on the Care of Creation, asserting that the earth belongs to God and that humanity is responsible to Him for it, reaffirming the Christian doctrine of stewardship, seeing environmental degradation as a sign of the limits of creation, with a need to repent of destructive attitudes and centre on faith.
- Activities since 1995 by the Alliance of Religions and Conservation, stimulated by the Assisi meetings, that aims to help religions develop environmental programmes through their beliefs ('sacred gifts'; for example, Sacred Gifts for a Living Planet conference in 2000), seeing them sharing the belief that nature is sacred and needing re-enchantment and responsible care.[11]
- Declarations by the Dalai Lama, Ecumenical Patriarch Bartholomew I (stressing natural destruction as 'ecological sin'), and Pope John Paul II (calling for 'ecological conversion'), in the Religion, Science and Environment, Symposia from 1994 to 2002, as well as other initiatives by them.
- Religious input in the UN-stimulated Earth Charter in 2000 (religion and ecology academic/activist Mary Evelyn Tucker being a member of the drafting committee), stressing ethical principles aimed at guiding humanity toward a sustainable future via a shared vision of living with reverence for the mystery of being, gratitude for the gift of life and humility concerning the human place in nature.[12]
- The creation of the Canadian Forum on Religion and Ecology to explore religious ethics, texts and world-views, in order to broaden understanding of the complex nature of environmental concerns within the Canadian context and promoting ecologically sustainable living.[13]
- Initiatives such as: Eco-Justice Ministries, encouraging churches to promote environmental sustainability;[14] GreenFaith, encouraging diverse spiritualities to rediscover the sacred in nature;[15] Religious Witness for the Earth, religiously oriented environmentalists, witnessing creation;[16] and Web of Creation, stressing personal/social transformation and eco-justice.[17]

Perhaps the most in-depth and influential recent engagement occurred from May 1996 to July 1998 in the Center for the Study of World Religions at Harvard University when a series of ten conferences under the title 'Religions of the World and Ecology' were organized, led by Mary Evelyn Tucker and John Grim. These involved the participation and collaboration of 600 scholars, religious leaders and environmental specialists, from around the world. Each conference covered a major religious tradition (Buddhism, Christianity, Confucianism, Daoism, Hinduism, Indigenous Traditions, Islam, Jainism, Judaism and Shinto) and explored it for images and views related to ecology. The aims were to provide a forum for reflection on reconceptualizing attitudes toward nature, stimulating the interest and concern of religious leaders, examining environmental perceptions of traditions (while recognizing cultural/historical complexity and context), identifying institutional grounds for change within them regarding attitudes to nature, and linking their transformative efforts to other ecological, economic, political or scientific, movements working towards global environmental ethics and aiming to reinvent industrial society (see Kalland 2005; Taylor 2004 2005c; Tucker 2003, 2006; Tucker and Grim 1997, 2001, 2005).

Following these conferences, and arising out of their dialogue, the Forum on Religion and Ecology was initiated, in 1998 (now affiliated to more than 800 academics and activists worldwide), with primary goals of establishing religion and ecology as an area of study and encouraging the exploration of environmental ethics within religious traditions in order to broaden understanding of and engage the complex nature of environmental issues.[18] Seeing a growing realization that religion can make important contributions to environmentalism the Forum aims to highlight the roles that traditions can play in constructing moral frameworks and orientating narratives regarding human interactions with nature. It sees these, in varying ways, as containers of symbolic language evoking nature's processes and revering its rhythms and sees a need to bring these insights to bear environmentally, highlighting the religious re-visioning of human–earth relations. In line with such ideas its goals include: identifying ecological attitudes and practices within cosmology, ritual, sacrament and scripture, analysing commonalities and identifying common ground on which to base environmental ethics; fostering analysis, official statements and sacred texts, on and by traditions (and intersecting areas such as gender, economics, policy, science); and encouraging grassroots environmental action inspired by and using religion, its scriptures, symbols and rituals, what are called 'engaged projects'. Such ideas and actions, then, have been conceived as a way to deepen and expand religious discourse as well as contributing to environmental ethics, exploring and using religion to nurture and influence environmental consciousness (see Taylor 2005c; Tucker 2003; Tucker and Grim 1997, 2001, 2005). As Mary Evelyn Tucker and John Grim state:

> religions need to be involved with the development of a more comprehensive worldview and ethics to assist in reversing [environmental degradation] . . . the attitudes and values that shape people's concepts of nature come primarily from religious worldviews . . . The moral imperative and value systems of religions are indispensable in mobilizing the sensibilities of people toward

preserving the environment . . . How to utilize the insights of the world's religions is [thus] a task of formidable urgency. Indeed, the formulation of a new ecological theology and environmental ethic is already emerging from within several of the world's religions. Clearly each of the world's religious traditions has something to contribute to this discussion.[19]

Alongside these initiatives the most recent addition to the field and acting somewhat as a focal point and central text (alongside a book series based on the Harvard conferences[20]) is the *Encyclopedia of Religion and Nature*, coordinated by Bron Taylor, that aims to explore the relationships between humanity, religion and nature, examine religious perceptions of nature, and assess if and how religions might be reshaping the environmental landscape.[21] Main questions animating it include: What are the perception of religions towards the earth and have they promoted eco-friendly lifestyles or otherwise? Are religions being transformed by environmental concern and do eco-beliefs lead to eco-practices? Are religions resources or barriers to 'green' transformation? Does environmentalism influence religion or vice versa and how have religions influenced each other in an environmental sense? Can environmental movements be considered religious? What are the perceptions in nature and political ideologies that shape nature religions? What are the impacts of globalization on nature-related religion and behaviour? How are nature-related religions reshaping the ecological, political and religious, landscape? (Taylor and Kaplan 2005:vii–viii). The *Encyclopedia*, then, analyses, collates and promotes, the major debates, events, figures, groups, theories and traditions, within the field (covering a wide variety of subjects and comprehensive geographic and religious range, major world religions, new religious movements, new cosmologies, environmental movements, with contributions from academics, environmental activists, nature writers, religious thinkers, scientists). In a sense, it demarcates a territory, an emerging and evolving discipline, covering nearly all of what is termed 'religious environmentalism', aiming to promote critical inquiry into religion and ecology and investigate what might constitute ethically appropriate relationships between humans and the places, including the entire biosphere, that they inhabit.

Such initiatives aim to reclaim and reconstruct religious traditions or stimulate new ones so as to promote flourishing human–earth relations, encouraging and utilizing religion as a legitimate, meaningful and powerful, tool for inculcating ecological consciousness (while recognizing possible disjunction between its principles and practices). The methodology seen as needed to achieve this is a critical, creative and empathetic, interpretative 'retrieval' (of tradition, regarding human–earth relations), 're-evaluation' (in the contemporary environmental context), and 'reconstruction' (adapting tradition): the historical and textual investigation of cosmology and scripture, identifying ethical codes and ritual customs that pertain to ecology; evaluating relevance of traditions and/or ecumenically using them; and making an amalgam of new ideas activating human imagination towards celebrating life and participating in its flourishing (Tucker and Grim 1997, 2001, 2005). For Tucker (2003:36–49) this involves self-reflexively analysing and/or adapting myths, prayers, rituals, scriptures or symbols, something envisaged as involving 'creative tensions' in key areas, challenging and inspiring traditions: in *dogma* the tension involves orthodoxy and dialogue, the former being challenged via interreligious dialogue to embrace the common good of the planet; in *rituals and symbols* the tension involves tradition and transformation, stressing dynamic renewal of the former through reconnection to the reality of nature (e.g. reassessing 'ecological' rituals such as the connection of liturgical and natural cycles); in *moral authority* the tension involves oppression and liberation through stressing egalitarianism not dominance, creativity not conformity (e.g. widening rights to nature, highlighting its divine pattern); in *soteriology* the tension involves worldly and otherworldly views, a creative dialectic of intimacy and distance, world-affirming as much as world-negating, combining transcendence and immanence via the presence of the divine in nature; and in *ethics* the tension involves anthropocentric, eco-centric and anthropocosmic, views, enlarging ethical concerns from human justice to justice for nature, recognizing its intrinsic (God-given) value, and accepting humanity as a reciprocal participant it.

Religious traditions, then, in this sense, are seen as able to (and needing to) tap into or reinterpret their meaningful, persuasive, cosmological languages and provide new primary values and sources of social direction, new religious-ecological cosmologies, challenging modern ideas and actions, dynamizing human creativity towards realigning its role within nature, stimulating moral growth and providing new rationales for behaviour, defining new possibilities and limitations, implying or prescribing new ethical principles and actions. As Tucker argues:

A key component that has been missing in much environmental discourse is how to identify and tap into the cosmologies, symbols, rituals, and ethics that inspire changes in attitudes and actions for creating a sustainable future (2006:401) . . . religious traditions of the world are repositories of cosmological worldviews reflecting particular views of nature. Investigating these cosmologies is a critical task because they point toward ways in which different cultures have seen their embedded-ness in and responsibility toward nature [and] . . . may be significant in the formation of ethical attitudes of respect toward nature . . . [we need to] reclaim the voices of religions in understanding the sacred dimensions of nature, appreciating the rich creativity of nature's cosmological processes and identifying our special role in fostering this continuing creativity for a sustainable future. (2002b:66–8)

For Tucker (2003:51–2), the fundamental challenge for religious traditions in the present environmental context (and the aim of the field of religion and ecology, in a sense), is to awaken a renewed sense of reverence for nature as a valuable numinous matrix of mystery and activate depths of resonance in humanity that can respond to it in a benign, healing, manner; to, as she puts it, '[crack] open the shell of our anthropocentric selves and . . . move toward more expansive religious sensibilities that embrace [nature] . . . new configurations of tradition and modernity . . . [reviving] a sense of wonder and celebration . . . regarding life itself' (and in doing so revitalize religion). No one religious tradition or new movement, one privileged hegemonic world-view, is seen as appropriate, however (the problem being global and caused by hegemony). What is seen as needed are multireligious perspectives in dialogue, what Callicott (1997) describes as an 'orchestral' approach, a harmonious interaction of different religious viewpoints each expressing their own view but conducted to produce a grand religious-ecological score. The aim is not only to stimulate new ecologically based religious thinking within traditions, then, but also to create shared religious-ecological vocabularies and actions. There is seen a need for mutually enriching cross-cultural comparisons of religious concepts of nature, human nature and human–nature interaction, a diversity of views in communication, used in a self-reflective not self-promoting way (recognizing the special insights but also the limitations of traditions). In this way truth claims are seen as respected but different avenues to truth explored (traditions being seen as partners not definitive agents of moral authority), the common ground being the earth itself which as an expression of creativity and the sacred is also seen as the common good (Nasr 1996, 2002; Oelschlaeger 1994; Tucker 2003; Tucker and Grim 1997, 2001, 2005).

> [T]he world's religions would generally cohere in affirming that nature has a sacred element. At the same time, that affirmation would be based on quite different cosmologies and symbol systems. By the same token, if asked whether nature should be protected, the world's religions would generally answer affirmatively, but their environmental ethics would be distinctive in each case. For these reasons, if we are to move towards a global environmental ethic, as many suggest we should, it is crucial that we are attentive to this variegated perspective of religious and cultural particularity. Like a great stained glass window in which light shines through different colors, views of nature and environmental ethics appear in distinctive shades among the various world religions. However, the resulting mosaic of light may lend direction and inspiration for human endeavours toward a sustainable future. (Tucker 2002b:78)

Like the travelers in *The Canterbury Tales*, each of the religions of the world has a story to tell about life as it is and life as it can be. And each of those stories has hope for the human race and for our endangered home. We have nothing to fear and everything to gain from hearing one another's stories. (Maguire 2000:9)

The field of religion and ecology thus encourages and initiates the eco-logical reassessment of religious traditions, exploring their differing concepts of nature with the aim of challenging the modern world-view (and traditions themselves) and creating a new diverse, dialogic and imaginative, religious-ecological language, leading to new (common) ecological (benign) behaviours. Questions that have been posed to stimulate such religious-ecological imagin-ation include: What cosmological dimensions in traditions help relate humans to nature? How do traditions and sacred texts challenge or support nature as a resource? What core values within traditions might lead to an environmental eth-ics? Is it possible to identify responsible ecological practices within traditions? (Tucker and Grim 2001:4). The aim of this, then, is to identify and evaluate dis-tinctive ecological values in traditions as well as commonalities between them, and constructively use them to articulate a common desirable mode of human presence within nature (Tucker and Grim 1997). Such cross-cultural explor-ation and comparison of different religious imaginations of nature (and their reassertion as legitimate forms of knowledge, challenging the domination of the modern world-view), for Nasr (1996:3, 6–7, 9–10), is crucial:

A need exists to . . . carry out a comparative study of the 'Earths' of various religions . . . Each tradition has both a wealth of knowledge and experiences concerning the order of nature, which, once resuscitated, can bring about a situation in which religions all over the globe could mutually enrich each other and also cooperate to heal the wounds inflicted upon the Earth on the basis of a shared perspective of the sacredness of nature . . . Furthermore such a resuscitation would not only make possible the serious implementa-tion of ethical principles concerning nature, but it would also affect deeply many in the modern secularized West who are searching desperately for a spiritual relation with nature . . . There must be a rebirth of the religious knowledge of nature, the traditional cosmologies and sacred sciences . . . Moreover a nexus must be created in this realm among the traditions, as has been carried out by the traditional proponents of the perennial philosophy for understanding of the Divine Principle and its numerous manifestations in various religious universes. One might say that in the same way that there is a *philosophia perennis*, there is also a *cosmologia perennis*, which in fact con-stitutes one of its elements and which shines through the multifarious trad-itional sciences of the cosmos . . . As man succeeds in destroying so much of the order of nature . . . it becomes necessary to turn to the other 'Heavens' and 'Earths' that have defined over the ages the *modus vivendi* of the many 'humanities' which to an ever-greater extent are now unifying their efforts in the destruction of the natural order . . . it is essential to turn to sapiential and metaphysical teachings of the religions.

Such exploration, interpretation and comparison, follows the Western initi-ated 'world religions' format based on unified 'religious traditions' mentioned earlier which, as also mentioned, may be challenged (especially when consider-ing the interpretations of Eastern traditions which are quite diverse) (see Asad 1993; Masuzawa 2005; Snyder 2006). Taylor (2005c), for example, highlights the limitations of the Harvard conferences in this sense, arguing that their multireligious world may not fit into tidy 'world religions' categories, while also seeing a lack of inclusiveness, seeing much nature-related religiosity left out and mainstream sections of mainstream traditions favoured (this obscuring diversity of views, religious bricolage/hybridization, popular interpretations or creative innovation; Kalland (2005) also sees selective interpretations ignoring beliefs harmful to nature). The field of religion and ecology itself is aware of and acknowledges such issues, recognizing its Western genesis and academic base, that religion is a contested category, as well as cosmological, ecological, historical, individual and social, diversity within and between religious tradi-tions and their dynamism and fluidity. Nevertheless, it still sees a use for the concepts of 'religion' and 'world religions' in discussions on religion and ecol-ogy, seeing these as providing concrete meaningful bases through which to critique the modern world-view, engage environmental issues, and stimulate and locate new ideas (seeing this as a way to create new roles for old traditions, while recognizing that they need to be used in a broad, dynamic and reflexive, sense) (see Tucker 2003; Tucker and Grim 2001, 2005).

The Forum on Religion and Ecology acknowledges the difficulties in strictly defining many of the terms used in its discussions. For example, the term 'reli-gion' [has] . . . many uses and meanings. To a large extent 'religion' is framed here in terms of the particular 'world's religions' . . . Obviously . . . these . . . have their own in-determinant references, yet, it can be said that there are historical processes that are self-identified as 'Buddhist,' for example, or 'Christian' . . . These ever-changing religious traditions transmit narratives and written records of interactions between human communities and local ecosystems. It is in this sense that we speak of investigations into religion and ecology as revealing attitudes toward nature within the religions of the world. Moreover, as a project the Forum on Religion and Ecology is concerned with understanding how the contemporary world's religions respond to the cur-rent environmental crises . . . [emphasizing] that [they] have reflected on the interactions of the natural world in coherent, often symbolic, and ordered ways. Thus, these 'ecological' reflections . . . provide the basis both for dia-logue with other disciplines attempting to understand the environment, as well as a moral force addressing contemporary environmental degradation.[22]

In this sense, then, for the field, there are coherent religious traditions, even if their interpretations may have been somewhat Western influenced, and they mean something to people, they provide personal and social beliefs and identities, connecting different peoples to wider realities. They are not just academic concepts but concrete practical actualities enabling people to address each other, the world and new developments. Interpretations of them can be challenged and deconstructed, their limitations highlighted, but they can also be constructively used (and thus challenged and reconstructed). The field thus stresses constructive as much as deconstructive ideas and insights: it is in essence a hopeful, future-oriented movement as much as a critical, tradition-bound, one, recognizing that religion, being diverse and dynamic, is able to (and constantly does) engage new issues, reinterpreting beliefs and traditions, providing meaningful environmental, personal and social, guidance. Thus it sees new religious-ecological visions as being legitimate, as well as of practical importance, able to positively assist individuals to construct their/new social and environmental realities (and address modernity's environmental discontents).

The religious-ecological ideas expressed in the field, then, while recognizing context and diversity and the dangers of reappropriating traditions, show how religion is creatively being readdressed in the modern context, how religious individuals and traditions (which are fluid living traditions) may be reassessing their views, recovering forgotten ecological themes or stimulating new ones, reinventing traditions and/or creating new forms in response to environmental issues (and thereby adapting to or challenging modern forms, becoming privately and publicly re-empowered). Such religious-ecological interpretations, what I term religious ecotopias, are thus new religious forms, selective ecologically based and inspired interpretations of diverse, historical and often context dependent, traditions, using them as constructive sources of environmental ideas, by environmentally aware individuals or groups. They are new religious creations, applying religious traditions to present realities and future possibilities, addressing evolving environmental issues and the human identities that go along with them, exploring new (common, future) ground.

Conclusions

In this chapter I have explored the perceived need for using religion as a resource to engage the environmental crisis. The latter is seen as an outward manifestation of a moral and spiritual crisis of (modern, anthropocentric) humanity, needing moral and spiritual challenge, an eco-centric reimagination of nature and humanity. Religion, with histories of ethical and social reflection, linguistic and ritual frameworks, and moral authority, stressing a diversity of world-views providing cosmic purpose and prophetic inspiration, is seen as able to provide this. The problem for this view is that religion is seen to

be in decline in modernity, lacking individual and social relevance and influence, challenged and overthrown by the (secularizing) modern world-view,
relegated to the private sphere, without public authority. Such ideas, however,
are themselves challenged through recognition of religion and secularization
being limited, static and universalizing Western concepts, imposed on diverse
and fluid practices. This thus allows for (recognition of) diversity and change
and possible religious revitalization. In particular, religion is seen as able to
challenge modern problems through (diversely, dynamically) engaging crucial global issues, such as the environmental crisis, that may be caused by or be
unable to be redressed by, the modern world-view. Such modern 'discontents',
seen as caused by a moral and spiritual lack, are seen as utopian spaces, arenas
of the contestation of meaning, which religion can fill.

In this sense, as much as religious decline there may be a green religious revitalization taking place with religion prophetically addressing environmental
issues, critiquing the modern imagination and providing new reimaginations
of nature and humanity (and in this challenging and changing traditions).
Thus a greening of religion is seen as taking place where religious traditions
embrace environmentalism, something consolidated, organized and stimulated, by the field of religion and ecology, a range of ideas and actions aimed
at preventing environmental degradation and revitalizing religion through
stimulating new personal and social religious-ecological thought and action.
The field, in this sense, seeks to provide a focal point, through which religious traditions can engage environmental issues, envision new environmental futures, and address the modern world, as well as re-envision and revitalize
themselves. It encourages constructive assessment and engagement of religious traditions with environmental issues, encouraging the construction of
new religious imaginations of nature and humanity, idealized future visions
of a better relationship between them, in the hope that such visions, individually and in mutual dialogue, may create or encourage more environmentally
benign behaviours than the perceived dominant and hegemonic, environmentally destructive, modern imagination.

In the following chapters, I further explore these ideas by analysing and
comparing the field's ecological reimaginations of several religious traditions,
the influential ecological metaphors and myths stressed, which I argue are
coalescing or being formed into new utopian eco-cosmological and ethical
accounts of how the world came into being, what its meaning and value is, and
what humanity's relationship to it is (or could or should be, connecting ought
and is), religious ecotopias (in Nasr's (1996) terms 'orders of nature'), envisaging alternative (evocative, hopeful, idealized) views of nature to modernity,
positing more environmentally friendly relations (aiming to refashion human
identity, changing its progress). I analyse several such religious ecotopia's
being developed in the field, concentrating on main world religions, those of
the 'Eastern' religions of Indian traditions (Hinduism and Jainism), Chinese

traditions (Confucianism and Daoism) and Buddhism, and the 'Western' traditions of Judaism, Christianity and Islam, exploring what they say about nature, humanity (and the divine) and their relationship.

Notes

1 Referenced to Caldwell, L. K., quoted in Miller, G. T., Jr, *Living in the Environment: An Introduction to Environmental Science* (Belmont, CA: Wadsworth, 1988), p. iii.

2 Environmentalism is seen to have a prophetic, spiritual dimension. Gardner (2002:8) sees 'spiritual' and 'sustainability' communities both seeing nature from a moral perspective, stressing wider obligations. Gottlieb (2006a, 2006b) sees environmentalism inspired by religion, stressing similar beliefs, experiences and rituals. Northcott (2000) sees environmentalists seeing nature as sacred, consumerism as spiritual malaise. Szerszynski (2005) sees nature always understood in religious terms (even in modernity), seeing radical environmentalism as secular Protestantism or post-modern religious bricolage. Taylor (2001a, 2001b) sees a 'pagan' environmentalism stressing (reverence of) nature's sacredness, evoking intuitive and mystical knowledge of it.

3 Referenced to Jay McDaniel, 'Spirituality and Sustainability', *Conservation Biology*, December 2002, p. 1461.

4 Referenced to Pedersen, P., Nature, Religion, and Cultural Identity: The Religious Environmentalist Paradigm, in *Asian Perception of Nature: A Critical Approach*, Bruun, O., and Kalland, A., eds (London: Curzon Press, 1995), pp. 258–76.

5 As Bowen (1998:5, 23) argues: 'what we call "religion" may look quite different from one society to another, in the relative importance of a shared belief system, in the degree to which religious practice involves strong emotions, and in the social functions and contexts associated with religious practices'. In this sense, secularization is often equated with European de-Christianization rather than decline of all religion. Recent definitions thus see narrow foci as too exclusive (and broad ones too inclusive), stressing complexity, dynamism and reflexivity, mixing substantive or functional definitions, stressing what religion is (e.g. patterns of belief) or what it does (e.g. symbols establishing motivations) with other dimensions such as cognitive belief, community, doctrine, ethics, experience, ideology, myth or ritual (Connolly 1999; Clarke and Byrne 1998; McGuire 1997).

6 Davie (2000) and Hervieu-Leger (2000) see religion as cultural memory. Thus secularization may be amnesia of the dominant Western, Christian memory, it existing vicariously, churches protecting it on behalf of wider society, and/or mutating into new diverse forms. In this sense, religious environmentalism may be creating a new religious-ecological memory, a shared perception of sacred nature.

7 Hervieu-Leger (2000) sees utopian religious innovation in base communities in Latin America and denominational feminism in the US. Similarly, Casanova (1994) sees deprivatization in Buddhism in Burma, Catholicism in Brazil, Poland and Spain, Evangelical Protestantism in the US, Judaism in Israel and Hinduism in India, while Beyer (1990, 1994) highlights the New Christian Right in the US,

the Islamic revolution in Iran, New Religious Zionism in Israel, Liberation Theology in Latin America and Religious Environmentalism.

8   See White, L., Jr, Continuing the Conservation, in *Western Man and Environmental Ethics: Attitudes to Nature and Technology*, Barbour, I. G., ed. (Reading, MA: Addison-Wesley, 1973).

9   Eastern traditions are often seen as eco-centric and environmentally friendly, stressing harmony between humanity and nature. However, they are also seen as world-denying, stressing spiritual escape from nature, holistically seeing destructive human action as 'natural', or accepting environmentally destructive political regimes (e.g. Marxist China). And, of course, any eco-centric views do not necessarily describe how adherents behave. There is seen a danger, then, of orientalizing, romanticizing or universalizing, them, seeing rational, scientific Occidentals and emotional, spiritual Orientals, imposing normative, static Western meanings on diverse dynamic Eastern forms ('eco-centric' is a Western term with little non-Western relevance). Nevertheless, it is also stressed that being diverse and dynamic Eastern traditions may have environmentally friendly elements adaptable to environmental concerns (see Asad 1993; Gottlieb 2006a; Johnston 2006; Kalland 2005; Masuwaza 2005; Snyder 2006; Tucker and Grim 2005; White 2002).

10 More recent influences are seen as including Wendell Berry, Murray Bookchin, Fritjof Capra, Frederick Elder, Matthew Fox, Wesley Granberg-Michaelson, John Hart, John Haught, Barry Lopez, Sally McFague and Theodore Roszak (Kinsley 1994; Nash 1989; Nasr 1996). Other authors exploring such greening include Callicott (1997), Foltz (2002b), Gottlieb (1996, 2006a), Kinsley (1994), and Taylor and Kapan (2005).

11 See www.arcworld.org, 20 Oct. 2008.

12 See www.earthcharterinaction.org/religion/, 20 Oct. 2008.

13 See www.cfore.ca, 20 Oct. 2008.

14 See www.eco-justice.org, 20 Oct. 2008.

15 See www.greenfaith.org, 20 Oct. 2008.

16 See www.religiouswitness.org, 20 Oct. 2008.

17 See www.webofcreation.org, 20 Oct. 2008.

18 See www.environment.harvard.edu/religion, 20 Oct. 2008.

19 From 'Religions of the World and Ecology: Discovering Common Ground', downloaded from www.environment.harvard.edu/religion/religion/index.html, 13 Apr. 2008.

20 See Chapple, C. K., ed. *Jainism and Ecology: Nonviolence in the Web of Life* (Cambridge, MA: Harvard University Press, 2002); Chapple, C. K., and Tucker, M. E., eds. *Hinduism and Ecology: The Intersection of Earth, Sky, and Water* (Cambridge, MA: Harvard University Press, 2000); Foltz, R. C., Denny, F. M., and Baharuddin, A., eds. *Islam and Ecology: A Bestowed Trust* (Cambridge, MA: Harvard University Press, 2003); Girardot, N. J., Miller, J., and Xiaogan, L., eds. *Daoism and Ecology: Ways within a Cosmic Landscape* (Cambridge, MA: Harvard University Press, 2001); Grim, J. A., ed. *Indigenous Traditions and Ecology: The Inter-being of Cosmology and Community* (Cambridge, MA: Harvard University Press, 2001); Hessel, D. T., and Ruether, R. R., eds. *Christianity and Ecology: Seeking the Well-Being of Earth and Humans* (Cambridge, MA: Harvard University Press, 2000); Tirosh-Samuelson, H.,

ed. *Judaism and Ecology: Created World and Revealed Word* (Cambridge, MA: Harvard University Press, 2002); Tucker, M. E., and Berthrong, J., eds. *Confucianism and Ecology: The Interrelation of Heaven, Earth and Humans* (Cambridge, MA: Harvard University Press, 1998); Tucker, M. E., and Williams, D. R., eds. *Buddhism and Ecology: The Interconnection of Dharma and Deeds* (Cambridge, MA: Harvard University Press, 1997).

21 Alongside this the *International Society for the Study of Religion, Nature, and Culture* and the *Journal for the Study of Religion, Nature, and Culture* have been initiated to further its aims (see www. religionandnature.com, 20 Oct. 2008).

22 Downloaded from www.environment.harvard.edu/religion/information/about/index. html, 13 Apr. 2008.

Chapter 3

Indian (Hindu and Jain) Visions

Ecological interpretations of Indian religions revolve mostly around the traditions of Hinduism and Jainism (these being seen as the oldest traditions, possibly related to/subsuming indigenous South Asian beliefs, possibly interconnected and mutually influencing; Buddhism is analysed separately, Sikhism and Zoroastrianism less analysed). These are seen as sharing (although interpreting differently) a stress on a sacred, living, universe, infused with the divine, which interconnects all life, with humanity needing to appreciate this, connecting to and caring for the wider organic and spiritual whole, in particular, via a righteous/dutiful (*dharma*), non-violent (*ahimsa*), lifestyle (this related to the cyclical notion of reincarnation, the effect of one's actions (*karma*), connecting the universe/life-forms) (Chapple 2002a, 2004; Foltz 2002b; Jacobsen 2005c).

Hinduism

[T]he Hindu viewpoint on nature . . . is permeated by a reverence for life, and an awareness that the great forces of nature . . . as well as various orders of life . . . are all bound to each other . . . The divine is not exterior to creation, but expresses itself through natural phenomena . . . This leads necessarily to a reverence for animal life . . . Ahimsa, or non-violence, is the greatest good, and on no account should life be taken . . . The Hindu tradition of reverence for nature and all forms of life, vegetable or animal, represents a powerful tradition which needs to be re-nurtured and reapplied in our contemporary context . . . Let us recall the ancient Hindu dictum – 'The Earth is our mother, and we are all her children.'

(Dr Karan Singh, The Hindu Declaration on Nature, WWF 1986:17–19)

One of the most striking aspects of the multitude of Hindu cosmogonic myths is [their] organic, biological visions . . . The . . . universe is imagined as a living organism . . . in which each part is inextricably related to the life of the whole . . . There is no such thing as objectified 'nature' or lifeless 'elements' for everything belongs to the living pattern of the whole . . . It is a view in which the universe, and by extension the land of India, is alive with interconnections and meanings.

(Bassett et al. 2000:59)[1]

Hinduism[2] is stressed as being a religion near to nature, seeing the divine manifested in every force, process or thing, the Hindu cosmos being alive with deities expressing themselves through natural phenomena: for example, earth (*Prthivi*), fire (*Agni*), rain (*Indra*), rivers (*Sarasvati*), wind (*Vayu*). Nature is thus deified and pilgrimages, prayers, rituals and texts, honour and celebrate its myriad manifestations, connecting humanity to it. This is something seen as formalized in the denotation of the 'five great elements' (*pancamahabhuta*, for Chapple (1994, 2001a) the building blocks of Hindu reality), air (*vayu*), earth (*prthivi*), fire (*tejas*), space (*akasa*) and water (*ap*), with meditative and ritual processes and daily worship entailing awareness of and evoking these, reminding of the sacred origins of matter and enabling a truthful and just earthly order (*rta*). Continuity is thus assumed between the human world and that of nature (Chapple 1994, 2004; Haberman 2000; Kinsley 1994; Narayan 2003; Narayanan 2005b, 2005c; Prime 1996; Seshagiri Rao 2000).

There is not an object in heaven and earth that a Hindu is not prepared to worship – sun, moon and stars; rocks, stocks, and stones; trees, shrubs and grasses; seas, pools and rivers; his own implements of trade; the animals he finds most useful; the noxious reptiles he fears . . . each and all come in for a share of divine honour or a tribute of more or less adoration. (Rukmani 2000:116)[3]

The Hindu religion, perhaps more than any other, is closely linked to a sense of place. It was born on the river banks of the Indus and the Ganges rivers, and in recent memory, if a Hindu left the subcontinent to travel across the sea, his or her religious status was compromised. Hinduism holds India's mountains, rivers, and trees sacred, regarding them to be infused with individual spirits (*jiva*) and suffused with an all-pervasive universal consciousness (*brahman*). (Chapple 1994:113)

Particularly seen as revered are rivers and trees. Rivers are sacred, living organisms, the abode of deities, even tangible forms of goddesses (the Ganges a mother, consort of god Shiva, the Yamuna a goddess associated with god Krishna, the Sarasvati the goddess of learning). They nurture (being compared to mother's milk), are fecund (manifestations of *shakti*, the creative power of the cosmos), and have loving, selfless, characteristics, being life-giving (and life-taking when angered). They are thus venerated, often personally (e.g. the Narmada being named 'one who absorbs but does not release sin'). They are moral purifiers, cleansing sin and providing auspiciousness (the Ganges absorbing India's moral dirt, something perceptible as physical dirt connecting immorality to pollution). They are sources of spiritual abilities, able to transform humans into divine love. Correspondingly sacred sites are situated along their banks (goddesses being present in these and their rituals, focusing attention on the rivers sacredness and purifying power).

They are centres of pilgrimage and ascetic practice, being *tirthas*, sacred crossings to another, divine realm. They are thus sacred space, involved in divine 'gift exchange', proving merit for devotion, symbolically reinforcing the human/nature/divine relationship. Haberman (2000) sees interconnected levels of reality in them (later levels encompassing earlier ones but only accessed by understanding their non-difference): the physical form; the spiritual form, allowing them to function as a holy site; and the divine form of a goddess, yielding highest joy. Rivers, in this sense, give access to the divine, if respected, revered and cared for (pollution may deny access) (Alley 2005; Chapple 1994, 2004; Craddock 2005; Deegan 2000; Haberman 2000; Maguire 2000; Narayanan 2001, 2005b, 2005c; Van Horn 2006).

Trees are seen as long revered, forests seen as the abode of deities and sages, woods surrounding villages as 'sacred groves' (*saran*, areas of spiritual integrity). Myths see the world as a Banyan tree, its branches representing life, the forest as Shiva's hair, or Krishna living simply in the forest, with the sacred Vedic literature thought to have been written in forests. Trees, therefore, are sacred (having protector deities), compared to humble devotees, tolerant and generous, providing auspiciousness (planting is divine, giving grace, felling is killing kin), something highlighted in ritual: for example, 'trees for life' a planting movement sees them blessed by holy men; pilgrims take cuttings of 'sacred' trees (*vriksha*, symbolically representing all trees) in temples and plant them as offerings (*prasada*), spreading the sacred forest; and the most widely recognized ecological examples, the 'Bishnois' and 'Chipko' movements, stressed (female) 'ritual defence' (against male power), sacrificing the human self for the wider good, women protecting trees from felling by forming human chains around them and tying sacred threads to them signifying their sanctity. Traditional Hindu villages are also seen to be based around five trees (*pancavati*), symbolizing the five elements sustaining life, such trees not being in the villages but the villages in them, unable to exist without them (and the world a village in, dependent on, its trees, needing to protect them to survive, declining if separated from them). The harmony and vitality of the forest is thus argued as guiding Indian civilization, Prime (1996:8–20, 87) seeing it as a 'forest culture': 'The Hindu idea is that this whole world is a forest. To keep this forest as it is we have to keep the world-forest intact . . . the forest symbolizes the divine attribute of "totality", combining all forms together in a single inter-dependent whole . . . You are also part of that forest . . . you can reorder it, but you cannot bypass it'[4] (thus humanity needs to protect trees to keep the world pollution free and habitable) (Aggarwal 2005; Apffel-Marglin and Parajuli 2000; Chapple 1994, 2004; Dwivedi 1996, 2000; James 2000; Nagarajan 2000; Narayan 2003; Narayanan 2001, 2005b, 2005c; Rukmani 2000; Shinn 2000; Van Horn 2006).

Trees are like good people who care for others (Vikram Caritam 65) . . . The whole life of these trees is to serve. With their leaves, flowers, fruits, branches, roots, shade, fragrance, sap, bark, wood, and finally even their ashes and coal, they exist for the purpose of others (Srimad Bhagavatam) . . . Trees have five sorts of kindness which are their daily sacrifice. To families they give fuel; to passer by they give shade and a resting place; to birds they give shelter; with their leaves, roots and bark they give medicines (Varaha Purana 162.41–2) . . . O tree! . . . you surrender yourself for others . . . with such devotion . . . please accept my heartfelt respects (Bhamini Vilasa 89). (Prime 1996:88–9)[5]

Hinduism is thus seen as offering imagery that values nature (stressing a 'sacred geography', symbolized by India and the 'sacred cow'), its cosmology being based on organic visions, seeing the universe as a dynamic, living network of relations filled with spiritual consciousness: for example, the cosmic sacrifice of a great being ('cosmic man', *purusha*), from which all things arise, a myth relating to the idea of the world being the body of the god Vishnu ('all pervasive', as the soul pervades body so Vishnu is thought to pervade nature: 'Everything rests on me as pearls are strung on a thread . . . I am . . . the life of all that lives', *Bhagavad Gita* 7.7–9).[6] Vishnu is also said to enter the world in animal or human incarnations (*avatara*) to overcome evil and establish righteousness (being transcendent and immanent, creating and withdrawing, something compared to evolution). Vishnu is thus the 'sustainer' upholding a divine balance and unity in nature, something that humanity has a duty to recognize and preserve, seeing and following his example; '(beholding) the Self in all beings and all beings in the Self . . . I am not lost to one who sees me in all things and sees all things in me' (*Bhagavad Gita* 6.29–30).[7] And, for Palmer and Finlay (2003:93–4), as Vishnu represents the heart, as opposed to Shiva, the 'destroyer', who represents the brain, it is the heart not the brain that is important to this, this suggesting intuition not reason as the appropriate means to engage nature (Chapple 1994; Dwivedi 2000; Jacobsen 2005b; Kinsley 1994; Narayan 2003; Narayanan 2001, 2005c; Nelson 2000; Prime 1996; Seshagiri Rao 2000).

[T]he rivers are the veins of the Cosmic Person and the trees are the hairs of His body. The air is His breath, the ocean is His waist, the hills and mountains are the stacks of His bones and the passing ages are His movements. (Srimad Bhagavatam 2.1.32–3, Prime 1996:28)

The earth is also seen as a goddess (*devi*) and mother (consort of Vishnu), compassionate, fertile and dependable, filled with sanctity (e.g. *Bharat-ma*, 'Mother India'). Humanity cannot survive without it and if it despoils it, it will diminish in its care for humanity (being offended by immoral activities). It was correctly created in harmonic abundance and humanity needs to ensure it stays that way (or suffer the consequences): 'nourish the *deva* . . . and let the *devas* nourish you' (*Bhagavad Gita* 3.10–12).[8] Nature, in this sense, is seen as embodying the feminine creative principle of the cosmos, *prakriti*, 'cosmic matter' or 'material cause', producing and nourishing life (in conjunction with Vishnu), the world dissolving into and manifesting from it, something linked to another feminine concept (and goddess), *shakti*, or 'dynamic energy', the material force of the universe, enabling cosmic procreation (related to *shakti pithas*, 'places of power' in nature, and present in humanity as a power increased through devotion). Hindu nature, then, is energetic and spiritual as much as material, inherently active, infused with a powerful, productive force creatively linking all things (tender but powerful, serving humanity but reacting when abused) (Callicott 1997; Craddock 2005; Dwivedi 1996, 2000; Haberman 2000; Jacobsen 2005e; James 2000; Kinsley 1994; Narayanan 2005b; Nelson 2000; Palmer and Finlay 2003; Seshagiri Rao 2000; Van Horn 2006).

> [M]other [earth], with your oceans, rivers, and other bodies of water, you give us land to grow grains, on which our survival depends . . . milk, fruits, water, and cereals as we need to eat and drink . . . please pour like a cow who never fails, a thousand streams of treasure to enrich me . . . May you, our motherland on whom we grow wheat, rice, and barley . . . be nourished by the cloud and loved by the rain. (Atharva Veda 12.1, Prime 1996:31)[9]

> [I]n Indian religious traditions nature is symbolized as the embodiment of a feminine principle . . . produced and renewed by the dialectical play of creation and destruction . . . 'The tension between opposites from which motion and movement arises is depicted as the first appearance of dynamic energy (Shakti). All existence arises from this primordial energy which is the substance of . . . everything. The manifestation of this power, this energy, is called nature (Prakriti).'[10] . . . In conjunction with the masculine principle (Purusa), Prakriti creates the world. (James 2000:516)[11]

In this sense, for Dwivedi (1996), Hinduism sees divinity as 'one-in-many' and 'many-in-one', God, the efficient cause, and (diverse) nature, the material cause, being in a harmonious relationship. Such 'oneness', incorporating 'manyness' is also seen as stressed in ideas of the identity of individual soul and Supreme Being seeing *atman*, or inner-self, a spiritual core reality of undifferentiated oneness within humanity (all beings), attained via self-awareness/ discipline, connected to (forming the body of) *Brahman*, the underlying universal reality or all-pervasive consciousness. In this scheme, Brahma, the creator, the energy of God (growing from the navel of Vishnu), is seen as entering into each object to create and maintain cosmic interrelationship: before creation all life is undifferentiated in *Brahman* but by the will of the Supreme Being this is manifested in the differentiated world. Thus a 'higher self', the Supreme Being, dwells in individual selves. All existence is one in essence. It is only an illusory power (*maya*) that causes the self to believe it exists independently, superimposing autonomous bias on unified reality. To fully realize humanness, then, humanity needs to get in touch with the wider, underlying essence, a spiritual quest and self-exploration achieved via attuning to the continuity and reciprocity within nature's rhythms (via meditation, yoga), seeing the self in all beings and all beings in the self (realizing that if humanity violates nature, it violates itself, if it protects it, it protects itself) (Callicott 1997; Chapple 1994; James 2000; Kinsley 1994; Narayanan 2001, 2005b, 2005c; Nelson 2000; Palmer and Finlay 2003; Prime 1996).

The human role in this cosmology is to maintain cosmic unity. This is *dharma*, or 'righteousness', a moral duty and cosmic law, a way of acting and a structure of reality, of equilibrium (from *dhr*, 'that which sustains'; a state of eternal balance and peace (*sanatana*); it also means 'religion', Hinduism is *sanatana dharma*, the 'eternal *dharma*'). It is doing justice to and acting for the wider good, in ways that sustain life and harmonious relationships. All species conduct themselves in accordance with *dharma* of their kind, supporting the whole, but humanity, virtue of free will, tends towards selfishness and needs to overcome this (through following *dharma sastras*, sacred texts, creating harmonic *dharmic* practices). The goal of Hindu humanity is thus to realize a state of peace, embracing, supporting and serving, the family of nature (to do otherwise is *adharma*, or 'unrighteousness', causing nature to suffer). Such a righteous path is achieved through centring life on the divine common good (*sarva-bhuta-hita*, the highest ethical standard, being altruistic toward the whole) following the example of God who came to earth as *avatara* for the purpose of upholding the *dharmic* cosmic order and uprooting *adharma* (thus acting with *dharma* is uniting with the divine). A *dharmic* person (*dharmikah*, one who follows the path of *dharma*) thus sacrifices self-interest for universal welfare, observing and creating mutual cooperation and respect (prosperity being the result) (Chapple 2004; Dwivedi 2000; Jacobsen 2005c; Maguire 2000; Narayanan 2001, 2005a, 2005b, 2005c; Nelson 2000; Palmer and Finlay 2003; Rukmani 2000; Seshagiri Rao 2000; Van Horn 2006).

> Sanskrit literature conveys the dominant worldview of *dharma*, which is *ecologically friendly* . . . an 'eco-person' . . . whom the Hindus call a dharmic individual [is] one who can live in harmony with nature as a whole. The stress here is on the inner transformation of an individual . . . [allowing] the sharing of the planet and its resources in a sense of mutuality . . . understanding oneself as being just one among many others in the 'whole' . . . even when the goal is economic gain (*artha*) or sensual gratification (*kama*), it can only be within the code of *dharma*. (Rukmani 2000:110–11, 113)

Dharma involves mastering baser characteristics and exploitative tendencies by centring the self on wider cosmic ordinances, leading to a higher communal state of self-realization. In this sense, it is seen as relating to ideas of rebirth (*samsara*), and *karma*, the 'effects of action': in this scheme, the soul is eternal, living many lifetimes in different forms (*purushas*), dependent on the quality of behaviour, moving 'upwards' or 'downwards' on the 'wheel of birth', a chain of events and incarnations (emphasizing humanity's kinship with and need to care for nature, it has been and may again be a 'lower' being). The moral quality of thoughts and actions thus determine station and fate, leaving good or bad *karma*, traces in character, sculpting destiny (and impacts can be delayed, past or present actions having future consequences). Beings thus reap what they sow (*karma-phala*, 'fruits of action') in a constant formation of self, every thought or action, selfish or selfless, counting as it impacts in the interconnected *karmic* web of life: 'An action, which has been committed by a human being in this life, follows him again and again' (*Mahabharata* 232:16).[12] This is seen as an endless flowing together of life, individual biographies forming the underlying unified reality, with the ultimate aim of liberation (*moksha*), from illusory (material, individual) self (and rebirth), unifying *atman/Brahman*, what is termed *sanatan dharma*, the eternal essence of life (fitting the soul to the eternal laws of the universe, achieving a state of peace). Thus humanity needs to sacrifice separate, worldly, ego-self and realize interconnected, spiritual *dharmic* self (Callicott 1997; Dwivedi 2000; Jacobsen 2005c; Kinsley 1994; Maguire 2000; Narayanan 2001, 2005a, 2005b, 2005c; Palmer and Finlay 2003; Regenstein 1991).[13]

> In our cosmic journey, we are involved in countless cycles of births and deaths. Life progresses into higher forms or regresses into lower forms . . . based upon our good or bad karma . . . Reincarnation warns us against treating lower forms of life with cruelty . . . According to Hindu philosophy, the goal of human life is the realization of the state of peace . . . a dynamic harmony among all the diverse facets of life . . . The Sanskrit for family is parivara and environment is parayavarana. If we think of the environment as our home and all of its members as our family, it is clear that the key to conserving nature is . . . giving and serving. (Palmer and Finlay 2003:95–6)

A main way to observe *dharma* is seen as being *ahimsa*, or non-violence (seen as India's premier ethical value and a moral impetus for conservation), a self-restraint emphasizing the inflicting of the minimum amount of violence, in thought, word or deed, to the community of life, respecting the rights of other life-forms to fulfil their lives (an active compassion based on the solidarity of interconnectedness): 'so long as man does not of his own free will put himself last among his fellow creatures, there is no salvation for him. Ahimsa is the farthest limit of humility'[14]). It is seen as leading to *satya*, truth (from *sat*, 'to be', and *rta*, the order of nature, thus stressing nature's processes as beholders of truth), something integral to proper *dharmic* existence, needing to be nurtured (*ahimsa* is the means to produce truthful ends, being an attribute of the divine Absolute Truth). *Ahimsa* is thus seen as the highest form of *dharma*, as Maguire (2000:72) notes: 'Non-malice to all beings in thought, word and deed; compassion and giving;

these are the eternal dharma (duty) of the good.' Thus it may free humanity from restricted notions of self and open it to an awareness of and sensitivity to the wants and needs (and moral value) of the larger community of nature (Callicott 1997; Chapple 1994; Dwivedi 2000; Jacobsen 2005a; Kinsley 1994; Narayanan 2001; Palmer and Finlay 2003; Regenstein 1991; Shinn 2000; Van Horn 2006).

A major influential exponent of *ahimsa* and *satyagraha*, or truthfulness, is seen as Mohandas Gandhi, stressing a hopeful, prophetic, ecological treatise of total commitment to a sustainable lifestyle, a 'Gandhian' ecology involving acting in non-violent ways with minimal needs, living a life of compassion and simplicity, allowing all life-forms to live in their own fashion (a non-anthropocentric self-restraint rather than self-assertion). Such *dharmic* behaviour is seen as anti-consumerist/materialist (a 'Gandhian' suspicion of *adharmic* exploitative industrialization), stressing use only at a rate that can be replenished, living in a cooperating network of decentralized, self-sufficient communities (a non-violent economy of simple, non-exploitative consumption and technology, argued as traditionally Hindu). This is seen as (individual and collective, the former underpinning the latter) 'self-rule' (*svaraj*), a self-abnegation and local eco-management or village-mindedness, minimizing wants and needs, respecting nature, living sustainably within its cycles, not pursuing 'growth-ism': as Prime (1996:118) argues 'The highest "standard of life" is the simplest; this has always been the Hindu way – the way of simple living and high thinking' (the most respected person in Hindu society is thus seen as the *sahdu*, or sage, who owns nothing and consumes little). Such 'Gandhian' ideas, then, are seen as based on an inner-logic of non-violence and self-sacrificial actions (*tapas*), leading towards the good of all ('Gandhian *sarvodaya*'; and, like tending a tree, nurturing this logic is seen a way to yield ecological fruit) (Apffel-Marglin and Parajuli 2000; Callicott 1997; Chapple 1994, 2004; Kinsley 1994; Lal 2005; Maguire 2000; Palmer and Finlay 2003; Prime 1996; Shinn 2000; Van Horn 2006).

Ultimately this way of acting is living a life of sacrifice (*yana*), performing acts that protect life, sacrificing oneself for the whole *dharmic* order of nature, something related to *dhana*, or giving, seeing wealth holistically, having less to ensure nature has plenty, contributing to the maintenance of the life cycle, seeing possessions as a sign of regress not progress (following nature's generosity in sustaining life). It is acting as individual *satyagrahis*, truth seekers controlling desire and passion (seen as able to reverse the 'inner-colonization' of Western consumerism), using asceticism, meditation or prayer, to rethink or purify the self, stimulating gentle and communal thinking and acting, delighting in the welfare of all beings. Such ideas are related to *karma-yoga*, desireless or dispassionate action, attained via 'meditative mastery' of the senses or five elements within the body that abandons egoism and embraces community, achieving *samadhi*, or non-difference with nature/spirit, reversing egocentrism and achieving the well-being of nature (*loka-samgraha*). Such action is seen as a form of devotional attachment to the divine (*dharma yuddha* or 'righteous battle'), exemplified by *sevaks* or servants of people, teaching Gandhi's methods, and the *sthitaprajna* or 'one whose mental attitude is disciplined' at peace with the surroundings (Callicott 1997; Chapple 2000, 2001a, 2005c; Jacobsen 2005b; Kinsley 1994; Maguire 2000; Nagarajan 2000; Nelson 2000; Palmer and Finlay 2003; Prime 1996; Shinn 2000; Van Horn 2006).

> The [*Bhagavad*] *Gita* . . . teaches . . . that full awareness of the spiritual dimension is indispensable for authentic happiness, and that such awareness cannot be attained without . . . limitations on the human tendency to live for the gratification of the desires . . . the *Gita* calls for more than a limitation of wants; it envisions a demanding asceticism in which desires and egoism are utterly renounced . . . the *Gita's* ideal is that we be 'devoid of any tinge of greed, desire to control, manipulate, or exploit.'[15] (Nelson 2000:131)

Such *dharmic* practice is seen in devotional rituals (*bhakti*) and ritual worship (*puja*) which connect human action/morality with natural cycles, using physical elements (earth, fire, plants, stone, water, wood) to remind of the sacred and provide purification and divine grace, creating awareness of the constituents of materiality and reciprocal connection to nature, enabling humanity to maintain the creative life cycle, being sacred activities creating the ordered cosmos. Nagarajan (2000) highlights *kolam*, or 'painted prayers', and 'marrying trees': the former is a daily ritual creating rice flour designs on the threshold of homes, temples or trees, symbolically inviting deities inside while also providing food for creatures, thereby initiating reciprocity and obtaining protection; the latter is a symbolic marriage of human and tree that reinforces the human/nature kinship as well as involving the tree taking on a burden of suffering (usually infertility) afflicting the human (trees having an abundance of fertility and a great ability to give). Such practices stress humanity entering a relationship of sacred exchange with nature, giving and receiving vitality, generating auspiciousness and positive intentionalities, expanding human and natural potential, creating mutual beneficence (environmentally friendly actions may thus create environmental auspiciousness, while destructive ones (or lack of ritual reverence; using plastic in *kolam*, not rice, thus not feeding animals, being ungenerous) may result in environmental inauspiciousness) (see Apffel-Marglin and Parajuli 2000; Chapple 2001a, 2004; Kinsley 1994; Narayanan 2001; Seshagiri Rao 2000; Van Horn 2006).

> It is about the *mutipani* [ozone layer], isn't it? The *kolam*, too, is disappearing. Do you see the connection? We are losing the ability to give to each other . . . We are forgetting that we need to practice giving constantly. I understand why the [ozone layer] is disappearing. We have forgotten to be generous . . . We used to give to each other . . . to the gods and goddesses. The *kolam* is about giving, do you know . . . I have the solution to problem of

the *mutipani* disappearing. We have to learn to give again. We have to marry trees again. (Nagarajan 2000:453–4)

[T]he Bhagavad Gita . . . [explains] in verses 3:14–16: Living bodies subsist on food grains, which are produced from rains. Rains are produced from the performance of yajna (sacrifice), and yajna is born of prescribed duties. Regulated activities are prescribed in the Vedas, and the Vedas are directly manifested from [God] . . . eternally situated in acts of sacrifice . . . one who does not follow in human life the cycle of sacrifice . . . lives a life full of sin. Living only for the satisfaction of the senses, such a person lives in vain. (Palmer and Finlay 2003:92)

Nagarajan (2000), in this sense, stresses (the need for) 'embedded ecologies', the subtle and complex relationships between cultural and natural worlds whereby each is able to expand (or diminish, if not properly cared for) the potential of the other. Apffel-Marglin and Parajuli (2000) sees such ideas in 'ecological ethnicities' and 'moral ecologies' displaying a practical 'ecological wisdom': small-scale local communities and practices exhibiting respectful, sustainable use of nature (exhibiting self-rule, being *dharmic* traditions, transmitting *dharma*). Such local ecologies stress ontological union between humanity and nature and ways of knowing embedded in place, including nature in their ethical frameworks. And they are, in this sense, linked to resistance to modernity, where knowing is disembedded from place and nature ethically discounted, being '*dharmic* protest' expressing self-rule. James (2000) and Callicott (1997) thus highlight the Chipko movement, where women embraced and protected trees for the sake of the local community in a spirit of self-sacrifice, seeing them as part of the sacred family of nature (tying sacred threads to them as sisters do to brothers in festivals). Such protest, often religiously sanctioned (led by ascetics, involving prayers/rituals), represents and creates a discourse on the ideal Hindu lifestyle of being at one with and serving nature, highlighting the need to maintain it, the well-being of communities integral to it, and the social reality that supports these, evoking moral duties rooted in *dharma* (see Chapple 1994, 2001a; Dwivedi 1996, 2000; Narayanan 2001; Prime 1996; Rukmani 2000; Shinn 2000; Van Horn 2006).

The village women . . . guarded the forest while listening to discourses from ancient texts . . . a forest officer [told them] . . . that the felling of trees was scientifically viable and economically indispensable . . . 'Do you know what the forest bear? Resin, timber, and foreign exchange!' . . . the women replied . . . 'What do the forest bear? Soil, water, and pure air! Soil, water, and pure air, sustains the earth and all she bears.'[16] (James 2000:511)

Such ideas and actions, then, are seen as highlighting Hinduism's connection to nature and expression of this in what Dwivedi (2000) calls '*dharmic* ecology', an environmental stewardship stressing *sarvodaya*, the serving of (the welfare of) all beings (combining the large-scale Hindu tradition with small-scale *dharmic* actions) (James 2000; Shinn 2000).[17]

> Hindus say 'Om shanti, shanti, shanti' – 'Peace, peace, peace' – before every prayer. The first 'shanti' means peace with nature, ecological peace; the second means peace in society, between human beings . . . the third means shanti within myself, spiritual peace. Ecological peace, social peace and spiritual peace – for the Hindus, environment embraces all three. (Prime 1996:76)

Jainism

> *Jain ecological philosophy is virtually synonymous with the principle of* ahimsa *(non-violence) which runs through the Jain tradition like a golden thread . . . a principle that Jains teach and practice not only towards human beings but towards all nature . . . The teaching of* ahimsa *refers not only to . . . physical acts of violence but to violence in the hearts and minds of human beings, their lack of concern . . . for the natural world. Ancient Jain texts explain that violence* (himsa) *is not defined by actual harm, for this may be unintentional. It is the intention to harm, the absence of compassion, that makes an action violent . . . Jain cosmology recognises the fundamental natural phenomenon of symbiosis or mutual dependence . . . all aspects of nature belong together and are bound in a physical as well as metaphysical relationship. Life is viewed as a gift of togetherness . . . in a universe teeming with inter-dependent constituents.*
> *(Singhvi 1990:6–7)*

> *The common concerns between Jainism and environmentalism can be found in a mutual sensitivity toward living things, a recognition of the interconnectedness of life-forms, and support of programs that educate others to respect and protect living systems. For the Jains this approach is anchored in a cosmology that views the world [containing] . . . life souls* (jiva) *that reincarnate repeatedly until . . . spiritual liberation . . . Jains adhere to the vows of non-violence to purify their* karma *and advance toward [this] . . . For Jain laypeople, this generally means . . . livelihoods deemed to inflict minimum of harm. For Jain monks and nuns, this means the need to avoid doing harm to all forms of life.*
> *(Chapple 2002b:xxxiii–xxxiv)*

Jainism[18] is stressed as a religious ecology that may have turned ecology into a religion, being a spiritual quest, an environmentally friendly value system and a code of conduct, of ecological harmony. It is seen as worshipping no God, nor acknowledging a first cause (seeing these as anthropocentric and counter to nature, interfering with 'true' communal perception of it), but rather seeing nature as uncreated and eternal, a constant cycle of birth, death and rebirth. It thus centres on life, its only sphere of meaning, sacralizing all aspects of worldly existence, seeing nature as a living, sensuous reality, emphasizing the integrity of every living thing. A fundamental tenet, then, is that all life is sacred and has inherent value, being viewed as a gift of mutual assistance in an interdependent cosmos: 'one another' means every living thing in nature: 'one who knows one comes to know all. One who knows all, knows one' (*Acaranga Sutra*).[19] Ecology, in this sense, may be implicit in the Jain way of life. To be Jain is to affirm the living biosphere and everything in it, this possibly resulting in ecological sensitivity (Chapple 2001b, 2002a, 2002c, 2005b; Cort 2002; Kumar 2002a, 2002b; Palmer and Finlay 2003; Shilapi 2002; Singhvi 1990; Tatia 2002; Tobias 1994).

Jainism holds that the entire world . . . is possessed of life . . . One is therefore expected to respect the land and its natural beauty. Jainism does so philosoph- ically by accepting the principle of the interdependent existence of nature . . . [considering] ecology as an indispensable part of both spirituality and mater- ial life . . . [realizing] the paramount importance of ecology and nature for spirituality and the value in protecting nonhuman life-forms for the sake of human welfare. Jainism tries to shape our attitude toward nature by prescrib- ing humane and non-violent approaches to everyday behaviour . . . [inspiring] its followers to safeguard what in contemporary discourse would be called the ecological perspective. (Jain 2002:172, 178)

The Jain definition of 'life', in this sense, is emphasized as being wide (comprising elements as well as organisms: 8,400,000 species, in air, earth, fire and water, bodied forms), Jainism stressing a unique 'bio-cosmology' linking life-forms in an interdependent life cycle, based on the number of senses possessed (seeing the seemingly inert world abounding with sensu- ousness). Elements, micro-organisms, and plants, are seen as possessing the one foundational sense of touch that defines 'life', developing life-forces of energy and respiration, craving for food and desire for reproduction, being subject to attraction and aversion, pleasure and pain. Two-sensed beings (e.g. leeches, molluscs, worms) add taste. Three-sensed beings (e.g. ants, insects, centipedes) add smell. Four-sensed beings (e.g. bees, scorpions, spiders) add sight. Five-sensed beings (e.g. birds, fish, reptiles, mammals, humanity (the only one with sentience)) add hearing. This view, where animals possess cog- nitive faculties and plants can respond in kind to humanity's presence, is seen as possibly leading to a deeper appreciation of biodiversity and of the need for human reciprocity with and care for nature: 'All breathing, existing, living, sentient creatures should not be slain, nor treated with violence, nor abused, nor tormented, nor driven away. This is the pure unchangeable, eternal law' (*Acaranga Sutra* 1.4.1)[20] (thus, for Jain (2002:171), some basic tenets of Jainism are: injure no creatures; do not command any creature; do not own any crea- ture; do not employ one as a servant) (Chapple 2001b, 2002c, 2004, 2005b;

Cort 2002; Jain 2002; Kumar 2002b; Regenstein 1991; Shilapi 2002; Soorideva 2003; Tatia 2002; Wiley 2002).

> 700,000 earth bodies, 700,000 water bodies, 700,000 fire bodies, 700,000 air bodies, 1,000,000 separate plant bodies, 1,400,000 aggregated plant bodies, 200,000 two-sensed beings, 200,000 three-sensed beings, 200,000 four-sensed beings, 400,000 divine five-sensed beings, 400,000 infernal five-sensed beings, 400,000 plant-and-animal five-sensed beings, 1,400,000 humans; in this way there are 8,400,000 forms of existence. Whatever harm I have done, caused to be done, or approved of, by mind, speech, or body, against all of them: may that harm be without consequence. (*Pratikramana* rite, Cort 2002:75)[21]

> An equality of all forms of life and reverence for them is [Mahavira's] central teaching. He taught, 'As you want to live, do so to others'. In that definition of 'others' he embraced not only all living beings that can move, but also the existence of earth, air, water and vegetation. He even expressed a reverence for the inert. By making people aware of the existence of life in earth, air, water and vegetation, he made a fundamental contribution to our understanding of ecology. He considered any injury to any of these a sinful act . . . [proclaiming] that anyone who neglects or disregards the existence of earth, air, water and vegetation disregards his own existence, which is intrinsically bound up with them. (Shilapi 2002:160)

Jainism is thus seen as stressing all life-forms possessing an enlivening, eternal, *jiva*, a life-force or soul, with such souls constantly reincarnated in different life-forms dependent on the accumulation of *karma*, 'gross' matter that clings to them from acts of (selfish) violence, binding them to the worldly cycle of birth/death/rebirth through clouding 'true' perception of life's interdependence. The aim of Jain life is seen as being to restrict this through selfless non-violence, enabling enlightenment and liberation from the worldly cycle (*moksha*). This is something only available via human form, although not all humans achieve it (which means human experience includes prior births as elements, micro-organisms or animals, and may again). However, lesser sensed beings are not more primitive, nor is there a linear progression from simple to complex. All souls are equally pure and perfect but differently affected by *karma* (they do not need to go through all senses to achieve liberation, but can bypass some, up or down, thus one-sensed beings may become human or humans them). Such ideas highlight that nature cannot be separated from moral order: all exists because it has earned its niche in the wider system of life and the intercausal *karmic* web; to see and understand nature is to acknowledge one's past and potential future, laying the foundation for seeing it with an empathetic, sympathetic eye (Jains being expected to pay attention to the positive or negative ways in which they affect life-forms, to ensure positive *karma* and because humanity is that which it harms) (Callicott 1997; Chapple 2001b, 2002a, 2002c, 2004, 2005b; Cort 2002; Jain 2002; Palmer and Finlay 2003; Regenstein 1991; Singhvi 1990; Soorideva 2003; Tobias 1994; Wiley 2002).[22]

Jainism, in this sense, is seen to exhibit a 'non-one-sidedness' or 'many-sidedness', an awareness of multiplicity and mutuality, accepting no single perspective as the definitive truth but rather seeing an ever-changing diversity of views depending on the time and place of viewer and viewed. In this scheme, knowledge of interdependent existence is intrinsic to the soul but covered by ignorance that differs from soul to soul. Nothing gets absolutely true knowledge of things but only a distorted, partial view. The world is not as it appears to be to any one life-form's (e.g. humanity's) limited perspective. Failing to respect other life-forms is thus rooted in mistaken knowledge, failing to see the wider picture: 'truth seekers' do not accept one truth but allow for divergent views, learning from others and constantly adapting ideas holistically (Callicott 1997; Koller 2002; Palmer and Finlay 2003; Singhvi 1990; Tatia 2002; Tobias 1994; Wiley 2002). Koller (2002) sees such ideas in the epistemological theory of 'viewpoints' (*nayavada*) and 'qualified perception' (*syadvada*) where different one-sided (qualified) viewpoints holistically interact to provide deep knowledge, allowing many-sided reality to be understood. This, then, is seen to stress a way of thinking about existence that is both being and becoming (not one or the other), recognizing that nature is both substance and change, highlighting dynamic complexity, enabling the other to be seen on its own terms as well as in common (all individual viewpoints being a partial search for truth which is the community of all viewpoints). Such ideas are seen as possibly providing an ontological base for a non-violent approach to nature through recognizing that claims from one perspective must be balanced by those from other perspectives, this legitimating and respecting diversity, allowing reconciliation of different views/life-forms through partial acceptance of all, overcoming individual (human) ignorance (and its environmental consequences).

'Jain ecology' is thus argued as based on equality and spirituality. All life-forms have inherent worth, the potential for liberation, being active and potent, affecting and being affected (with humanity one soul among many). Creation is dependent on their efforts with their function being to assist one another within its ecological (spiritual) balance (to do otherwise, one soul dominating, causes imbalance/problems, for example, environmental degradation). A Jain term for ecology is thus seen as being *sarvodayavada*, or 'concern for lifting up all life-forms', supporting different souls to ensure (they can support) natural balance. This, for Tobias (1994), is 'conscious (universal) love' (*mettim bhavehi*): the striving for harmonious coexistence, a purposeful, soul-supportive, evolutionary instinct of nature, including human nature. And humanity, in this scheme, as a sensate, thinking being, has been given the special opportunity and task of cultivating this via ethical behaviour, acknowledging nature as suffused with souls that warrant care and respect. The core of Jainism in this respect is seen to involve conscience and stewardship, a direct concern for the pain and welfare of life. Thus instead of depleting nature the aim is to only take enough and to give back, to make nature (the whole) greater. Only through this can humanity find fulfilment and liberation (*siddha loka*, thus to become Jain is to affirm every organism and connection in nature) (Chapple 2002c, 2005b; Jain 2002; Koller 2002; Kumar 2002b; Shilapi 2002; Singhvi 1990).

Recognizing an intertwined place in nature in this way is something achieved through conquering inner temptations and acting carefully: Jainism derives from *jina* meaning 'peaceful conqueror of self', with this seen as highlighting a need to overcome egoism and embrace and protect wider nature. Thus (adherence to) fundamental Jain principles are stressed: for example, the 'three jewels' of *right knowledge*, understanding how *karma* binds the soul, *right faith*, belief in the essentials of Jainism, and *right conduct*, behaving sensitively; the 'five vows' (*vratas*) of non-violence (*ahimsa*), truthfulness/not lying (*satya*; not distorting interdependent reality), not-stealing (*asteya*; avoiding greed), love without lust (*bramacarya*; not demeaning the body, human or natural) and non-possession (*aparigraha*; living simply); the 'rules of conduct' (*samitis*) of care in walking, accepting things, picking up/putting down things and excretion, and other principles such as compassion (*jiva-daya*), equanimity (*samyaktva*), forgiveness (*kshama*), purification (*tapas*; fasting, freeing from moral dirt), simplicity (*samyama*) or universal friendliness (*maitri*); and the basic need to refrain from 'obnoxious habits', such as alcohol, gambling, hunting or meat-eating, or 'violent actions', such as, digging, drinking non-filtered water or ploughing, as well as the abuse of animals, the breaking of oaths or harming others livelihood. In line with such ideas Shilapi (2002) highlights the Jain daily prayer as containing a word of forgiveness for pain caused to all life-forms while Wiley (2002:46) highlights the practice of asking forgiveness from nature: 'I ask pardon of all living creatures, may all of them pardon me, may I have friendship with all beings and enmity with none' (*Pratikramana-sutra* 49)[23] (Chapple 2002a, 2002c, 2005b; Cort 2002; Jain 2002; Koller 2002; Kumar 2002a, 2002b; Regenstein 1991; Shilapi 2002; Singhvi 1990; Tobias 1994; Wiley 2002).

Essentially these principles highlight the need to be responsible in life, to be thoughtful and careful (for Shilapi (2002) carefulness in all actions is the norm for the Jain way of life). And of these, Kumar (2002b) and Singhvi (1990) argue that the fundamental principle and central teaching is *ahimsa* (avoiding harmful or negligent thought, speech or action, in the past, present or future), what they see as a way of life more than a dogma (*Ahimsa parma dharmah*, 'nonviolence is the supreme religion'). Callicott (1997) sees this as the moral core of Jainism, Soorideva (2003) sees Jaina culture based on it, Shilapi (2002) sees it as the root of the Jain path of purification, and Koller (2002) sees it as a fundamental ecological principle (of respect for all life-forms).

> Of all the world's religions, none is more strict in its commitment to avoid harming living creatures that Jainism ... The Jains' reverence for life is so strong that devout Jainist monks go to extreme lengths to avoid harming even insects and 'lower' life forms such as mold and yeast. They sweep the path in front of them so as not to walk on insects and refrain from tilling the soil or brewing beverages. The Jainists truly live their religion, adopting a life-style intended to avoid killing any of the earth's other life forms. (Regenstein 1991:229)

> The earliest known Jaina text, the *Acaranga Sutra*, lists in detail different forms of life and advocates various techniques for their protection ... [discussing] avoiding harm not only to animals, but also to plants, by not touching them, and to the bodies that dwell in the earth, the water, the fire, and the air. For instance Jaina monks and nuns must not stamp upon the earth, or swim in water, or light or extinguish fires, or thrash their arms in the air. (Chapple 2002c:284)

Ahimsa, in this sense, is an avoidance of the negative (detrimental to the whole) and an embracing of the positive (beneficial to the whole), maximizing not diminishing nature. It involves experiences that unify the cosmos, creating identity between self and other. It is souls supporting souls, enabling the true communal self to be experienced, allowing experience of totality (thus dispersing *karma* and liberating the soul from the birth/death/rebirth cycle) (Bassett et al. 2000; Callicott 1997; Cort 2002; Jain 2002; Koller 2002; Kumar 2002b; Regenstein 1991; Shilapi 2002; Singhvi 1990; Tatia 2002; Tobias 1994; Wiley 2002).

> The *Acaranga* [*Sutra*] ... explains ... 'You are the one whom you intend to kill, you are the one you intend to tyrannize, you are the one whom you intend to torment, you are the one you intend to punish and drive away. The enlightened one who lives up to this dictum neither kills nor causes others to kill' ... 'Bondage and emancipation are within yourself.'[24] (Tatia 2002:7)

To achieve this asceticism is stressed, ascetic Jain holy men/women being seen as models of right livelihood, meditating to create awareness of actions, avoiding anger, desire and harm to all forms of life in all thoughts and actions, and living simply, with minimal consumption, not owning possessions (Kumar (2002a) and Shilapi (2002) highlight the importance of nature in assisting this, providing beauty, communion, food and shelter). Such asceticism is also seen influencing a lay quasi-ascetic lifestyle, a 'temporary asceticism' of fasting, minimal production/consumption, and vegetarianism, with no brewing, farming, fishing, hunting or mineral exploitation. And it may be more widely influential than that, Jainism being seen as a 'radical ecological lifestyle' able to stimulate a global ecological lifestyle, caring for nature rather than abusing it, restraining modern industrialization: Jains are seen addressing pollution, advocating vegetarianism, campaigning against nuclear weapons, providing animal sanctuaries and supporting peace organizations, as well as providing ecological education and inspiring legislation to protect nature, with the *Anuvrat* movement, a series of 12 vows, ranging from 'I will not kill' to 'I will do my best to avoid pollution', dedicated to stimulating people to adapt their lifestyle to create a more non-violent world (Callicott 1997; Chapple 2002a, 2002b, 2002c; Cort 2002; Jain 2002; Kumar 2002b; Regenstein 1991; Shilapi 2002; Singhvi 1990; Tatia 2002; Tobias 1994; Wiley 2002).

Jainism is thus seen as able to remind the world of the complexity and sacredness of nature and the moral advantage of living peacefully and simply within it, stressing the need for individual transformation to enable social transformation. It is seen as able to stimulate environmentally friendly behaviour, stressing ways to resist the temptations of consumerism that lead to a disregard for nature and create a 'light' living in it, with Tatia (2002) stressing guidelines for this: relinquish anger and hatred, do not kill or let others kill, but find whatever means possible to protect life; speak truthfully and resist injustice even if it may threaten your own safety; make every effort to resolve conflicts, peacefully, by consensus; do not make accumulation an aim of life but live simply and share; do not force others to adopt your views but remain open to theirs; be aware of the existence of suffering and find ways to help those who suffer. Such ideas, for Kumar (2002a), unlike Western ideas of 'I think, therefore I am', stressing exploitative individual action on an objective world, stress 'You are, therefore I am' (*so'ham*), highlighting interdependence and mutual care, stressing reciprocal action with a subjective world. In a similar vein, Chapple (2001b) sees Jainism offering a world-view that both decentralizes and universalizes ethics, going beyond anthropocentric concerns, bringing into vivid relief the urgency of life in its elemental, vegetable and animal forms, what Cort (2002) sees as a combination of a 'context-sensitive ethic' of differentiated souls and a 'universal ethic' of the potential of each.

Conclusions

Ecological interpretations of Indian religions, based around the traditions of Hinduism and Jainism, see them valuing and revering nature, seeing it as alive and interdependent, a dynamic, diverse yet harmonious, whole, with humanity an integral part, needing to recognize this and affirm the whole, not act selfishly: Hinduism is seen as deifying nature, stressing organic visions seeing the universe as a dynamic, living, organism, made up of interconnected parts, a sacred topography, seeing the divine manifested in all forces, objects and processes; Jainism is seen as a religious ecology stressing no god or first cause but rather seeing the universe as uncreated and eternal thus sacralizing worldly existence, stressing a livingness of the world where all things desire and possess life and soul and thus are sacred, having inherent value and integrity; humanity in these schemes is related to nature and needs to act with non-violence and live respectfully, responsibly and simply, within it, facilitating its diverse harmony.

Hinduism is stressed as revering and valuing rivers and trees, seeing them infused with the divine, symbolizing humanity's sacred reciprocal relationship to nature, rivers being tangible forms of the divine, moral purifiers and sources of spiritual abilities, with life-giving potential, trees symbols of fecundity, generous and tolerant, the forest, diverse yet harmonic, being a model for Indian civilization, symbolizing divine totality. Nature, in this sense, is seen as the body of god (Vishnu) who encompasses and sustains it (being incarnated in it as *avatara*), or inhabited by goddesses who compassionately nourish it, being the embodiment of a divine creative principle/dynamic energy (*prakriti/shakti*). Reality, in this sense, is a oneness incorporating manyness, a divine/nature union, the aim of life being to unify inner-self (*atman*) with wider (divine) reality (*Brahman*), uncovering and maintaining the harmonious cosmic order (*dharma*, righteousness, a structure of reality and a way of acting of eternal balance, *sanatana*). In this sense, the moral quality of thoughts/actions affect the whole and determine fate (*karma*, effects of action, *samsara*, rebirth), either self-sacrificially liberating from the life cycle (uniting with the divine) or egotistically binding to it (separating from the divine), with a main way to achieve the former being non-violence (*ahimsa*), restraining limited ego-self (which causes all nature and thus the self to suffer) in favour of wider (*dharmic*) self, a life of self-sacrifice (following the cosmic sacrifice), acting for the common good of all. A major influential exponent of this is seen as Gandhi stressing a non-exploitative self-rule, acting communally, locally and simply, an ascetic, desireless, action (*karma-yoga*), highlighted in devotional rituals, local ecologies and non-violent protest, reciprocally engaging nature, expanding its potential.

Jainism is stressed as envisaging a living cosmos, widening the concept of life, including sentient and non-sentient forms, based on the number of senses (including 'non-living' in a Western sense; in its barest form, breath, bodily strength and the sense of touch), this seen as leading to a deeper appreciation of biodiversity and the inherent value of nature, stressing its care. All nature, in this sense, has integrity, life-forms possessing a soul (*jiva*) reincarnated in different forms dependent on moral actions (either selfish, clouding true perception of life's interdependence, accumulating *karma*, gross matter binding to the life cycle, or selfless, recognizing and enhancing interdependence, banishing *karma*, achieving liberation from the life cycle). Reality is thus holistically moral: everything exists in the interdependent life cycle. Such ideas stress 'many-sidedness', a diversity of partial perspectives combining to form a whole, knowledge of this being intrinsic to souls but distorted by egoism, the world not being as it appears to be to any one life-form's (e.g. humanity's) limited perspective, different claims to knowledge (e.g. nature's) needing to be recognized. Such a view sees humanity's failure to respect nature as unnatural, stressing it needing to recognize and cultivate its intertwined place in nature, realizing that life is dependent on the efforts of different life-forms and that they and the whole they support need to be cared for, what is seen as the lifting up of souls, a striving for harmonious existence (*sarvodayavada*). In this light, various principles, such as, non-violence (*ahimsa*, seen as the moral core of Jainism), truthfulness, non-possession or simplicity, guiding caring and responsible thought and action, are stressed (with asceticism the purest lifestyle) and Jainism stressed as demonstrating a positive ecological lifestyle of context-sensitive reverence and gratitude.

Notes

[1] Referenced to Diana Eck, Ganga: The Goddess in Hindu Sacred Geography, in *Devi: Goddesses of India,* John Stratton Hawley and Donna Wulff, eds (Berkeley: University of California Press, 1995), p. 141.

[2] Hinduism is stressed as being a variety of beliefs/practices, named after the Indus bioregion (by Persians, British colonizers): 'Vedic' literature (Samhitas, Brahmanas, Aranyakas, Upanishads; 'Code of Manu' laws); epic poems (*Mahabharata, Bhagavad Gita, Ramayana)*; deity worship (*Vaishnavism; Shaivism*). Thus it is seen as difficult to define, covering a 'great tradition' of scripture, a 'little tradition' of village beliefs, an urban 'neo' Hinduism, oral traditions and popular customs, with no single teacher/text. It is thus seen in a broad, inclusive, sense ecologically, something Prime (1996) sees as apt as Hindus do not separate religion from daily life or other faiths but see all stressing the unity of God, humanity and nature (seeing India as *Bharat*, way of life common to all, linked to *Sanantan Dharma*, the eternal essence of life, a possible legitimate name for Hinduism) (see Callicott 1997; Chapple 1994, 2000, 2001b, 2004; Foltz 2002b; Narayanan 2001, 2005b, 2005c; Regenstein 1991; Rukmani 2000; Van Horn 2006).

[3] Referenced to Monier Monier-Williams, *Brahmanism and Hinduism* (New York: Macmillan, 1891), p. 350; from *Cultural heritage of India,* vol. 4, Haridas Bhattacharya, ed. (Calcutta: Ramakrishna Mission, Institute of Culture, 1983), p. 479.

[4] Referenced to *Hindu Principles of Protecting and Organising the Environment* (Banwari, New Delhi, 1991).

[5] Referenced to verses gathered from Hindu scriptures by Balbir Mathur.

[6] From Prime (1996:26).

[7] From Nelson (2000:134).

[8] From Nelson (2000:132).

[9] Referenced to Dwivedi, O. P., and Tiwari, B. N. *Environmental Crisis and Hindu Religion*, New Delhi: Gitanjali, 1987.

10 Referenced to Vandana Shiva, *Staying Alive: Women, Ecology, and Development* (London: Zed Books, 1989), pp. 38–9, 48.

11 Nelson (2000) sees ecological valorization of *prakriti* as not traditionally Hindu but a new appreciation of it. Jacobsen (2005e), similarly, sees Hindu theologians (ecologically) dissolving the dualism of *prakriti* and *purusha*, or consciousness.

12 From Dwivedi (2000:15).

13 Hindu liberation is seen as possibly world-denying, seeing nature as an illusion covering spiritual reality: Nelson (2000:135–50) sees the *Bhagavad Gita* stressing *hierarchical dualism*, self not nature, *antinomian and deterministic tendencies*, holistic amoralism accepting destructive action, *apatheia*, abandoning attachment and *static social vision*, favouring the status quo. Others stress industrialization in India and different 'conservation' to the West, seeing sacred purity not exclusive from physical pollution. However, some literature is seen as world-affirming, renouncing consumerism, stressing holistic liberation and Indian eco-activism and eco-friendly subsistence contexts (Agarwal 2000; Alley 2005; Callicott 1997; Chapple 1994, 2000, 2001b; Dwivedi 1996; Jacobsen 2005c; James 2000; Kinsley 1994; Narayanan 2001, 2005a, 2005b, 2005c; Regenstein 1991; Rukmani 2000; Van Horn 2006).

14 From Jacobsen (2005a:31), referenced to Gandhi, Mohandas, K., *An Autobiography: The Story of My Experience with Truth* (Boston: Beacon Press, 1957), p. 505).

15 Referenced to Sadhusangananda dasa, 'The Search for Ecology in the Bhagavad-Gita: Critical Examination of an Academic Study', *On the Way to Krishna*, Spring, Summer, Winter, 1998, 6–7, 6–8, 6–8.

16 Referenced to Thomas Weber, *Hugging the Trees: The History of the Chipko Movement* (New Delhi: Penguin Books, 1988), p. 53.

17 For Chapple (2000:xxxiii–xxxv, xliii–xlv) this needs a '*Dharmic* administrative model' based on a 'Gandhian ethos' integrating tradition with secularism, addressing different groups through different ecological commitments.

18 Jainism is stressed as traced to 'Mahavira' or 'Jina', the most recent of 24 '*jinas*' (Tirthankaras, 'path-finders' helping others enlightenment), who widely defined life and stressed non-violence and spirituality sustaining it. It is seen as having no missionary tradition but stressing lay cultivation, its oldest text, *Acaranga Sutra*, seen as stressing non-harm to animals/plants, and *Tattvartha Sutra* seeing souls weighted by *karmic* material but able to be liberated (later literature developing stories, poetry and philosophy) (see Callicott 1997; Chapple 2002b, 2002c, 2005b; Kumar 2002a; Palmer and Finlay 2003; Regenstein 1991; Shilapi 2002; Singhvi 1990; Tobias 1994).

19 From Jain (2002:171), referenced to *Pavayanasaro Sutta, Gatha* 47 in *Sramana Siddhanta Pathavali* (Jaipur: Kunthuvijaya Granthamala Samiti, 1982), p. 268.

20 From Chapple (2002c:284).

21 Referenced to *Sraddha-Pratikramana Sutra* (*Prabodha Tika*), Pannyas Bhadrankarvijaygani and Muni Kalyanprabhvijay, eds (Bombay: Jain Sahitya Vikas Mandal, 1977), pp. 2, 120–1.

22 Jain liberation is seen as possibly problematic, stressing non-violence for self not nature, with humanity, through which liberation is achieved, prioritized. Thus Jains may not protect nature in a Western sense (damaging it through being influential in business or seeing some eco-actions as spiritually unacceptable) and to say it is inherently eco-friendly may be a misinterpretation. However, for

Cort (2002) liberation may include responsibly acting within nature, while Jain (2002) sees (charitable) Jain businesses as goals for it, stimulating environmental ethics (see Callicott 1997; Chapple 2001b, 2002b, 2005b; Cort 2002; Regenstein 1991).

[23] Referenced to Williams, R., *Jaina Yoga: A Survey of Mediaeval Sravakacaras* (London: Oxford University Press, 1963), p. 207.

[24] Referenced to John M. Koller and Patricia Koller, *Asian Philosophies* (Upper Saddle River, NJ: Prentice Hall, 1998), p. 37.

Chapter 4

Chinese (Confucian and Daoist) Visions[1]

Dao-De Jing [states] . . . 'The Tao gives birth to the One. The One gives birth to the Two. The Two gives birth to the Three. The Three give birth to the Ten Thousand.' These words describe how the Tao, the essence of all, gives birth to Nature – the One – which in turn gives birth to Yin and Yang – the Two. Yin is female, moist, cold, the moon, autumn and winter, shadows and waters. Yang is male, dry, hot, the sun, spring and summer, brightness and earth. From the perpetual striving of Yin and Yang arises the Three – Heaven, Earth and Humanity. Humanity must try to balance the opposites of Heaven and Earth.[2]

The virtue of the universe is wholeness. It regards all things as equal. The virtue of the sage is wholeness. He too regards all things as equal . . . Can you always embrace Oneness without the slightest separation of body and mind . . . love your people and serve your state with no self-exaltation . . . Give birth to and nourish all things without desiring to possess them . . . Give of yourself, without expecting something in return. Assist people, but do not attempt to control them. This is to realize the integral virtue of the universe . . . Tao, the subtle energy of the universe, is omnipresent . . . All things derive their life from it . . . Yet it takes possession of nothing. It accomplishes its purpose, but it claims no merit. It clothes and feeds all, but has no ambition to be master over anyone. Thus it may be regarded as 'the Small'. All things return to it, and it contains them. Yet it claims no authority over them. Thus it may be recognized as 'the Great'.

(Tao Te Ching, *Lao Tzu* 1996:67–70)

Ecological interpretations of Chinese religions revolve around the traditions of Confucianism and Daoism,[3] seeing them differing in specific teachings but sharing a world-view that is holistic, organic and vitalistic, seeing the universe as a dynamic, interdependent whole, diverse parts making up a balanced, harmonious community (of which humanity is a part and thus connected to nature): Kinsley (1994:69–70) and Weiming (2002:210–16) stress *continuity*, a continuous dynamic web of relations, *wholeness*, self-containment and all-encompassment, and *dynamism*, a 'vigorous' open system with no closure. In this scheme, there is no creation and no external creator God or heaven to be sought, rather the universe is complete unto itself, there is no reality outside it (nature is thus the source of all value and spirit and matter are unified). It is a mutually reinforcing orchestral whole without a conductor (based on a creative force, *Dao*, enlivened by a vital energy, *qi*, expressed in polarities, *yin/yang*), a spontaneous, self-generating, process (dynamic energy-fields rather than static matter) connecting all things, characterized by union not disunion, synthesis not separation (*sheng-sheng*, 'production and reproduction', or fecundity of life, emphasizing value lying in the creative transformation of nature). Relational change is the basis of reality and humanity rather than trying to return to an original external state needs to model itself on the ceaseless vitality of natural processes, creating harmony with nature, what is seen as the 'continuity of being' (thus there may be little world-denial, rather the world is affirmed as the proper place for existence, damaging nature would damage self and would make little sense, and perceiving it as static and external obstructs true vision and undermines humanity's natural capacity to form union) (Callicott 1997; Cheng 2002; Kinsley 1994; Maguire 2000; Snyder 2006; Tucker 1994, 2001, 2002a, 2004, 2005b; Tucker and Berthrong 1998; Weiming 2001, 2002).

> [T]he Chinese worldview tends towards inclusiveness . . . Among the notions central to [this] is that of order and harmony in the universe. Heaven, Earth, and humans are seen as coexisting, interdependent, and interconnected through their ongoing relationships with each other [determining] . . . how the balance and harmony of the cosmos is maintained. This worldview suggests constant . . . harmonious interaction. (Foltz 2002b:208)

Such ideas are seen as non-anthropocentric (although not indifferent to humanity as it is integral to the universe), impartially allowing things to exist within the 'Great Harmony', the *Dao* ('the Way', of heaven and earth), a primordial wisdom of reality and spontaneous well-spring of creativity and harmony. The *Dao* is the origin and essence of everything, undefinable, existing beyond form. It follows no principle other than its own being, being both what there is and how it is, the principle and the being of existence, transcendent, the creative source, and immanent, a vital power (*de*, also seen as virtue), eternal and ineffable yet fecund and creative (the governing principle of nature is thus in it). It is the unmanifest, nameless, generating power and sustaining process, beyond distinction (only able to be approached through image, paradox or intuition), empty yet full of potentiality, a nothingness that becomes a somethingness, pre-existence and existence, making no effort but having infinite effect, doing nothing (*wu-wei*) but leaving nothing undone (*wu bu wei*). It is thus seen as natural creative spontaneity (*tzu-jan*), an underlying source and movement, working via a process of 'self-so-ing' (*ziran*, naturalness), a

'reversing and transforming', continuously folding back on and being preg-
nant with itself in a superfluity of vitality and power (not imposing but allowing things to spontaneously come into being of their own accord) (Ames
2001; Bassett et al. 2000; Callicott 1997; Cheng 1998; Jiyu 2001; Kalton 1998;
Maguire 2000; Miller 2005a, 2005b; Palmer and Finlay 2003; Paper 2005; Ro
1998; Tucker 1994; Weiming 2002; Xiaogan 2001).

> The Great Harmony . . . underlies all counter processes of floating and sink-
> ing, rising and falling, and motion and rest. It is the origin of the process of
> fusion and intermingling, of overcoming and being overcome, and of expan-
> sion and contraction. At the commencement these processes are incipient,
> subtle, obscure, easy, and simple, but at the end they are extensive, great,
> strong, and firm. It is *ch'ien* (Heaven) that begins with the Knowledge of
> Change, and *k'un* (Earth) that models after simplicity . . . Unless the whole
> universe is in the process of fusion and intermingling like fleeting forces
> moving in all directions, it may not be called Great Harmony. (Weiming
> 2002:212–13)[4]

An essential component of the *Dao*, arising from the undifferentiated 'Great
Vacuity' and functioning as the manifested 'Harmony', is *qi* a 'vital material
energy' or primordial substance that enlivens the universe (materially, morally
and spiritually, objects and spaces, differences being variations in form). *Qi* is
seen as creating the movement and reciprocity of the universe, being the basis
of the interaction and continuation of life, the spontaneous arising and decay-
ing of things. Everything is pervaded by it and thus has vitality, the universe
likened to an organism enlivened by flowing blood and rhythmic breathing
patterns of *qi*. It is one and many, coherent things but also change, like water:
a thing (water), action (to water), attribute (watery) and modality (fluid); 'As
a metaphor for Dao in the world, It is like the streams and creeks flowing to
the rivers and seas' (*Daode jing* 32).[5] *Qi* is thus seen as the principle by which
micro and macro dimensions of being interrelate and coevolve, 'resonating' in
different forms of energy/matter within a 'cosmic resonance' (*kan-ying*, something able to be nourished, giving a moral dimension situating the ethical
vitality of individuals against the dynamic pattern of *qi* in nature). Although
impermanent or indeterminate by itself *qi* is thus not purposeless but an inherently ordering force (related to *li*, principles or patterns of change), leading
to proportionate evolution of different life-forms which have moral meaning
and purpose through comprehending its resonant flow (this implying a need
to balance particular life resonances with cosmic resonance, correct human
existence being the process of flowing with rather than resisting *qi*, such ideas
being seen as possibly providing a basis for a this-worldly spirituality encouraging human reciprocity with nature) (Adler 1998; Ames 2001; Callicott 1997;
Cheng 2002; Kalland 2005; Kalton 1998; Kinsley 1994; Lai 2001; Maguire 2000;

Miller 2001, 2005a; 2005b; Tucker 1998, 2005a; Weiming 2002; Weller and Bol 1998).

> The fact that the things of the world, whether rivers or mountains, plants or animals . . . provide beneficial support for all things is the result of the natural influence of the moving power [*qi*] . . . And as it completely provides for the flourish and transformation of all things, it is all the more spatially unrestricted . . . it operates in time and proceeds with time . . . there is no time at which it does not operate. (Weiming 2002:213)[6]

Qi makes everything flow together, connecting spirit and matter through constant diffusion and fusion, consisting of opposites working in dialectical unison (polar but not dualistic), symbolized by two primal energies, *yin* and *yang*. These correspond to complementary dualities that constantly transform into each other in a balanced cosmic heartbeat of expansion and contraction of *qi* (*yang* is active, bright, fire, hard, heaven, hot, masculine; *yin* is passive, dark, water, soft, earth, cold, female). This gives rise to the phenomenal reality of nature (via five generative or destructive phases (*wu-hsing*), wood to fire to earth to metal to water), things manifesting *yin* and *yang* in different combinations, with change being the waxing and waning of each, a projection (*yang-qi*) and reception (*yin-qi*) of energy, which, when in harmony, fuses into the *Dao* and creates the energy of life (*sheng*, birth, constant reversion of emptiness and fullness: 'the myriad things shouldering yin embrace yang, And blending the qi together make it harmonious', *Daode jing* 42[7]). Existence is thus the harmonic process of flowing with transformation, yielding rather than resisting, reciprocal communication rather than competitive opposition (the supreme vision, the 'Great Peace', is of mutual communication, and to resist this futile and dangerous, causing conflict and disorder: humanity, associated with 'Central Harmony-*qi*', is seen as needing to balance *yin-qi* (heaven) and *yang-qi* (earth)) (Ames 2001; Callicott 1997; Cheng 1998, 2002; Jiyu 2001; Kinsley 1994; Kuwako 1998; Lai 2001; Miller 2001, 2005b; Palmer and Finlay 2003; Ro 1998; Weiming 2002; Weller and Bol 1998).

> The functioning of heaven and earth occurs through the Five Phases of yin and yang qi. Being generated by the Five Phases, all the myriad things are considered as their children. If human beings understand the way of heaven and earth, the operation of yin and yang qi, as well as the sequence of Five Phases, they will be able to perceive the rise and decline of society, the life and death of themselves and all the myriad things. (Jiyu and Yuanguo 2001:114)[8]

There are thus good and bad ways of channelling *qi*, causing harmony and growth or disorder and destruction, the aim being to create the former, partnering not exploiting nature. Chinese gardens, for example, are seen as demonstrating the harmony of *qi* (and human/nature relationship) being human cultivation responding to natural essence/patterns, evoking deeper reality, serving as ideals of natural perfection and places to experience a deeper dimension of existence (giving multiple perspectives forming a coordinated whole instead of a single experience, expressing diversity in animals/plants and unity in stone/water). Chinese painting, similarly, is seen as capturing the *qi* of natural objects and arranging them to show relational balance, demonstrating the diverse harmony of nature (and that human presence is relational not dominant), something achieved through the artist communing with nature to overcome the delusion of separateness and create naturally, spontaneously (*ziran*), conveying deeper natural reality (also *ziran*, thus creative spontaneity and nature are the same). Painting and gardening, in this sense, are seen as '*ziran*-oriented activities' spontaneously capturing and embodying the (natural) *Dao* in image and form so as to create windows into it for others. *Fengshui* is seen as similar, placing objects harmoniously in line with nature's *qi* ensuring health ('auspicious *qi*', the productive *yang* phase; obstructing it is 'baneful *qi*' the destructive *yin* phase), as is Chinese medicine (e.g. acupuncture, herbal remedies) seeing health as harmonious bodily exchange of *qi*, 'illness' disturbing this and 'healing' harmonizing it (which as body *qi* is connected to cosmic *qi* involves human harmony with nature in a balanced lifestyle, seeing health holistically) (Barnhill 2005a; Bruun 2002; Field 2001; Kinsley 1994; Kohn 2001; Meyer 2001; Miller 2001, 2004, 2005b; Paper 2005; Weller and Bol 1998).

For Callicott (1997), Foltz (2002b), Kinsley (1994) and Tucker (1994), Confucianism and Daoism interpret the above Chinese world-view in different ways, the former actively, stressing harmony within society, reflecting cosmic harmony, the latter passively, stressing living in accordance with the *Dao*/nature, as opposed to cultivating or striving against it. The former is thus seen to stress secondary causality of humans, the need to responsibly create a harmonious, just society in harmony with nature, via personal/social cultivation and commitment, seeing a moral ruler and humane government, promoting education and responsible ethical practice, as the highest examples, enabling peaceful and productive existence. The latter, by contrast, is seen to stress primary causality of the *Dao*, the need to be in accordance with it, stressing simplicity and spontaneity, a withdrawal from social/political affairs and cultivation of closeness to nature, seeing the hermit in a mountain retreat as the ideal, protecting nature not by overt involvement but by detached, subtle, indirection, stressing non-egocentric action (*wu-wei*), following the unfolding of natural processes. For Tucker (1994), such perspectives may be fruitful for environmental ethics: humanity may need greater Confucian understanding of the importance of moral leadership, education and a sense of responsibility to nature, rethinking individual–society–nature connections, while at the same time it may need greater Daoist understanding of the subtle unfolding of the principles/ processes of nature, attuning to its complexities, radically rethinking human–earth relations.[9]

Confucianism

Confucianism is fundamentally different from anthropocentrism because it professes the unity of man and Heaven rather than the imposition of the human will upon nature. In fact the anthropocentric assumption that man is put on earth to pursue knowledge and, as knowledge expands, so does man's domain over earth is quite different from the Confucian perception of the pursuit of knowledge as an integral part of one's self-cultivation [where] . . . human transformation of nature [is] . . . an integrative effort to learn to live harmoniously in one's natural environment.

(Taylor 1998:44–5)[10]

Confucianism[11] is stressed as stressing 'anthropocosmism' or 'cosmic humanism' rather than anthropocentrism, recognizing the embeddedness of humanity in cosmic relationships, and thus its wider responsibilities, stressing holistic moral education and a social system cultivating hierarchical loyalties, these seen as offering stability and moral rectification, contributing to social and environmental order through establishing just and sustainable societies. Such ideas, based on Confucius's teachings devoted to establishing order via human virtues, are seen by Bassett et al. (2000) and Weiming (1998, 2001) as being built on four interrelated principles, 'self', 'community', 'nature' and 'heaven', which stress that the self is never isolated but always a centre of relationships: mutuality between self and community, harmony between humanity and nature, and communication between humanity and heaven, are defining characteristics and supreme values in the human project (to be sacred is to be in tune with one's surroundings; humanity thus needs to collaborate as a coparticipant with nature and heaven, mutual responsiveness between the human 'heart-mind' and the 'Way of Heaven' being the ultimate path). The focus is on human roles and responsibilities, to family and society (and environment; linked to cosmic rhythms and values, hence anthropo*cosmism*). The human ideal is a 'superior/noble' person (*chun tzu*) re-creating the order of the cosmos in individual character and social (and environmental) action, what is seen as a 'concern-consciousness', an inner character centred on the Way of Heaven. Self-identity and human society thus need to harmonize with cosmic patterns/ principles (human virtues having cosmological components: humaneness, righteousness, propriety and wisdom, corresponding to fecundity, flourishing, advantage and firmness). Such ideas affirm relationality, humanity being seen in kinship (continuous) with other life, related via the 'parents' Heaven and earth (the correct attitude to nature is thus one of filial responsibility) (Bassett et al. 2000; Berthrong 1998; Callicott 1997; Cheng 1998; Kinsley 1994; Snyder 2006; Tucker 2002a, 2004, 2005c; Tucker and Berthrong 1998; Weiming 1998, 2002; Wensveen 2005).

Heaven is my Father and earth is my mother, and even such a small creature as I find an intimate place in their midst. Therefore that which fills the universe I regard as my body, and that which directs the universe I consider as my nature. All people are my bothers and sisters, and all things are my companions. The great ruler (the emperor) is the eldest son of my parents (Heaven and Earth), and the great ministers are his stewards. Respect the ages – that is the way to treat them. Show deep love toward the orphaned and the weak – this is the way to treat them. The sage identifies his character with that of the Heaven and Earth. Even those who are tired, inform, cripples, or sick; those who have no brothers or children, wives or husbands, are all my brothers and sisters who are in distress and have no one to turn to. In life I will honor and serve Heaven and Earth. ('Western Inscription', Maguire 2000:83)

The highest Confucian ideal, the most authentic manifestation of humanity, involves forming a trinity with earth and heaven. Humanity thus has a special role. It is seen as the 'eldest sibling' in nature, with the most refined expression of *qi*, with most sentience and sensitivity, and thus able to comprehend, and being impelled to fulfil, the interconnectedness of reality: through moral, spiritual and social cultivation, realizing a wider identity, bringing personal morality into harmony with the lager cosmic pattern, humanity is able to form 'one body' with the cosmos, an inclusive 'sympathetic resonance' with heaven and earth, fulfilling the harmony of nature. Humanity, in this sense, is the agent of cosmic transformation, entering and nurturing the cosmological process of change, transcending anthropocentrism through recognizing and experiencing the world as one body and realizing the cosmic harmony (the cosmos suffering without this). It is, then, charged with enhancing and refining nature, which, as human nature is interrelated with this, means enhancing and refining itself. There is an innate goodness in humanity that needs to be realized to fulfil nature's harmony, the power of 'sincerity' (*ch'eng*, also seen as 'authenticity') emanating from the human heart to the cosmos (humanity's authentic, sincere, nature affects the rejuvenating forces in nature through realizing a 'betweenness' or mutual identification of it with heaven and earth). Self and social cultivation are thus needed to realize humanity's inherent 'heart-mind', its reciprocal partnership with heaven and earth (Bassett et al. 2000; Cheng 1998; Kinsley 1994; Ro 1998; Tucker 2002a, 2004; Tucker and Berthrong 1998; Weiming 1998, 2002).

Only those who are most sincere . . . can fully realize their own nature. If they can realize their own nature, they can fully realize human nature. If they can fully realize human nature, they can fully realize the nature of things. If they can fully realize the nature of things, they can take part in the transforming and nourishing process of Heaven and Earth. If they can take part in the transforming and nourishing process of Heaven and Earth, they can form a trinity with Heaven and Earth. ('Doctrine of the Mean', Weiming 2001:249)[12]

Such a view envisages the mind forming a union with nature, merging the self into an expanded reality via reciprocal participation (not objective appropriation). Humanity is thus situated within the dynamic, organic processes of nature and exists in expanding, concentric circles of relationships, from self to family to community to nation to nature (to heaven, with moral cultivation regulating self, family, community, and so on). This stresses the importance of relationships and cooperation, a 'mutual reciprocity' of obligations and support and larger sense of common good, including indebtedness to past generations and obligations to descendants (the individual is supported by and supports the other circles, an exchange of mutual obligations). Humans are thus defined by their relationships, having a socially constituted self needing constant cultivation (education, meditation, spiritual discipline; overcoming inappropriate selfish desires and structures and creating appropriate communal ones). In this sense, Confucianism has been termed a 'social ecology' and a 'political ecology' as well as a 'moral ecology' involving carefully integrated programmes of self-realization, harmonized family life and well-ordered states (Callicott 1997; Cheng 1998; Kalton 1998; Maguire 2000; Ro 1998; Tucker 1994, 2002a, 2004, 2005a, 2005b, 2005c; Weiming 2001, 2002).

The ancients who wished to illuminate their 'illuminating virtue' to all under Heaven first governed their states. Wishing to govern their states, they first regulated their families. Wishing to regulate their families, they first cultivated their personal lives. Wishing to cultivate their personal lives, they first rectified their hearts and minds. Wishing to rectify their hearts and minds, they first authenticated their intentions. Wishing to authenticate their intentions, they first refined their knowledge. The refinement of knowledge lay in the study of things. ('The Great Learning', Weiming 2001:248)[13]

For Weiming (2001), then, the 'Mandate of Heaven', or moral law, enjoins humanity to take part in cosmic transformation (it is predicated on it), cultivating the self to embody the creative life process ('Heaven, earth, and humans are the basis of all creatures. Heaven gives them birth, earth nourishes them, and humans bring them to completion', Tung Ch'shu).[14] To realize this involves 'moral responsiveness' or 'relational resonance' in tune with 'cosmic resonance' (*kan-ying*), a non-linear causality whereby different things and events influence each other (via *qi*, the coming and going of vital essence, connecting thoughts and actions). Such resonance involves mutual/reciprocal response to myriad things (to movements of *qi* in the world, which responds to 'vibrations' from things and events). This is a 'companionship' with all things, recognizing that the feelings of grass and humanity, for example, are of the same nature. Humanity, then, is interconnected with nature, part of the 'internal resonance' of its vital forces (*Dao/qi*), something it can enhance through an 'aesthetic' experience of mutuality and immediacy, suspending sensory and conceptual apparatus to embrace nature via sensitivity (intuitively). Reality thus involves a web of 'resonant affinities' and experiencing this affinity sends positive 'resonant vibrations' and brings harmony, while not doing so brings disharmony (thus every action has wide-ranging effects, everything has 'resonant influences') (Adler 1998; Maguire 2000; Taylor 1998; Tucker 2002a; Weiming 2002; Weller and Bol 1998).

In line with these ideas there is seen an appropriate human response to nature in accordance with *li*, principles or emergent patterns amidst the flux of the cosmos that give structure to *qi* (*qi* causes things, *li* direct their evolution; the universe is thus an open yet regular system). There is natural foundation for moral conduct, a proper moral response determined by the relationship between things. Each has an appropriate place and function in the web of life and needs to act and be treated accordingly, governed by *li* (linked to the 'universal principle' of the *Dao*). Thus humanity is biologically endowed with principles for structuring thought and action which if realized (in communal, harmonious action: *yi*, appropriateness) result in an integrated world ('survival of the fittest' involves holistically fitting in with the cosmic pattern, something requiring humanity which has the 'fullest' *li*). Such a human 'investigation of *li*', understanding complex relational reality and acting with harmonious conduct fitting with it, is seen exemplified by the 'sage', the 'superior person' who has 'integrative wisdom', spontaneously and properly responding to all things, instantiating the perfection of natural order in thought and action, combining heaven and earth. The sage is able to merge with the *Dao* through curbing selfish desires and acting as a 'refined' person, understanding and creating natural harmony. He is 'authentic' (morally responsive, reciprocal), fully developing his nature and the nature of others, assisting the *Dao*, actualizing in moral activity the true harmonious nature of reality (being consonant with *li*, fully manifesting the natural principles of *qi*) (Adler 1998; Cheng 1998; Kalton 1998; Kinsley 1994; Ro 1998; Tucker 2005a, 2005c; Weiming 2002; Weller and Bol 1998).

> The sage . . . reflects the universal character of the feelings of all things . . . because he views things . . . from the viewpoint of things. Since he is able to do this, how can there be anything between him and things . . . We can understand things as they are if we do not impose our ego on them. The sage gives them every benefit and forgets his own ego. (Kinsley 1994:79)[15]

To obtain sagehood requires self-cultivation and in particular practising and enhancing virtue (*de*), especially *jen*, or 'humaneness', the essence of true humanity and the way of heaven and earth, the way to form one body with all things (a primordial concern for others and the embodiment of cosmic creativity). To practise *jen* is to go beyond differences, natural or social, and identify with the harmonious whole, attuning to nature and the Mandate of Heaven (realizing the basic goodness of humanity, creatively manifesting heaven and earth in human life). It is seen as analogous to origination in nature with its growth having the fecundity of nature as its counterpart. In this sense, it is bound up with reciprocally participating in the creativity and harmony of the *Dao*, being a compassion that is like a vital energy nourishing the life-force of all things, recognizing that life is interconnected and that fulfilment/success depends on helping others to be fulfilled/succeed (Adler 1998; Bassett et al. 2000; Berthrong 1998; Callicott 1997; Cheng 1998; Kuwako 1998; Maguire 2000; Tucker 2005c; Wensveen 2005).

[There is] innate goodness in the human mind-and-heart . . . the feeling of commiseration in the human which would naturally flourish in the practice of humanness (*jen*) extended to other humans and toward all living and non-living things.[16]

The great man . . . regards the world as one family . . . his humanity (*jen*) forms one body with [animals, people, nature] . . . when he observes the pitiful cries and frightened appearance of birds and animals . . . sees plants broken . . . tiles and stones shattered . . . he cannot help . . . feeling . . . regret. (Weiming 1998:18)[17]

In this sense, humanity, for Cheng (1998), can create a 'cosmo-eco-ethics' uniting the cosmology of heaven and the ecology of earth. In this light, others stress principles of a Confucian ecological vision or 'eco-wisdom' that may contribute to the formation of new eco-ethics. Berthrong (1998:244–5, 259) sees the creativity of the *Dao*, as symbol for all that is or could be, *jen* as the embodiment of *Dao* creativity via a primordial concern for others, *hsin*, or 'trustworthiness', as the 'mind-heart' functioning as the locus of the experiential unity of concern-consciousness, *hsing*, or '(human) nature', as the cultivation of 'mind-heart', participating in the *Dao*, and *Tao wen-hsueh*, or 'pursuing study', as a way of discerning human conduct in line with the *Dao*. More generally, Tucker (2002a, 2004, 2005c) sees the stress on social/political order seeing nature as inherently valuable and morally good, stressing care of it as correct destroying it problematic, as fostering cooperation, sublimating self to the common good, stressing responsibilities over rights, while Weiming (2001) sees cosmic humanism and self-cultivation, the stress on human 'heart-mind' expanding to nature in a self-strengthening mutual responsiveness, as able to stimulate harmonious interaction between humanity and nature.

Daoism

Daoism[18] is stressed as defining humanity in reference to the world in which it is embedded, stressing a 'relational world-view' deriving from and reflecting relationships in nature, centring on the *Dao*, seen as the reliable origin and flourishing of nature (they are one and the same, natural spontaneity or 'self-so' (*ziran*), not needing human activity). The ultimate aim of Daoists, in this sense, is to merge with the *Dao*, human activity being judged by how well it correlates or harmonizes to activity in nature (thus it seen as distrustful of 'civilization'). The universe is seen as essentially mysterious and the proper way to relate to it is not to improve it but to attend to its essential nature and rhythms, 'flowing' with it, mirroring natural spontaneity. A central theme, then, is that there is more to nature that can be imagined and so it should not be conformed to humanity's limited perspective but left alone, celebrated in its naturalness (a 'non-heroic' action; nature is thus not distrusted, nor does it need a redemptive 'heroic' human action, this being dangerous as it interferes with the *Dao* leading to unintended yet avoidable problems). Thus Daoism is seen as possibly being ecological as it is based on the negotiation of humanity with nature, recognizing humanity as inextricably woven into its fabric and needing to realize this not disrupt it, intuitively embracing the totality (*de*, virtue) (Ames 2001; Girardot et al. 2001; Kinsley 1994; Kirkland 2001; Lishka 2005; Miller 2001, 2004, 2005a, 2005b; Snyder 2006).

> Dao is the highest object of pursuit for the Daoists. A Daoist believes in Dao, relies upon Dao, cultivates Dao, and practices Dao. *De* refers to the particular conduct of the believer as she practices Dao. One may say that *de* is the practice of Dao in the believer's life. Hence to the extent that one follows the practice of *de*, one is in fact paying homage to Dao. Thus the core of Daoism consists of respecting Dao and giving high value to *de* . . . *Daode jing* 25 says: 'Humankind models itself after the Earth. Earth models itself after Heaven. Heaven models itself after Dao. And Dao models itself after the natural'. *Daode jing* 55 says: 'to know harmony means to be in accord with the eternal (Dao). To be in accord with the eternal (Dao) means to be enlightened.' (Jiyu 2001:362, 364)

Daoism is thus seen as following the *Dao* (naturalness) above all else, understanding and following its complementary, harmonious, rule of movement; not exploiting or controlling it but learning from and cooperating with it, practising restraint, avoiding selfish consumption (which can run counter to the balance of nature), seeing affluence in biodiversity and success in harmony. Miller et al. (2001) thus argue that certain 'ecological themes' are central to Daoism: the cosmological interdependence of heaven, earth and humanity, and the harmonizing role of humanity in cosmic ecology (refraining from obscuring the flow of the *Dao*, allowing mutual flourishing); the view of the body as a spiritual ecosystem, part of the same *Dao* process as nature, whereby nurturing it, harmonizing its *qi* (creating *de* or virtue) nurtures/harmonizes nature (with ecology thus a 'psycho-physio-energetic' problem); and a respect for nature, seeing it as being beyond human categories, with humanity only being able to achieve salvation through joining and caring for it not separating and dominating it (joining the creative process of nature to fulfil human nature). In this sense, whereas Confucianism is argued as stressing cultivation of self and nature, Daoism is seen as stressing the value of nature for its own sake, distrusting education, social structures and the imposition of human morals (seeing them creating an inadequate limited perspective obscuring the dynamic, holistic, nature of reality), seeing simplicity, spontaneity, intuitive knowledge and non-interference, as appropriate (stressing the stripping away of intellectual and social beliefs and structures that impose on nature and the realization of a spontaneous 'transparent communication' with it: as Miller (2004:3) argues 'The goal of all higher Daoist practice is to mirror unobtrusively the dynamic spontaneity of one's environment, to become imperceptible and transparent as though one were not at all' (Callicott 1997; Girardot et al. 2001; Kinsley 1994; Miller 2001, 2005a; Palmer and Finlay 2003; Tucker 1994).[19]

> As for the Dao, the Way that can be spoken of is not the constant Way; As for the names, the name that can be named is not the constant name. The nameless is the beginning of the ten thousand things; The named is the mother of the ten thousand things. Therefore, those constantly without desires, by this means will perceive its subtlety; Those constantly with desires, by this means will see only that which they yearn for and seek. These two together emerge; They have different names yet they're called the same; That which is even more profound than the profound – The gateway of all subtleties. (*Daode jing*, Girardot et al. 2001:xxxvii)[20]

Such a spontaneous, unobtrusive, way of acting is seen as *wu-wei*, or 'non (assertive) action' (related to *wu-chih/yu*, 'not knowing/desiring', the opposite being *yu-wei*, 'assertive-action'). This involves letting everything grow according to its own course without interference, acting in a 'weak' way that meets no resistance but rather flows in harmony with nature, a non-dominating action, devoid of desire: 'The stiff and strong are Death's companions, the soft and weak are Life's companions . . . the strong and great sink down, the soft and weak rise up' (*Daode jing* 76).[21] This is not seen as rejection of the world or passive relinquishing of responsibility but rather a responsible 'higher' action that is cautious, indirect, respectful and non-goal-oriented, a conscious detachment that acts from within the balance of nature rather than imposing on it. It is seen as acting 'appropriately', in tune with the *Dao*, producing the best results from minimum effort, avoiding 'overdoing' that might cause serious mistakes.

The aim is to be like water, soft and yielding yet powerful, a 'potentiality' of generative action and power. This follows the *Dao*, which is empty yet full of potentiality, allowing things to develop in their own ways in harmony: 'empty, yet its usefulness is inexhaustible . . . the origin of all things . . . It has no form, yet it . . . harmonizes all things' (*Daode jing* 4).[22] The aim is to penetrate the primordial essence of *Dao*, the dialectical nature of being ('self-so'), where yielding is the creative function, where 'being' is the product of 'non-being', and mirror this, so that 'non-doing' is 'doing'. Being and non-being, doing and not-doing, then, are not fixed, or the former favoured, as in Western thought, but part of the same process: 'things of the world originate in Being (*you*). And Being originates in Not-Being (*wu*)' (*Daode jing* 40).[23] Thus non-action is seen as able to facilitate (not dictate) the emergence of spontaneous novelty, nurturing natural growth and fulfilment of things ('self-so-ing'). This is seen as following the *yin* or female side of nature, the generative power of 'feminine fecundity' that springs from openness and receptivity, allowing activity (*yang*). *Wu-wei* is thus creative participation in the cosmos in a manner that coheres to nature not controls or resists it (balancing 'mutual stealing among the three powers' where myriad things of nature harmoniously 'steal' energy from heaven and earth to live) (Ames 2001; Callicott 1997; Hall 2001; Jiyu and Yuanguo 2001; Kinsley 1994; Kirkland 2001; LaFargue 2001; Miller 2001, 2005b; Snyder 2006; Tucker 1994; Xiaogan 2001).

Daoism is thus stressed as seeing a harmonic universal reality beyond human comprehension not needing a human saviour: Daoist practice does not involve 'heroically' overcoming a fallen/wild nature but allowing its harmony (thus it may not propose happy solutions but rather difficult choices, accepting harmonic totality rather than selfish desires; if things run counter to nature they must be abandoned even if they are in human self-interest). Daoists, in this sense, rather than being morally obliged to intervene in nature are morally obliged to refrain from intervening (an 'enlightened restraint': non-action is compassionate whereas action can cause unintended problems by upsetting the harmony). The practical result of this is an ascetic self-cultivation, acting like a 'craftsman', laying less stress on technique and more on facilitating inner-form, activating nature's latent potential (its 'naturalness', *ziran*), spontaneously highlighting the harmony already present, facilitating the *Dao* in nature (human *de* assisting nature's *de*, 'self-so-ing'). Humanity, in this sense, 'cultivates' nature to perfection via 'spontaneous mutual adjustment' to it, going beyond, or emptying the self of, reason, reversing human bias, 'learning to be unlearned' (not avoiding acting on an untouched nature but assisting its harmony without working at it). Thus the Daoist 'sage', the 'perfected/ numinous' person (a model of *de*), is translucent to nature, in harmony with the *Dao*, claiming no authority or possession, desireless, non-discriminatory, not quantifying or thinking in terms of cause and effect, but intuiting, having only temporary, fluid goals, avoiding competitive, rash, large-scale, actions in favour of cooperative, prudent, small-scale, ones, limiting destructive action while positively supporting natural balance. Such a 'wise' person understands the harmonic creativity of nature, and transparently, non-forcefully, facilitates it (respecting the myriad *de's* of natural life-forms and allowing them to prosper) (Girardot et al. 2001; Hall 2001; Jiyu and Yuanguo 2001; Kinsley 1994; Kirkland 2001; LaFargue 2001; Lishka 2005; Miller 2001; Palmer and Finlay 2003; Raphals 2001; Xiaogan 2001).

> [T]he sage takes no action (*wuwei*) and therefore does not fail. He grasps nothing and therefore he does not lose anything . . . The sage desires to have no desire . . . He learns to be unlearned, and returns to what the multitude has missed (Dao). Thus he supports the naturalness of ten thousand things . . . The sage . . . lets all thing arise, but claims no authority. He creates the myriad, but claims no possession. He accomplishes his task, but claims no credit. (*Daode jing* 64, 2, Xiaogan 2001:328, 331)[24]

> Do not be an embodier of fame . . . a storehouse of schemes . . . an undertaker of projects . . . Be empty . . . The Perfect Man uses his mind like a mirror – going after nothing . . . return to the essential . . . do not let what is human wipe out what is Heavenly. (*Zhuangzi* 7, 17)[25]

In this sense, 'Daoist ecology' is not seen as an intellectual principle but rather an experiential negotiation. Daoism is seen as sceptical of rational understanding, seeing it as an arrogant, limited imposition on nature, unbalancing and harming it through ignoring its underlying dynamic spirituality (thus Daoism is seen as a critical process, challenging social/political beliefs, as much as an ecological 'resource'). There is more to nature, in this sense, than can be recognized, imagined or conveyed, by human knowledge. Nature is metaphysical and physical, ontological and axiological, descriptive and prescriptive, beyond thoughts, words or deeds. Thus it needs to be alluded to in terms of the inconstant, unusual, extraordinary: Daoist 'knowing' is seen as holistic, alchemical and ecological, involving comprehending transient existence via revelatory experience though bodily relationships to other things, transcending ordinary experience. Ames (2001) sees this as giving priority to process over form, narrative over analysis, *mythos* over *logos*, centring on the continuous emergence of novelty rather than a fixed, foundational, position, integrating subjective/objective, things being defined correlatively not as discrete agents, stressing not 'what is the truth' but 'what is the way', experiential 'know how' rather than 'know what'. In this sense, 'knowledge' or 'truth' are not abstract standards but relational realities, not ontological explanations of the world but guidance on how one ought to act. There is no discrete 'discovery' only 'participation', a negotiated, indeterminate, harmony (not a deterministic teleology), autopoietically and correlatively maximizing the creative possibilities of situations in novel not predicted ways. Daoist actions are thus seen as aiming to respect and enhance the integrity and relatedness of life, acting in ways that create a negotiated, beneficial harmony (Girardot et al. 2001; Kinsley 1994; LaFargue 2001; Miller 2004; Snyder 2006; Xiaogan 2001).

For Hall (2001) such understandings of nature are 'aesthetically' ordered, denying ontological privilege to any one thing (i.e. humanity), stressing normless, non-theoretical experience, being based on 'deference'. Instead of 'referential' language classifying nature, stressing 'presence' and objective being separate from absent non-being (like Western logic models) such Daoist deference is seen as depending on allusion, yielding to the transient perspective of things, stressing 'absence' and giving way to non-represent-able subjects (there is no notion of being as ontological ground and no contrast between being and non-being). This is seen as an 'a-cosmotic' cosmology, a non-coherent, decentred, world of particulars, an 'aesthetic' order dependent on experiential perspectives mutually deferring to each other (not to a single perspective). Action is 'of the moment' rather than based on discriminatory recall/anticipation. It does not mirror an unchanging essence but transitory particulars. It is 'unprincipled knowing' (*wuzhi*), a denial of logical clarity and acceptance of vagueness, understanding the totality from a particular focus. The Daoist vision is thus seen as referent-less, based rather on things capable of being deferents (it is more relational, acting and knowing with deference to the particular *de's* of things). Daoists (sages) are thus seen as able to see beneath layers of artifice that mask the naturalness (*ziran*) of things and respond/defer to their 'intrinsic excellence', recognizing the dynamic continuity between self and other, the relational creative process, something that calls forth a deferential or yielding response so as to promote harmonic and complementary well-being.

Girardot et al. (2001) thus see Daoism as a dynamic ecological system that links 'lower-outer-physical', or earthly, and 'higher-inner-spiritual', or cosmic, levels of life, where interpenetrating 'bodies' of individuals, society, nature and 'celestial', spheres constitute a cosmic landscape pulsating with life (although not necessarily conforming to Western notions of 'ecological' as it recommends the transformation of individuals to penetrate beyond physicality). They thus see a 'Daoist eco-theology' reinterpreting traditional Daoist values to contemporary problems ('global consciousness and cooperative methodologies informed by (Daoist) cultural insights'): understanding the environmental whole and its 'ten thousand' parts, fostering respect for the totality of the cosmic environment and the reciprocal interrelationship of its parts.[26] Similarly, for Tucker (1994:155–6), 'While an extreme Taoist position might advocate complete non-interference with nature, a more moderate [one] would call for interaction . . . in a far less exploitative manner . . . [a] cooperation with nature.' For Girardot et al. (2001:lix), then:

Daoists may not always be the first to act in times of crisis, nor are they likely to work out elaborate theories of engaged social action, but they have always known that it is imperative to take up a way of life that responds in a timely and imaginative fashion to the dangers of neglect, imbalance, distortion, and degradation that inevitably affect human relations with the natural and cosmic worlds . . . all things – including the natural world itself – require attentive cultivation and responsive care. This, after all, is the 'natural' way of things . . . which might be called a 'Daoist' . . . way – to live gracefully, reciprocally, and responsibly within the cosmic landscape of life.

Conclusions

Ecological interpretations of Chinese religions stress Confucianism and Daoism sharing a world-view that sees no creator or creation but a dynamic, holistic, self-generating universe; a world-affirming view, unifying spirit/matter, stressing the need to exist in worldly harmony (not return to an otherworldly state). In this scheme, continuity of being stresses harmonious creativity based on ongoing relationships, a fluid, orchestral whole of energy fields not matter entities (*sheng-sheng*, production and reproduction/fecundity). This relates to the *Dao*, the Way or Great Harmony, the primordial essence, enlivening and directing nature in a mutually adjusting dynamic order, empty yet spontaneously creative, nowhere and everywhere (self-so or *ziran*, naturalness; nature is thus the dynamic source of creativity). All things exist in this via *qi*, a material energy that assumes tangible forms (connecting micro and macro, life-forms *qi* proportionately resonating with cosmic *qi*), providing relational motive power via two complementary, oscillating, energies, *yin* and *yang*, creating different things in the universe. Existence is thus harmonic transformation and humanity needs to realize not resist this, connecting to the *Dao*, channelling *qi*, and balancing *yin/yang*, creating wider relational (cosmic) balance. Confucianism and Daoism are seen as interpreting this in different ways, the former stressing cultivation of the individual, society and nature, seeing peaceful harmony in society as a reflection of/creating cosmic harmony, the latter stressing passive, simple non-interference with nature, a social withdrawal and subtle, spontaneous closeness to it, letting it unfold in its own way.

Confucianism is argued as stressing anthropocosmism/cosmic humanism, focusing on human virtues and society, linked to cosmic values, seeing humanity having an active role to play in nature, the highest ideal being to form a trinity with heaven and earth, being one body with the cosmos, something achieved through moral, social and spiritual practice, involving a relational or sympathetic resonance with all things, in tune with a cosmic resonance (a moral responsiveness or relationality responding to movements of *qi* in the world: each thing has an appropriate place and function in the dynamic whole, with humanity's being to bring these together, facilitating the balanced functioning of the cosmic process). There is, in this sense, an innate goodness (sincerity) in humanity that needs to be cultivated, an appropriate response to nature in accordance to *li*, principles or cosmic patterns that give structure to *qi* (being the reason why things are), a natural foundation for moral conduct. Humanity is thus biologically endowed for relational action, with personal/social cultivation enhancing this, such virtue (*de*) being exemplified by humaneness (*jen*), a primordial concern for others, identifying with the whole, something exemplified by the sage with integrative wisdom, able to discipline selfish desires and merge with nature/ *Dao*, responding spontaneously, in a morally responsive way (naturally, consonant with *li*).

Daoism is argued as stressing following the *Dao* above all else, valuing nature intrinsically, stressing detachment, intuition and spontaneity, a non-action (*wu-wei*) involving passive yielding rather than assertive imposing, acting like water, indirect and unforceful yet a generative potentiality, facilitating the emergence of spontaneous novelty (trusting nature's creative harmony, avoiding overdoing, which is seen as dangerous). Daoist practice, in this sense, is seen to stress enlightened restraint, embracing difficult choices not interventional solutions (morally obliging non-interference). This is seen as acting like a craftsman (a model of virtue), understanding and following nature's ways, facilitating inner-form: going beyond controlling human reason and acting with spirit, reflecting the totality, assisting latent naturalness, bringing out what is already present not imposing (self-so-ing). Daoist knowledge is thus not seen as intellectual understanding (seen as a limited, unbalancing, imposition) but revelatory experience of underlying harmony, giving priority to process over form, 'know how' over 'know what' (dynamic participation not abstract standards), based on relational deferents in communication, not a single referent, respecting harmonic diversity (naturalness not artificiality).

Notes

[1] Chinese terminology involves two systems, the 'Pinyin' (e.g. *Dao*, Daoism, *Daode jing*, *qi*) and 'Wade-Giles' (e.g. *Tao*, Taoism, *Tao Te Ching*, *ch'i*), used by different Daoist and Confucian scholars (Girardot et al. 2001). For clarity I mostly use the former, except in quotes or translations where I leave original terminology to reflect the literature.

[2] Downloaded from www.arcworld.org/faiths.asp?pageID=35, 15 Sept. 2006.

[3] Confucianism and Daoism are seen as diverse traditions. Snyder (2006) highlights problems relating them to ecology, such as non-contextual interpretation, whether Westerners can 'authentically' practice them (this possibly being colonialism), or scepticism of them protecting nature, highlighting failure in China, arguing that

although environmentally friendly beliefs may occur, Chinese practice may not be ideal (Bruun (2002) sees Chinese anthropocentrism stressing nature relevant only as a resource or possibly aesthetically). Nevertheless, he also sees other areas (economics, politics) driving degradation, stressing that no religion develops in a vacuum, and argues for reflexive use of traditions, stressing (a not inauthentic) contextual reinterpretation.

4   Referenced to Chang Tsai, 'Correcting Youthful Ignorance', in *A Source Book in Chinese Philosophy*, Wing-tsit Chan (Princeton: Princeton University Press, 1963), pp. 500–1.

5   From Ames (2001:268).

6   Referenced to Wang Fu-chih, in *A Source Book in Chinese Philosophy*, Wing-tsit Chan (Princeton: Princeton University Press, 1963), pp. 505:698–9.

7   From Ames (2001:268).

8   Referenced to Li Quan, *Huangdi yinfu jing shu* (A Commentary on the Yellow Emperors *Yinfu jing*), *Daozang* 110:2.1a–3a.

9   Cheng (2002:234–5) sees a Chinese metaphysics of nature emerging from the *Dao*: *self-transformation*, the *Dao* as dynamic relationships; *creative spontaneity*, reality being emergence of life; *interpenetration*, life as relational; *harmonization*, natural harmony stressing harmonic humanity. Correspondingly he sees 'environmental principles' returning to the *Dao*: *harmonization*, humanity harmonizes by conserving life; *interpenetration*, humanity develops relationally; *creative spontaneity*, humanity spontaneously harmonizes; *self-transformation*, humanity transforms into holistic reality. Such views are seen as 'depth' meanings grounding morality in nature (unlike Western 'surface' meanings grounding morality in human mind): humanity, via the *Dao*, unites with nature, acting benignly, without it, is separated, acting destructively (see Jiyu 2001; Xiaogan 2001).

10 Referenced to Weiming, T., The Value of the Human in Classical Confucian Thought, in *Confucian Thought: Selfhood as Creative Transformation*, Weiming, T., ed. (Albany: State University of New York Press, 1985), p. 75.

11 Confucianism is stressed as founded by K'ung Fu-tzu (Confucius) and developed by Mencius, Hsun tzu and Chu His (delineating four central texts, 'Great Learning', 'Doctrine of the Mean', 'Analects', 'Mencius'), the term generally referring to the 'classical' period up to the '*Han*' and '*T'ang*' dynasties (551 BCE–907 CE); 'Neo-Confucianism' is seen developing from the tenth century; 'New Confucianism' is seen developing from the twentieth century in Hong Kong, Taiwan and US. It is thus seen as a broad living tradition with environmental potential (e.g. valuing nature as the origin of life), especially in East Asia where it is seen as having historical legacy and influence. Thus it is used broadly in relation to ecology (while acknowledging a gap between theory and practice and China not always being environmentally friendly) (see Bassett et al. 2000; Bruun 2002; Girardot et al. 2001; Kirkland 2001; Paper 2001; Snyder 2006; Tucker 2004; Tucker and Berthrong 1998).

12 *Zhongyong*, XXII, referenced to Tu Weiming, *Centrality and Commonality: An Essay on Confucian Religiousness* (Albany, NY: State University of New York Press, 1989), p. 77.

13 Referenced to Wing-tsit Chan, *A Source Book in Chinese Philosophy* (Princeton: Princeton University Press, 1963), p. 86.

14 From Tucker (2004:2).

15 Referenced to Wing-tsit Chan, *Sources of Chinese Civilization* (New York: Columbia University Press, 1960), vol. 1, p. 465.

16 Downloaded from www.environment.harvard.edu/religion/religion/confucianism/texts/index.html, 15 Sept. 2006.

17 Referenced to Wang Yang-ming, *Inquiry on the Great Learning*, in *A Source Book in Chinese Philosophy*, Wing-tsit Chan (Princeton: Princeton University Press, 1963), pp. 659–60.

18 Daoism is stressed as diverse beliefs/practices, named after the *Dao*, traced to the *Daode jing* (attributed to Lao Tzu) and popular culture, based on: ancient texts (*Laozi, Zhuangzi*); the *Han* dynasty, the *Tianshi*, or 'Celestial Masters', *Shangqing*, or 'Highest Clarity', and *Lingbao*, or 'Numinous Treasure', traditions; sectarian groups of *Daozang*, or 'Treasury of the Dao'; reformist movements of 'inner alchemy'; the *Zhengyi* (Orthodox Unity) and *Quanzhen* (Complete Perfection) traditions; and new American/European forms. Daoism and ecology is thus seen as a complex realm and simply seeing them as natural partners may be a Westernization, ignoring Chinese ecological neglect, and universalizing Daoism's diverse traditions (Chinese, Chinese Diaspora, Western, scholars, popularizers; none being seen as able to fully capture its imaginative truth). Thus a broad, flexible, ecological approach is stressed, respecting contextual ethics, rituals, social forms and texts, while expanding Daoism's understandings of life's interdependence (Bassett et al. 2000; Bruun 2002; Girardot et al. 2001; Kirkland 2001; Paper 2001; Snyder 2006; Tucker 1994, 2004).

19 Kirkland (2001) sees a pre-modern Daoist social ethic supporting public service while others note 'precepts' in early Daoism ordering society, suggesting social cultivation as much as individual asceticism, although these are seen as exercises for inner-harmony rather than political actions (see Miller 2001, 2005a; Snyder 2006).

20 Referenced to (Mawangdui, B.), chapter 1 (amended Hendricks).

21 Downloaded from www.environment.harvard.edu/religion/religion/daoism/texts/index.html, 15 Sept. 2006; referenced to Stephen Addis and Stanley Lombardo, *Tao Te Ching: Lao-Tzu* (Indianapolis, IN: Hackett Publishing Company Ltd, 1993), p. 7.

22 From Lao Tzu (1996:67–8).

23 From Hall (2001:250–1).

24 Referenced to Wing-tsit Chan, *A Source Book in Chinese Philosophy* (Princeton: Princeton University Press, 1963), pp. 170, 140.

25 Downloaded from www.environment.harvard.edu/religion/religion/daoism/texts/index.html, 15 Sept. 2006; referenced to Burton Watson, *Zhuangzi or Chuang Tzu: Basic Writings* (New York: Columbia University Press, 1964), pp. 94–5, 104.

26 Girardot et al. (2001:xlviii–lii) sees this stressing: *cosmic ecology*, spontaneous generation from primal emptiness; *ecology of the body*, interpenetration of being;

ecology of time, cyclic not linear time; *local ecology*, respecting grassroots life; *reversion and spontaneity*, mirroring of natural spontaneity; *constructing nature*, inner not external attitude. Jiyu (2001) sees a 'Daoist ecological agenda' continuing a 'Daoist ecological tradition' of non-action, non-violence, and harmonious human/nature relationship.

Chapter 5

Buddhist Visions

Buddhism . . . attaches great importance towards wild life and the . . . environment . . . they too are sensitive to happiness and suffering . . . We should therefore be wary of justifying the right of any species to survive solely on the basis of its usefulness to human beings . . . We regard our survival as an undeniable right. As co-inhabitants of this planet, other species too have this right for survival. And since human beings as well as other non-human sentient beings depend upon the environment as the ultimate source of life and well-being . . . the restoration of the imbalance caused by our negligence [must] . . . be implemented . . . Such destruction of the environment and the life depending upon it is a result of ignorance [and] greed . . . [thus] it is very important that we examine our responsibilities and commitment to values, and think of the kind of world we are to bequeath to future generations.

(*Venerable Lungrig Nomgayal Abbot, The Buddhist Declaration on Nature, WWF 1986:5–7*)

As a boy studying Buddhism, I was taught the importance of a caring attitude toward the environment. Our practice of non-violence applies not just to human beings but to all sentient beings, any living thing that has a mind. Where there is a mind, there are feelings such as pain, pleasure, and joy . . . In Buddhist practice [such] . . . non-violence and the ending of all suffering [means] . . . we become accustomed to not harming or destroying anything indiscriminately . . . we share a sense of universal responsibility for both mankind and nature. Our belief in reincarnation is one example of our concern for the future. If you think that you will be reborn, you are likely to . . . preserve such and such because [your] . . . future reincarnation will be able to continue with these things.

(*Dalai Lama, Bassett et al. 2000:61*)

Buddhism,[1] interpreted ecologically (what is seen as 'green Buddhism' or the 'greening of Buddhist practice'),[2] is stressed as being at essence an ecological religion or religious ecology having concern for (worship of) nature as its most important element, a central part of its morality: as Prasad (2003:41–2) argues 'Buddhism . . . extends the idea of interrelationships and interactions to [eco] systems . . . For Buddhists all ecosystems with their inhabitants and organisms – humans, animals, birds, insects, plants etc. mean religion . . . Respect for . . . life . . . is . . . integral'. It is seen as stressing a dynamic, inter-dependent, cosmos, and prescribing a cooperative, non-violent, simple, way of living, able to counter destructive modern views, stressing ego-extinction and spiritual development, teaching that separateness from nature is an illusion, that one existence is no more important than another, that simplicity and moderation, respecting natural cycles, avoiding harm to nature, are needed to diminish destructive greed and create an ecologically respectful lifestyle (Badiner 1990; Batchelor and Brown 1994; Gross 2002; Johnston 2006; Kaza 2002a, 2002b; Kraft 1996; Prasad 2003; Sponberg 1997; Swearer 2005, 2006).

> 'The fruit of Buddhism – mindful living cultivates a view of human beings, nature, and their relationship that is fundamentally ecological . . . If we have any real identity at all in Buddhism, it is in ecology itself – a massive interdependent, self-causing dynamic energy-event against the backdrop of ceaseless change'[3] . . . 'Stating the traditional Buddhist attitudes of not injur-ing (*ahimsa*), benevolence (*metta/maitri*) and compassion (*karuna*) to entail an "ecological" behaviour is surely justified in so far as these attitudes . . . include also other living beings.'[4] (Swearer 2006:125, 130)

> [W]ith its philosophic insight into the interconnectedness and . . . inter-dependence of all . . . things . . . its thesis that happiness is to be found through restraint of desire . . . its goal of enlightenment through renunci-ation and contemplation and its ethic of non-injury and boundless loving kindness for all beings, Buddhism provides all the essential elements for a relationship to the natural world characterized by respect, care, and com-passion. (Callicott 1997:65)[5]

Such a relationship between Buddhism and ecology, for Palmer and Finlay (2003:78–82), is summed up in three contexts, seeing nature in different ways: *nature as teacher*, stressing cyclic change, mutual interconnection and suffering, as essences of life, stimulating relational understanding; *nature as spiritual force*, stressing a balance of ecology, morality and spirituality, enhancing the ability of humanity to live in tune with nature; and *nature as way of life*, stressing skil-ful living of non-aggression, sensitivity and simplicity. Swearer (2001:226–30, 234, 2004:1–5) sees such ideas as an 'ecology of human flourishing' empha-sizing holism, mindful awareness and simple lifestyle, a responsibility rooted in compassion, conjoined on four levels: *existential*, understanding the univer-sal condition of suffering and the need for cessation of it; *moral*, sharing this understanding and highlighting the virtue of compassion and non-violent alleviation of suffering; *cosmological*, stressing a shared condition of cyclic rebirth for all life and thus relational consequences of action, arguing for care and cooperation; and *ontological*, stressing unity and interdependent causality of life. Maguire (2000) sees this as 'Buddhist wisdom' downsizing wants and unrealistic needs, critiquing self-centred, destructive humanity, while Kaza (2002a, 2002b) sees it as possibly providing respect, restraint and spiritual stability, an ecologically loving presence (inner strength and moral courage), in the face of environmental destruction, based on human interdependence with nature, a non-anthropocentric, non-heroic, action not motivated by ego but by mutual support and spiritual friendship with nature.

In line with such ideas the life of Buddha is highlighted (stressed as occurring in intimacy with nature (e.g. attaining *bodhi*, or awakening, under the bo-tree), this seen as emphasizing it bearing witness to him). Stressed here is that Buddha on encountering the reality of suffering strove to understand life's meaning and via a lifestyle of compassion, meditation and simplicity, attained enlightenment, understanding and teaching that all phenomena are transitory, mutually arising, interacting and passing, sharing fundamental conditions of birth, suffering and death, and that understanding this cycle of change (the human place in it) frees one from egoistic desire (ignorance, the projection of ego as a self-directing centre, separate from nature) that causes disharmony and suffering (and rebirth into this, seeing a causal relationship between current and future affairs and past actions). Buddha is thus seen as assessing the human condition in relation to the interdependent continuum of life, teaching that nature highlights a balance and spiritual force and that respect for it is essential, that living gently and meditatively develops self-understanding and 'oneness' with it, enabling a life of mutual benefit and liberation from suffering (seen important to this are the 'Jataka' (moral) tales Buddha told about his previous lives as animals/nature, highlighting correct behaviour and human/nature connection, something also stressed in injunctions teaching that the moral community should include all forms of life as they are related and can transform into each other, exposing humanity's selfish ignorance and encouraging self-sacrificial behaviour). Buddha, then, is seen as exemplifying a paradigmatic way of life based on a reflective enquiry into the nature of reality aimed at alleviating suffering (not an otherworldly transcendence but a this-worldly way of living without desire). Thus Buddhism encourages people to 'act like Buddha', going beyond selfish desires and embracing the whole (Brown 1994; Chapple 2005a; Gosling 2001; Halifax 1990; Jacobsen 2005d; Kaza 2002b; Palmer and Finlay 2003; Regenstein 1991; Schmithausen 2005; Swearer 2001, 2005).

Especially stressed are Buddha's 'Four Noble Truths' (seen as the core of Buddhist teaching): the universal reality of suffering in life, that (in 'conventional living', for example, Western consumerism) though humanity strives for pleasure it receives pain (e.g. a degraded world); the cause of suffering being ignorance and desire, the illusion of a lasting self, independent from nature, instead of a transient self, interdependent with it, this creating (unsatisfactory) attachment to existence, tying to (rebirth in) the suffering birth/death cycle; freedom from ignorance/desire being freedom from suffering, overcoming the delusion of and extinguishing the need for permanent selfish existence (and realizing peace and satisfaction) through realizing that all phenomena arise from interdependent causes and conditions; freedom from ignorance/desire/ suffering lying in a life of moral discipline and spiritual depth, a middle way avoiding excessive pleasure or hardship. The base of any Buddhist 'eco-ethics', then, is argued as being the recognition that suffering (*dukkha*, for example, environmental degradation) is caused by *trishna*, a delusional, attachment to existence and selfish desire for autonomy ('I-self'), where the object of desire is more in control than the desiring subject (the mistaken view that getting 'something' (e.g. wealth) will bring happiness, instead of accepting what 'is'), and that to alleviate the former requires overcoming the latter through realiz- ing the interdependent nature of reality (a cooperative cosmos or 'we-self') via moral/spiritual learning. Thus peace and satisfaction (enlightenment) come through piercing illusory *trishna*, accepting impermanence and interdepend- ence, what is seen as 'non-self' (*anatman*), a 'self-forgetting' or 'emptiness' (*sun- yata*), realizing that there are no individual 'selves' but only 'selves-in-Self' (a supportive 'non-heroic' self, unimpeding the interrelated reality, rather than a dominating 'leader' requiring selfish satisfaction) (Barnhill 2001; Batchelor, S. 1994; Brown 1994; Callicott 1997; Chapple 2005a; Gosling 2001; Gross 2002; Johnston 2006; Kaza 1993, 2001, 2002a; Maguire 2000; Swearer 1997, 2004, 2005).[6]

> Buddhist believe that the reality of the interconnectedness of human beings, society, and Nature will reveal itself more and more to us . . . as we gradually cease to be possessed by anxiety, fear, and the dispersion of the mind . . . we must recover ourselves, one must be whole . . . [a] lifestyle that is free from the destruction of one's humaneness . . . in a state of equilibrium[7] . . . When we accept that . . . every being has the nature of Buddha – then we will . . . make peace.[8] (Palmer and Finlay 2003:77–8)

Also stressed, in line with such ideas, are *karma*, or law of cause and effect, where past actions shape present station and present actions shape future sta- tion, and *samsara*, or rebirth, where beings are constantly reborn in different forms as a result of their actions, these seen as linking life in a '*karmic* con- tinuum', all life sharing a common problematic and promise, suffering and enlightenment, difference being relative not absolute (all beings have been parents, siblings or children, of each other and can be again). Life is thus interconnected and mapped morally, place in the continuum being depend- ent on moral actions (selfless, more desirable rebirth, selfish, less desirable, with enlightenment attained via human form, animals/plants needing to go 'up' through this, although humans can be reborn 'down' as animals/plants). In this sense, humanity is bound up with nature as a whole, all things exist- ing virtue of other things, life being a complex aggregation, not autonomous isolation, and needs to be compassionate, non-violent and responsible, in relation to it to better shape the future (to attain enlightenment) (Batchelor, M. 1994a; Brown 1994; De Silva 1994; Harris 1997; Kaza 2002a, 2002b; Prasad 2003; Schmithausen 2005; Swearer 2006; Thakur 2003).[9] To achieve this, for Swearer (2001, 2004, 2005), involves a 'particular-general-principle' process, following Buddha's enlightenment example, understanding (particular) personal karmic history, then (general) karmic history of humanity, and finally the (principle) underlying cause of suffering (generalized as a law of causality: 'on the arising of this, that arises; on the cessation of this that ceases'), this seen as not only a vision of causal interdependence but also a model for moral reasoning.

> A belief in reincarnation is basic to Buddhism . . . In the 'Jatakas' . . . Buddha told about his previous lives . . . [as] an animal, including an elephant, a tiger, a fish, or different species of birds. There are also stories where he is the spirit of a tree . . . The Jatakas make clear that in Buddhism the moral community should include all forms of life, and that all species of living beings are not only related but can transform into each other and are essentially one. (Bassett et al. 2000:60)

> A Buddhist believes that he or she has been other than a human in the past and may be other than a human in the future. Thus, a Buddhist human is not intrinsically superior to any other sentient being; he feels as if other beings are his relatives. In fact, since time, according to Buddhism, has no beginning, a Buddhist recognizes that he has been re-born an infinite number of times as every other sort of being . . . [which has] at one time or another been his mother . . . thus we seek to repay their kindness.[10] (Regenstein 1991:237)

Such *karmic* enlightenment process is seen as a Buddhist soteriology exposing the interdependent nature of reality, nothing standing forth of its own power but being a function of other factors. It is seen as a movement towards the cosmic body of Buddha (*dharmakaya*, in all beings), an all-inclusive, non-differentiating 'suchness' (*tathata*), an innately pure consciousness of integral totality (present as embryonic *tathagatarbha* needing to be realized). These ideas are linked to *dharma*, '(path to) truth', the sacred law and teachings of Buddha, as well as meaning things in nature, highlighting that all inner and outer phenomena are inseparable and intertwined: to recognize the interdependent nature of reality is to see the *dharma* (and to see the *dharma* is to see the Buddha). All beings (or nature in general), in this sense, are *dharmas* or have '*dharma*-nature' (also termed 'Buddha-nature', *buddhakaya*), the 'One Mind' or 'True Self', the truth of reality, an essential substance in all life (all beings are different expressions of a common reality, interconnected not separate). Nature, in this sense, is also seen as the body of Buddha, with life-forms 'mandalas' or images symbolizing the dynamic flowing of *dharma*-nature. All beings are thus embryonic Buddha's and have the potentiality to attain enlightenment, although this fact is obscured by desire/ignorance, needing to be realized through acquiring the (enlightened) 'Buddha-eye' and awakening to *dharma*-nature through cultivating an awareness of interdependence and a right (harmonious) way of acting (practising *dharma*, this leading to *sangha*, or community) (Badiner 1990; Barnhill 1997, 2005b; Batchelor, M. 1994a; Brown 1994; Harris 2002; Kaza 2002a; Kinsley 1994; Lancaster 1997; Swearer 2006).

In this light animals and plants are seen as positively highlighted in Buddhism (reverence for them being seen as integral to it), having *dharma*-nature, with potential for 'Buddhahood', being fellow voyagers within the *karmic* cycle of life, aspiring to and working towards enlightenment. Thus they are seen as needing to be treated with compassion and kindness, not hated or harmed. Chapple (1997) stresses the awareness, compassion and wisdom of animals (and their hosting of different life-forms via rebirth, explaining present day life), in the Jataka tales, seeing them demonstrating right (and wrong) morality (highlighting vegetarianism and condemnation of animal sacrifice). Poceski (2005a), similarly, sees the Buddhahood of grasses, rocks and trees, highlighting inherent worth of mundane things, while LaFleur (1990) stresses *sattva*, an embracing commonality and beneficence, for plants and trees (all nature), stressing their abilities for (creating) (co)enlightenment: 'animals move faster than plants, and plants move faster than soil, and soil moves faster than mountains. But all move' (Chan-jan). Nature in this sense, has sentience and shares 'beingness', being a companion in enlightenment, and although not able to practise Buddhism its intrinsic impermanence and interdependence may demonstrate wisdom, testifying to *dharma*, being the loci of the sacred, or sacred itself (especially forests with trees sanctified, even 'ordained'), existing in its being as Buddha, being a natural supportive *sangha*, or community, what is seen as 'original enlightenment' (Barnhill 2005b; Batchelor, M. 1994a; Gross 2002, 2005; Habito 2005; Harris 2002; Ho 1990; Kaza 2002a; Kinsley 1994; Regenstein 1991; Swearer 1997, 2001, 2004; Waldau 2005).

For Ingram (1997) such holistic, organic ideas (what he sees as a 'Buddhist environmental paradigm') are summed up in (ritualistic) Shingon, 'esoteric', ideas stressing the (harmony of) 'Six Great Elements', the (inseparability of) 'Four Mandalas', the (manifestation of) 'Three Mysteries', and (interrelation of) 'Indra's Net'.[11] In this scheme, the 'Six Great Elements' – earth, water, fire, wind, space and consciousness – highlight the timeless harmony of nature, existing within 'dependent co-origination' (*pratitya-samutpada*): life, sentient and non-sentient, arises simultaneously and mutually via their constant interaction, a 'together-rising-up-of-things' (the 'Great Wheel of Causation'), where all things affect each other, each being the cause and condition of others and of the whole (when one thing arises all arise, what happens to one happens to all, thus there is no static creation or creator but a constant creative life process). This relates to the doctrine of emptiness (*sunyata*) and non-self (*anatman*) seeing nothing as self-existing but dependent on other things, a totality. To be is to be of, with and for, others. Existence is thus a collaborative process, a context of relations, a synthesis. All things, humanity, animals, plants, even inanimate objects, are not just related but identical (part of the body of Buddha). Each phenomenon thus takes on unqualified value, the universe depends on it: as Barnhill (2001:89) argues, 'to throw away even a single chopstick as worthless is to set up a hierarchy of values which in the end kills us . . . everything counts'[12] (Badiner 1990; Batchelor, M. 1994a; Batchelor, S. 1994; Brown 1994; Gross 2002; Johnston 2006; Kaza 2001, 2002a, 2002b, 2005; Loori 1997; Schmithausen 2005; Sponberg 1997).[13]

Buddha said, 'This is because that is; this is not because that is not; this is born because that is born; this dies because that dies'. The health of the whole is inseparably linked with the health of the parts, and the health of the parts is inseparably linked with the whole. Everything in life arises through causes and conditions. (Palmer and Finlay 2003:77)

All lands are my body And so are the Buddha's living there; Watch my pores, And I will show you the Buddha's realm. Just as the nature of the earth is one While beings each live separately, and the earth has no thought of oneness or difference So is the truth of the Buddha. (Avatamsaka Sutra, Batchelor, M. 1994a:11)[14]

Life, in this sense, is dynamic interdependence, and the aim of existence, the path to enlightenment, is to be aware of and experience this (thus it is a mistake to see fulfilment in terms of personal development alone), something achieved, for Ingram (1997), through meditation via the 'Four Mandalas' (ritual images): 'Great Mandalas', of Buddha/deities in colours representing the six elements, symbolizing (Buddha in) the interpenetrating universe; 'Samaya-Mandala', expressing ontological unity underlying diversity (in Buddha's body); 'Dharma-Mandala', a sphere of (Buddha's) revelation of truth; and 'Karma Mandalas', symbolizing change as interconnected action (of Buddha). These, then, symbolize and encourage movement towards Buddhahood, integrating the 'Three Mysteries' of (Buddha's) 'Body' (Buddha's 'such-ness' incarnate in nature), 'Speech' (Buddha's revelation of *dharma* through every thing/event) and 'Mind' (Buddha's enlightenment of the suchness of nature), within human body, speech and mind, creating enlightened compassion. Such ideas are correlated with 'Indras Net' of many-sided jewels, each reflecting the other: as one jewel changes so the others reflect this change; if one becomes cloudy (polluted) or broken (species loss) this is reflected in all others *ad infinitum* (or if one jewel is cleaned up so are the others). Thus humanity's true being is not separate from but is part of, affecting and being affected by, wider nature, a reciprocal relation-centred ontology and cause for positive action, seeing all life-forms, no matter how humble, as valuable, affecting and being affected within the whole. Thus everything we do affects the whole of nature (and returns to affect us) and all nature, blades of rice to tips of hairs, has a place in and demonstrates the truth of the whole (see Barnhill 1997, 2001; Batchelor, M. 1994a; Callicott 1997; Halifax 1990; Kaza 2002a, 2002b, 2005; Kinsley 1994; Poceski 2005b; Swearer 2001, 2005, 2006).[15]

> Buddhists believe that all life forms are interrelated and part of a much larger unified life-force. Thus to do harm to any part of this entity is to harm one's own self, and *all* life: 'In reality there is only one life force in the universe. All of us are part of this great Life Force. Whenever we cause suffering to any other being we are causing suffering to this great Life Force. There is nothing that we do that affects only ourselves. The entire Universe is helped by our acts of compassion but is harmed by our acts of violence and unkindness.'[16] (Regenstein 1991:237)

> The entire cosmos is a cooperative. The sun, the moon and the stars . . . humans and animals, trees, and the earth. When we realize that the world is a mutual, interdependent, cooperative enterprise . . . then we can build a noble environment. If our lives are not based on this truth, then we shall perish. (Swearer 2004:3)[17]

Reality, in this sense, is 'non-dual': all 'parts' are at once the 'whole', all phenomena being identical in their constituent self-identity (all participate in *dharma*; thus there is no absolute difference between humanity and nature). For Barnhill (2001) this is a differentiated integration, where each different element is necessary for the whole to exist, different forms of life being distinct but integrated: they need to be in a whole to exist and the whole needs them to exist (like waves, distinguishable but integral parts of whole oceans). This affirms both particularity and whole; both have ontological integrity in their interfusion; both thus need to be respected (this overcoming dualistic dominance, enabling mindful negotiation, respecting but encompassing boundaries). For Barnhill, such ideas stress a 'relational holism', an alternative to atomism, holism and communalism, that stress parts, wholes or relationality, being particularistic, holistic and relational, highlighting relationships between particulars but also between each particular and the field of relationships, a view of the self that is seen as a 'Self-with-selves-in-Self-as-selves', affirming individuals as well as the whole and the relationships between them.

> Differences exist between matter and mind, but in their essential nature they remain the same. Matter is no other than mind; mind no other than matter. Without any obstruction, they are interrelated. The subject is the object; the object, the subject. The seeing is the seen, and the seen is the

seeing. Nothing differentiates them. Although we speak of the creating and the created, there is in reality neither. (Ingram 1997:77)[18]

'In One is All, in Many is One, One is identical to All, Many is identical to One'[19] . . . '[T]he one and the many establish each other. Only when one is completely the many can it be called the one, and only when the many can be completely be called the one can it be called the many. There is not a separate one outside the many . . . it is one within the many'[20] . . . To the enlightened mind, the interpenetrating world is experienced as a single whole that is characterized by multiplicity. (Barnhill 2001:87–8, 96)

For Sponberg (1997) such ideas suggest a 'hierarchy of compassion' where 'progress' is an evolution of consciousness toward the awareness and cultivation of interdependence, something involving complementary dimensions of (vertical) development and (horizontal) relationality, where more evolved beings have greater awareness of interdependence and correspondingly greater compassion for and responsibility towards life. Instead of a 'hierarchy of oppression' where as one evolves interrelatedness is denied and decreases, leading to domination (linearly moving upward through power over others, satisfying selfish need) in a 'hierarchy of compassion' as one evolves (the only way one does so) interrelatedness is accepted and increased, leading to equality/community (spirally moving upward through empowering others, relinquishing selfish needs). This, then, is a progress away from selfishness, a 'virtue ethic' involving the 'threefold learning' (*trisiksa*) of morality, meditation and insight, practising self-restraint, reducing desires and simplifying needs, a path leading to the spiritual perfection of the *bodhisattva* or enlightened being on the way to being a Buddha but who holds back to help others in this quest, vowing to serve others until suffering is extinguished (see Batchelor, M. 1994a; Gosling 2001; Halifax 1990; Kaza 2002a, 2005; Kinsley 1994; Schmithausen 2005; Sponberg 1997; Swearer 2004, 2005).

For Kaza (1993) this is living with a peaceful heart, 'planting seeds of joy, peace and understanding', practising 'compassion' (*karuna*) and 'loving kindness' (*metta*), the former arising through natural spontaneous response to suffering, the latter through prayer towards it. This is seen as a 'policy of kindness' (seen as the heart of Buddhist practice, beyond doctrine), involving a deep awareness of interdependency and cultivation of intimacy with nature (spiritual friendship, *kalyana mitta*), a 'relational richness' penetrating the objectifying mind and meeting nature directly (subjectively), being a 'presence', sharing its suffering: 'Great compassion makes a peaceful heart. A peaceful heart makes a peaceful person. A peaceful person makes a peaceful family. A peaceful family makes a peaceful community. A peaceful community makes a peaceful nation. A peaceful nation makes a peaceful world.'[21] In a similar way to such ideas other concepts emphasizing the valuation and protection of life are stressed, such as, *ahimsa*, or non-violence (a primary precept, not destroying life, not even to sustain it, especially not for pleasure), equanimity (*upekkha*), gratitude (*katannu*) or sympathetic joy (*mudita*). These are seen as demonstrating a wish to alleviate suffering, intentionally (e.g. not hating or injuring) or unintentionally (e.g. avoiding drinking unstrained water or ploughing a field) something extended to plants, who are seen as 'like friends', having intelligence and sensitivity, seeking a life of peace and security. Such life-affirming ideas are seen as demonstrating a self-sacrificial identification with the feelings of animals, plants, even rocks, respecting their intrinsic value and capacity for experience (see Batchelor, M. 1994a; De Silva 1994; Harris 2002; Kinsley 1994; Maguire 2000; Palmer and Finlay 2003; Regenstein 1991; Swearer 2001, 2004, 2005, 2006; Thakur 2003).

> [T]he Buddha described how one should cultivate loving kindness . . . 'Let none betray another's trust Or offer any slight at all, Or even let them wish in wrath Or in revenge each other's ill' . . . Thus as a mother with her life Will guard . . . her only child; Let him extend without bounds His heart to every living being. (Sutta-nipata I, 8, Batchelor, M. 1994a:4)[22]

> [P]erform eight deeds to show kindness . . . To benefit sentient beings; to gladden sentient beings; not to hate sentient beings; to be straight-forward; not to discriminate among sentient beings; to be compliant with sentient beings; to contemplate all dharmas; and to be as pure as space.[23]

In this light Loori (1997) highlights traditional 'precepts', the minimum code of ethics every lay Buddhist is expected to follow. First, are the three 'treasures', *Buddha, dharma* and *sangha*, the virtues of 'supreme enlightenment', 'purity' and 'harmony'. Second, are the three 'pure precepts' of *not creating evil, practising good* and *actualizing good for others*, the first based on the assumption of inherent purity, evil being of humanity's making, needing to be overcome, from which the second and third follow. Third, are the ten 'grave precepts': *affirm life – do not kill,* which ecologically means not decimating nature, creating a vacuum which affects other life; *be giving – do not steal,* means not seeing nature as a resource, stealing life from it; *honour the body – do not misuse sexuality,* means honouring the body of nature, not interfering with natural order; *manifest truth – do not lie,* means not 'green-washing', pretending to be ecologically friendly but not actualizing this; *proceed clearly – do not cloud the mind,* means not clouding perception with greed but respecting nature through living with less; *see the perfection – do not speak of others' errors or faults,* means not altering nature based on an ideology that stresses it being in error; *realize self and other as one – do not elevate the self and put down others,* means not elevating humanity and putting down nature but recognizing their interdependency; *give generously – do not be withholding,* means understanding giving and receiving are one, that if something is taken from nature something should be returned to it; *actualize harmony – do not be angry,* means not abusing but protecting natural cycles, thinking holistically, long term; *experience the intimacy of things – do not defile the Three Treasures*, stresses abusing nature as separating from it, defiling the three treasures which are its body (see De Silva 1994; Kaza 2002b; Maguire 2000; Schmithausen 2005).

Also stressed, in this sense, is the 'eight-fold path' of self-transformation, changing attitudes and ways of living, beginning with ignorance (e.g. the environmental crisis) and ending in enlightenment (healing nature): the first step involves *right understanding* and *right intention/thought*, understanding interdependence and non-self and controlling (selfish) thoughts/actions; the second step involves *right speech* and *right action*, taking responsibility for body, speech and behaviour, respecting nature and being grateful to it, recognizing its suffering; the third step involves *right livelihood* and *right effort*, developing a non-dualistic notion of reality, enhancing dialogue, setting moral boundaries through kindness; the fourth step involves *right mindfulness* and *right concentration*, emphasizing learning, meditation and ritual, deepening awareness and uprooting destructive tendencies (realizing *karmic* effects of action), grounding intention in understanding not desire. This path, then, is seen as a way to increase awareness of nature and underlying assumptions that may cause abuse of it. It is, for Badiner (1990:xv), the 'mystical rain' described in the Lotus Sutra that fosters the growth of life (similar to Buddha who is seen as a great cloud covering all things, bringing fullness and satisfaction, like a rain spreading its moisture everywhere): 'This rain is our practice . . . the quality of life for all beings, is cultivated by correct practice'. It is thus seen as able to inspire a green Buddhist virtue ethics simplifying needs and desires, inspiring 'mindful' action, reducing nature's suffering. As Batchelor and Brown (1994:ix) state: 'solutions to the global crisis [begin] within each of us. To transform the world, we must [transform] ourselves . . . Enlightenment . . . is not some mystical state where visions of unearthly bliss unfold but a series of responses to the question: how am I to live in this world' (Batchelor, M. 1994a; Kaza 1993, 2002a, 2002b; Sponberg 1997).

These ideas are linked to the 'Middle Way' (*majjhima patipata*), an ethic of moderation, avoiding extremes of self-indulgence/denial (attachment to the world or ascetic rejection of it, both of which may be destructive), providing an equanimity of mind and body necessary to pursue enlightenment. This is a 'right effort' of not too little, not too much, something related to 'mindfulness', being aware of humanity's destructive tendencies and life's interdependence, looking at the wider, long-term, picture (rather than being unmindful, which is a form of violence). This involves awareness of, and controlling, body, breath, feelings and mind, being clear and positive, moderating harsh/rash speech/action, being gentle, truthful and useful, a 'silent one' (*muni*), in control of inner and outer speech. It is self-mastery (rather than a mastery over others), relinquishing the need for control (e.g. over nature), stressing restraint over indulgence, quelling the 'fire' of desire for self-satisfaction, reducing wants, being frugal, humble and non-exploitative, creating a 'wise' lifestyle in harmony with nature (following Buddha, a humble monk with a simple lifestyle) (Batchelor, M. 1994a; Callicott 1997; De Silva 1994; Gross 1997; Kaza 2002a, 2005; Kinsley 1994; Maguire 2000; Sivaraksa 1990; Swearer 2004, 2006).

In line with such ideas, meditation, prayer and ritual, are stressed, these seen as able to stimulate self-analysis and reduce egoism, fostering appreciation for nature, cultivating 'oneness' with it, something seen as especially stressed in 'Zen' practice, that is seen as developing a sense of place, stimulating a selfless 'flowing with' nature, a 'sensitizing' to it: for example, 'breathing mindfully', before, during and after, action, creating calm, clear (spiritual) awareness and understanding, stimulating deeper powers of perception, leading to illuminative (ecological) insight, realizing one's true interdependent nature, overcoming the wall of separation dividing what is seen and the subject that sees. This is seen as enabling identification with all phenomena through immersing the self in awareness of interdependence, creating a 'policy of kindness' from which compassion and wisdom flow naturally. It is seen as the means through which enlightenment oneness comes to be realized, grounding one in the continuum of life, cultivating an inner (spiritual) peace, a full 'presence', existing in the present moment, beyond earthly pursuits (a 'zero point', simply being rather than doing or having). And when added to exposure to suffering this is seen as allowing a 'suffering with' others, being aware that nothing is outside concern (experiencing the present as including the past and future, the one and the many, leading to ecological commitment) (Badiner 1990; Batchelor, M. 1994b; Codiga 1990; Habito 1997, 2005; Ho 1990; Kaza 1993, Kinsley 1994; Kraft 1996, 1997).[24]

> Breathing in, I know that I am breathing in. Breathing out, I know that I am breathing out. Breathing in, I see myself as a flower. Breathing out, I feel fresh. Breathing in, I see myself as a mountain. Breathing out, I feel solid. Breathing in, I see myself as still water. Breathing out, I reflect on things as they are. Breathing in, I see myself as space. Breathing out, I feel free. (Kraft 1996:485–6)[25]

Such mindful and meditative Buddhist action is seen as highlighted by Buddhist monks and in monasteries/temples which are seen as ideal *sangha's*, communities of mutual support abandoning selfish individualistic notions, situated in nature away from the self-preoccupation of modern life, inculcating a sense of harmony, opening the 'two doors' to *dharma* of internal peace and reverence for life. A *sangha*, in this sense, is seen as a critical moral example and ideal for all Buddhists, an 'eco-centric' place where one is located in a community, responding to the larger web of relationships, where spiritual practice is a practice of place, living ethically with other people and nature, teaching and practising a 'slowing down', reducing time spent with objects and fostering intimate, mutually supporting, friendship with nature's subjects (bearing ecological responsibility, being a place where all forms of life, human, animal, plant, live as a cooperative microcosm of a larger ecosystem). It is thus seen as a countercultural 'green society', a small, egalitarian, cooperative community, stressing non-violence, self-restraint and limited consumption, centred on and 'witnessing' the bioregion, affirming the rights of other species, extending moral boundaries, practising a 'mindful dwelling' grounded in compassion, equanimity and non-acquisitiveness, intimate with and serving nature, cultivating oneness with it (and such ideals and actions are seen as able to be enlarged globally, providing the ideals and impetus for the creation of a 'Great Earth *Sangha*', an environmentally friendly way of being embracing global society and the ecosphere of the planet) (Barnhill 1997; Batchelor, M. 1994b; Devall 1990; Gosling 2001; Kaza 1993, 2002b; Sponsel and Sponsel 1997; Swearer 2001, 2004, 2005, 2006).

> The lives . . . and . . . relationships in the Sangha convey to people in the larger society certain 'messages' . . . which deny or resist the prevailing values . . . [pointing] to the true value of life, indicating that development of inwardness is more important than wealth and power, that the life of tranquillity and material simplicity is more rewarding and fulfilling . . . [enabling] people to stop and reflect upon their lives, leading them to seek themselves rather than material gain or glory. Such messages are especially revolutionary for a society blindly obsessed by impoverished values. To have [sanghas] . . . is to have *communities of resistance*. (Sponsel and Sponsel 1997:50)[26]

Such ideas are also seen as represented in (leading to) Buddhist environmental activism (with environmentalism, for Johnston (2006), having a Buddhist identity almost from its genesis). Particularly stressed are *ecosattvas*, or Buddhist environmental activists, who advocate non-delusion/greed/hatred and 'skilful', gentle and sensitive, living in all human pursuits, avoiding pollution/waste (e.g. Buddhist monks only taking other's leftovers as food or wearing robes stitched from rags). Buddhism is thus seen as able to act as a (globally influential) counterculture, critiquing and resisting mainstream modern views and practices, their self-indulgent materialist consumerism and striving for power or wealth, causing violence or waste, able to break through the mental and social habits (and denial) that cause environmental problems. This is seen as practical 'engaged Buddhism', bringing Buddhist teachings to bear upon the problems of the world (rather than shunning mundane existence), seeing it possible to advance the spiritual path to enlightenment (of oneself and others) in the midst of life's travails (and, in this sense, enlightenment/liberation may be communal, having social/political dimensions, something that may have been realized and practised throughout Buddhist history) (Batchelor, S. 1994; De Silva 1994; Kaza 1993, 2002b, 2005; Kraft 1996; 2005; Regenstein 1991).[27]

In all the foregoing precepts, eight-fold path, meditation and activism, however, what must be kept in mind, for M. Batchelor (1994a:7–8), is that the morality upon which Buddhist ideals and practice is based does not come from following rules without question but out of love and respect for all life, creating the conditions for the realization of spiritual fulfilment. It comes from personal spiritual development, from good (non-violent) thought: 'Not to commit evil But to practice all good And to keep the heart pure; This is the teaching of the Buddha' (The Dhammapada); 'When a man gives his merit will increase; No enmity can grow in the self-restrained. The skilled shun evil; they attain nirvana By ending greed and hatred and delusion' (Digha Nikaya 16; Udana VIII).[28] The world, in this sense, is created from intentions, the situation humanity finds itself in now, and that which it will find itself in in the future, is the consequence of how it chooses to act, by arrogance and greed or humility and compassion, with Buddhism stressing the latter as appropriate. In line with such ideas 'true development', in Buddhist terms (as opposed to Western ideas of development), for Sivaraksa (1990), means challenging consumerism and materialism, providing the ideals and morals to critique, reject or subvert, the dominant, harmful and wasteful, modern status quo, and change hearts and minds, creating awareness of the wider reality of natural relationships and the need for humanity to be in tune with these rather than separate from them, leading to less anthropocentrism, exploitation and harm, and more eco-centrism, compassion and care, something expressed in a threefold way of self-knowledge of correct speech, actions and relations (*sila*, morality), inner-truth (*smaadhi*, meditation) and enlightenment (*panna*, wisdom), that stress respect for the wider community and the *quality* (not quantity) of life (see Batchelor, S. 1994; Kinsley 1994; Sponberg 1997).

> From the Buddhist perspective, development must aim at the reduction for craving, the avoidance of violence, and the development of the spirit rather than material things. As each individual progresses, he increasingly attends to the needs of others, without waiting for the millennium or for the ideal socialist society. Cooperation is better than competition, whether in a capitalist or socialist context. In Buddhism, true development is attained in stages as unwholesome desires are overcome. The goal of increasing the quality of life is understood differently. From the materialist standpoint, when there are more desires, there can be further development. From the Buddhist standpoint, when there are fewer desires, there can be further development. (Sivaraksa 1990:171)

Conclusions

Buddhist ecological interpretations stress it as being ecologically sensitive, having respect and concern for nature as its core, stressing a balanced, holistic and relational, cosmos, and prescribing human selflessness, simple lifestyle and spiritual development. It is seen as stressing life as essentially interdependent, seeing independence as an illusion caused by selfish desire, which disrupts the interdependence and causes suffering. Thus it is seen to stress a need to diminish craving and greed and be selfless and cooperative to alleviate suffering (to attain liberation from it), encouraging human self-restraint and care for nature, respecting natural life cycles, seeing one existence as no more important than another, avoiding harming others (a non-heroic action motivated not by ego but by mutual/spiritual connection). Such ideas are seen to fit with an 'ecological' vision, being ecologically empowering, promoting an eco-centric vision of compassionate relatedness, critiquing and correcting harmful modern anthropocentrism.

Buddha is used as an exemplar for this, his experiences/understanding of nature (of its interdependence/spirituality), that all things are transitory and mutually influencing, and the need to recognize this, abandoning egoism/ desire, acting gently and simply (nature bearing witness to his Four Noble Truths: the reality of suffering, its cause of desire and the need to overcome this, via self-discipline). Environmental degradation (suffering) is thus related to a delusional, selfish, attachment to independent existence (*trishna*), with this seen as needing to be overcome via moral/spiritual learning, realizing the interdependent nature of reality (*anatman/sunyata*, detachment from autonomous ego-self and embracing cooperative interbeing, something linked to *karma*, cause and effect, and *samsara*, rebirth, linking life (morally) through stressing thoughts/actions having good or bad consequences, selfless creating the former, selfish the latter). Such interdependence (the attaining of it; 'suchness') is also seen in the concept of *dharma*, or '(path to) truth', all beings having *dharma*-nature, a universal essence, being embryonic Buddha's, capable of enlightenment/liberation from suffering. Thus nature has intrinsic value and conveys spiritual insight, its elements being companions in the *karmic* cycle, testifying to harmonic *dharma*, with humanity needing to be aware of this and act likewise (with compassion and non-violence), something enhanced by the concept of 'co-origination' stressing life as mutually affecting, each thing being the cause of all others and the whole (nothing is self-existing but rather depends on everything else: for example, 'Indra's Net' of many-sided jewels, reflecting each other and the whole, if one is abused (or protected) so are all others and the whole).

From such ideas it is inferred that humanity's true nature is not separate from but in reciprocal union with everything else, a 'relational holism' stressing identity-in-difference, the whole being the interworking of its parts, parts needing each other/the whole to function and the whole needing them. Understanding and achieving this (enlightenment) is seen as involving compassion, loving kindness and non-violence, a 'progress' away from separateness

and towards cooperation, evolution being greater awareness of interdependence and responsibility toward life, existentially experiencing the suffering
of others (exemplified by the *bodhisattva* or enlightened one). To stimulate
this ethical 'precepts' are stressed, such as, not creating evil, practising good,
affirming life, being giving, avoiding selfishness or honouring the body, as is
the 'eightfold path' of self-transformation of 'right' understanding, thought,
speech, action, livelihood, effort, mindfulness and concentration. These are
seen to emphasize a 'middle way' moderate lifestyle, avoiding self-indulgence/
denial, keeping balance and harmony, based around 'mindfulness': being conscious of and overcoming humanity's destructive tendencies, something highlighted by 'Zen' meditation developing a sense of place, cultivating 'oneness'
with nature, creating immersion in interdependence, leading to a community
of mutual support that lives simply and practises harmony with nature (*sangha*,
needing to be extended globally in a 'Great Earth *Sangha*': for example, *ecosattvas*, Buddhist environmental activists, and 'engaged Buddhism', stressing
'true development', holistic knowledge based on the quality not quantity of
life, leading to sensitive, simple living in tune with nature).

Notes

[1] Buddhism is stressed as a variety of beliefs/practices (American, East Asian,
    Indian, Japanese, Thai, Tibetan; interpreted as a coherent tradition by the West)
    with no definitive perspective on nature. However, it is also seen as a dynamic,
    living tradition, reinterpreting heritage to new situations, with applying it to
    ecology thus possibly authentically representing it (see Gosling 2001; Johnston
    2006; Kraft 1996; Masuzawa 2005; Sponberg 1997; Swearer 2005, 2006; Williams
    1997). The aim, for Williams (1997), should be to explore a wide range of Bud-
    dhist ecological views via a variety of methodologies – critical, descriptive,
    engaged, interpretive, prophetic – leading to creative adaptation of Buddhist
    concepts (by ordained/lay Buddhists, academic 'Buddhologists', Buddhist
    sympathizers).
[2] Johnston (2006), Kaza (2002a, 2002b) and Swearer (2006:125–37) analyse Bud-
    dhism and ecology historically/thematically (by Buddhists/Westerners; seeing
    environmentalism influenced by it), the latter dividing it into *eco-apologists*, see-
    ing it as inherently eco-friendly, *eco-critics*, seeing this as Western distortion of
    values seeing nature negatively, the site of suffering, *eco-constructivists*, critiquing
    appropriation but stressing critical analysis, *eco-ethicists*, seeing an eco-friendly
    ethic of moderation, and *eco-contextualists*, concentrating on grassroots meanings
    of nature.
[3] Referenced to Badiner (1990:xiv–v).
[4] Referenced to Schmithausen, L., *Buddhism and Nature* (Tokyo: International
    Institute for Buddhist Studies, 1991), p. 32.
[5] Referened to Bhikku Bohdi, 'Foreword', in *Buddhist Perspectives on the Ecocrisis*,
    Klas Sindel, ed. (Kandy, Sri Lanka: Buddhist Publication Society, 1987), p. vii.

6 For Kaza (1993) the Four Noble Truths can be applied to environmental issues via four questions (addressing suffering, providing an alternative to political/ technological approaches de-emphasizing it): What is the problem or suffering? What are the causes of the suffering? What would put an end to the suffering? What is the path to realize this goal?

7 Referenced to Thich Nhat Hanh.

8 Referenced to Maha Ghosananda.

9 Kraft (1997) posits ecologically extending *karma* from individuals to groups, East to West, religious to secular, low-tech to hi-tech societies, suggesting *eco*, *group* or *techno-karma* (applying compassion to ecosystems, examining global warming *karmically*, for example, will humanity get the fate it deserves, and which sections, individuals/nations, rich/poor).

10 Referenced to Roger Corless, *The Concern for Animals in Buddhism* (Silver Spring, MD: International Network for Religion and Animals, no date).

11 Referenced to Kukai, *Attaining Enlightenment in This Very Existence (Sokushin jobutsu gi).*

12 Referenced to Francis Cook, *Hua-yen Buddhism* (University Park: Pennsylvania State University Press, 1977), p. 19.

13 De Silva (1994:18–21) sees Buddhism stressing nature's (transformational) interconnection via physical, biological, psychological, moral and causal, laws (*panca niyamadhamma:* season, seed, mind, action, phenomenal), through which elements condition biology influence thought patterns determine moral standards and affect nature. Brown (1994:125) also notes Buddha's teaching of nature as clusters of five psycho-physical elements: *rupa*, material, *vedana*, feelings; *samjna*, perceptions, *samskara*, dispositions, and *vijnana*, awareness.

14 Referenced to Thomas Cleary, *The Flower Ornament Scripture*, vol. 1 (Boston: Shambhala, 1984), pp. 184, 302.

15 Barnhill (1997) highlights Gary Snyder connecting Indra's Net to the food-web, seeing it as gift exchange for the continuation of life, and stressing the need for interlinked, bioregional, communities (ecologizing the Buddhist notion of interpenetration and Buddhacizing the notion of ecosystem).

16 Referenced to Rev. Iru Price (Shik Po Chih), 'Compassion', Humanitarian Literature Distribution Service San Francisco.

17 Referenced to Buddhadasa Bhikku.

18 Referenced to Kukai, *Sokushin jobutsu gi* (Attaining enlightenment in this very existence), in Yoshito S. Hakeda, *Kukai: Major Works* (New York: Columbia University Press, 1972), pp. 229–30.

19 Referenced to Uisang, in Odin, S., *Process Metaphysics and Hua-yen Buddhism* (Albany: State University of New York Press, 1982), pp. xix–xx (de-italicized).

20 Referenced to Fazang, in Odin, S., *Process Metaphysics and Hua-yen Buddhism* (Albany: State University of New York Press, 1982), p. 25.

21 Referenced to Maha Ghosananda, Cambodian Prayer, in *The Path of Compassion*, Fred Eppsteiner, ed. (Berkeley: Parallax Press, 1985), pp. 24–5.

22 Referenced to the Pali Text Society, London.

23 Downloaded from www.environment.harvard.edu/religion/religion/buddhism/ texts. index.html, 15 Sept. 2006; referenced to Maharatnakuta Sutra, 'Dwelling in the Forest'.

[24] M. Batchelor (1994b:104–7), Ho (1990:133–5), Kaza (1993:141–4) and Kraft (1996:485–90) stress ecological *gathas* or 'mindfulness verses' aiding meditation: for example, 'This plate of food, so fragrant and appetizing, also contains much suffering'; 'Hearing the crickets at night, I vow with all beings, to keep my practice simple'; 'A lotus to you, A Buddha to be'.

[25] Referenced to Thich Nhat Hanh, *Touching Peace*, pp. 11–12.

[26] Referenced to Phra Phaisan Visalo, The Forest Monastery and Its Relevance to Modern Thai Society, in *Radical Conservatism: Buddhism in the Contemporary World*, Sulak Sivaraska et al. ed. (Bangkok: Thai Inter-Religious Commission for Development and International Network of Engaged Buddhists, 1990), pp. 293–4.

[27] For S. Batchelor (1994) a Buddhist solution to environmental problems is to explain how modernity is not in humanity's self-interest, challenging structures blinding to its destructive actions. Kaza (2002b) sees this in resistance actions (protests, rituals), critique of social structures (animal rights, nature preserves) and cultural transformation (bioregionalism, vegetarianism). Johnston (2006), Kaza (2002b, 2005), Kraft (1996, 2005) and Regenstein (1991) note the growth of Buddhist-oriented environmental activism: for example, Buddhist Perception of Nature Project; International Network of Engaged Buddhists; monks ordaining trees to protect from development (Thailand); Sarvodaya Shramadana self-help movement (Sri Lanka); Schools of Zen, Soka Gakkai, Rissho Koseikai (Japan, US); and the Dalai Lama, poet Gary Snyder, scholar Joanna Macy, monks Buddhadasa (his forest monastery exemplifying *sangha*) and Thich Nhat Hanh, expounding environmental responsibility.

[28] Referenced to the Pali Text Society, London.

Chapter 6

Jewish Visions

The Talmud . . . tells us (Shabbat 151b) that heaven rewards the person who has concern and compassion for the rest of creation . . . the righteous Jew, is not a pillar saint who has withdrawn from the world . . . [Jewish] festivals . . . celebrate, in joy, the cycle of the seasons of nature . . . The highest form of obedience to God's command-ments is to do them not in mere acceptance but in the nature of union with Him. In such joyous encounter . . . the very rightness of the world is affirmed. The encounter of God and man in nature is thus conceived in Judaism as a seamless web with man as the leader and custodian of the natural world. Even . . . when Jews were most involved in their own immediate dangers and destiny, this universalist concern has never withered . . . Now, when the whole world is in peril . . . it is our Jewish respon-sibility to put the defence of the whole of nature at the very centre of our concern . . . man was given dominion over nature, but he was commanded to behave towards the rest of creation with justice and compassion . . . We have a responsibility to life, to defend it everywhere, not only against our own sins but also against those of others.
(Rabbi Arthur Hertzberg, The Jewish Declaration on
Nature, WWF 1986:29–31)

Judaism has never seen man as separate and apart from nature, as the licensed plun-derer of a planet; Judaism calls on us to cherish and revere all that has been created in sacredness. In Jewish tradition, man and his world are one, inseparable, inviol-able . . . both good and dependent on each other.

(Regenstein 1991:207)[1]

Jewish ideas concerned with ecology are seen to have been dealt with inciden-tally rather than directly, integral to relationships between God, humanity and the world, Judaism being seen as a complete way of life, based on specific con-crete obligations as much as intellectual theological pursuit. Nevertheless, des-pite a stress on what is seen as traditional Jewish concentration on practice, on the integration of people, land and spirituality (which itself may be seen as an ecological statement), there is also seen arising a 'Jewish theology of nature' where Judaism is being reflected on and explored (and promoted) for envir-onmentally friendly ideas: as Waskow (2002:306) argues 'there are unique wisdoms and unique energies that [Judaism] can bring to [earth] healing. In doing so we can renew the deepest and most powerful energy of Judaism' (see Tirosh-Samuelson 2002a).[2]

> Jewish tradition makes a distinctive and important contribution to our under-standing of contemporary environmental ethics . . . While the Bible . . . as well as post-biblical exegesis, contains not one normative view of nature but a variety of views, many ancient and medieval Jewish texts both express and are consistent with a strong environmental ethic. Far from providing a blan-ket endorsement to man's domination of nature . . . Judaism imposes numer-ous restrictions on how, when, and to what extent people can use [it]. Rather than simply expressing anthropocentric views, many of its ideas and principles either explicitly or implicitly evoke themes that are consistent with eco- or bio-centric understandings of the relationship between people and nature. Indeed, the latter ethos, rather than representing a major new departure in or challenge to western religious thought, is actually prefigured in both ancient and medieval Jewish religious texts. (Vogel 2006:1)[3]

> The Old Testament is full of the wonders of nature, of knowledge of nature. The book of Psalms is a collective hymn to God and to nature. The prophet Isaiah raised the description of the land, rivers, trees, flowers, animals, to a sublime level . . . *chayim*, meaning life, *Shabbat*, meaning Sabbath, and *sha-lom*, meaning peace. These words summarize the Jewish approach to our environment . . . Life is to be enjoyed . . . environment needs rest . . . peace [involves] . . . respect for all forms of life, recognizing their interdepend-ence. (Rose 1992b:11–12)

Particularly stressed is that the origins of Judaism are intimately related to a sacred relationship to the earth: that is, the Jews as the 'chosen people' inhabit-ing the 'chosen land' of Israel (with its prosperity depending on their moral integrity), the Bible being about a people knowing and caring about their land, seeing it as God's gift, their lives reciprocally bound up with it, what is seen as a vision of *shlemut*, harmony, peace and wholeness (something seen as a proto-type of the ecological behaviour of humanity in general; in line with such ideas Israel, its animal sanctuaries, innovative irrigation and reclamation of barren lands, nature reserves and solar energy programmes, is highlighted in 'environ-mentally friendly' terms). The Jewish people and the land of Israel are, in this sense, seen to be in symbiosis: it is seen as blossoming when (correctly) inhab-ited by them and declining when not (as are they). In a similar way, Zionism is seen as an ecological statement, not just a return to a historical landscape but a return to nature as whole, as well as to a true Jewish 'self', a proper divinely intended human relationship with nature, rooted in the divinely inspired soil, with land cultivation a sacred task of the Jews in Israel, with their and the lands health tied to it (this being opposed to the Diaspora, which is a 'turning (being turned) away' from nature and self, creating a 'non-people', separated from their intended natural/spiritual home, resulting in (human/nature) suffering, something used as a parable of the modern alienation from nature and its environmental suffering) (Fink 2004; Katz 1994; Rose 1992a, 1992c; Schwartz 2002; Solomon 1992; Swartz 1996; Tirosh-Samuelson 2002a, 2005b; Waskow 2002).

In line with such ideas stress is placed on the (first) account of creation in Genesis or on prohibitions and restrictions in Exodus, Leviticus or Deuteronomy, that show the paramount importance of nature and the need for humanity to harmoniously fit into it. In this scheme, the world (including humanity) owes it existence to God, the creator, who saw that creation was good and, therefore, has regard for it. Nature is thus important as it was created by God's action, for example, 'In the beginning God created the heavens and the earth'. Furthermore, this is seen as an ongoing process, God renewing creation/nature daily, meaning that it is constantly bound up with His benevolent creative action, constantly filled with His breath of life (*ruah*, showing a divine regard for its continuance). The 'beginning' is thus with God and then nature and later humanity and there is (God's wilful, loving) order and integrity to nature and thus an important existence to it apart from humanity's desires or needs. It is owned by God ('The earth is the Lord's and all that is in it, the world and those who live in it', Ps. 24.1[4]), which He does not forsake to humanity but merely allows it tenancy (it cannot own the land, it is God's and for all its created inhabitants, something that commandments and ritual action reinforce through stressing the need for humanity to require God's permission to use His creation: 'the land is not to be sold in perpetuity for [it] is Mine . . . you are strangers and sojourners before Me', Lev. 25.23[5]) (Bassett et al. 2000; Katz 1994; Maguire 2000; Palmer and Finlay 2003; Solomon 1992; Tirosh-Samuelson 2001).

Where wast thou when I laid the foundations of the earth? Declare, if thou hast understanding. Who hath laid the measures thereof, if thou knowest? or who hath stretched the line upon it? . . . Who hath divided a watercourse for the overflowing waters, or a way for the lightning of thunder; To cause it to rain in the earth, where no man is; on the wilderness, wherein there is no man; To satisfy the desolate and waste ground; and to cause the bud of the tender herb to spring forth? (Job 38:4–5; 25–27) . . . 'The untamed world beyond the frontiers of human society is fraught with the numinous, it is a constant reminder that man is not master in the world but only a privileged and therefore responsible inhabitant of it.'[6] God's message to Job is that . . . humans will be fulfilled if they accede to the interests and demands of God . . . This is the message of Job: do not believe the rain falls for you. (Katz 2001:153, 164)

The world, in this scheme, was not created for humanity, which is finite, not omniscient, and is not for its interests alone but for all. There is thus seen to be a 'non-anthropocentrism' in Judaism: it is seen to offer a theocentric universe where meaning, purpose and value, emerge from God's creative activity (the value of nature lying not in its usefulness to humanity but in its existence as part of God's plan). In this sense, also, God is argued as having created everything 'according to its kind', this being seen as assigning unique value to species and arguing for their conservation (e.g. Noah and the ark, conserving species irrespective of usefulness), highlighting that biodiversity needs to be cherished as it relates to the rightness of God's pattern for creation, establishing boundaries, and the human relation to it (of which animals/nature may teach, humanity needing to observe and learn, for example, differentiation of clean/unclean, non-mixing of species). All species are intended for their own sake, having a purpose, being their own projects, precious and irreplaceable, intrinsically valuable, and thus due just deserts. They are ontological loci of value through being purposeful parts of God's ordered plan for creation, requiring understanding, respect and care, based on their God-given 'being' (Fink 2004; Goodman 2002; Hutterman 2002; Jacobs 2002; Katz 1994, 2001; Maguire 2000; Regenstein 1991; Solomon 1992; Tirosh-Samuelson 2001).

> The Talmud even shows the wisdom to appreciate the lowliest, most obscure of creatures, many of which are largely considered pests: 'Thou thinkest that flies, fleas, mosquitoes are superfluous, but they have their purpose in creation, as a means of a final outcome . . . Of all that the Holy One, blessed be He, created in His world, He did not create a single thing without purpose' (Shabbat 77b).[7] (Regenstein 1991:189)

Nothing, then, is created in vain, all conveys meaning, something seen as further stressed in humanity not being created until the sixth day, with nature, plants, animals, even insects, preceding it (and in God appearing to Moses in a lowly bush). Nothing is without God's presence, everything points to Him: as Palmer and Finlay (2003:115) note 'Every sprout and leaf of grass says something . . . every stone whispers some hidden message in the silence, every creation utters it song'.[8] God is also seen as commending nature for its beauty, while descriptions of it in Jewish texts are seen as expressing its value, particularly its orderliness, with Isaiah, Psalms and Song of Songs, especially, being seen as hymns to it, extolling its sacredness, stimulating awe, reverence and wonder, at it (and, in this sense, also, it is seen as having a beneficial effect on human consciousness, able to connect it to a wider spiritual reality): 'Behold my works, how fair and lovely they are. All that I have created, I have created for [you] . . . do not corrupt and destroy my universe, for if you [do] . . . there is no one to repair it after you' (Eccl. Rabbah 7:13)[9] (Hutterman 2002; Palmer and Finlay 2003; Regenstein 1991; Rose 1992b; Swartz 1996; Tirosh-Samuelson 2005a). Such Jewish 'creation spirituality' ideas, for Solomon (1992), thus articulate an 'original blessing' of goodness (rather than stressing original sin), where nature meets God's intent, being perfect with respect to its purpose of sustenance and flourishing, independent of human concerns, an allusion to His glory, pervaded by Him. Schwartz (2002) and Kaplan (2002) see such ideas inspiring a 'radical amazement' model of human action with respect to nature, based on the wisdom literature of Job and Ecclesiastes, engaging it through awe and reverence at its complexity, mystery and sacredness (this tempering egoism), Kaplan arguing for a 'depth theology' approach to it, engaging it subjectively via intuition rather than objectively via reason, discerning and partaking of (caring for) its divine communion.[10]

Nature is thus seen as filled with meaningful (spiritual) life and not to be abused or wasted: 'He did not create it as a waste but made it to be lived in' (Isa. 45.18).[11] It is not meant to be empty or diminished, but filled with fulfilled life (what is seen as the vision of Genesis). In line with this, the concept of *bal tashchit*, meaning 'do not destroy', is stressed, emphasizing nature as something to be respected and conserved, that humanity is to complement and protect it, not destroy it (a positive preventing of harm as much as negative stopping of destruction). This is seen as relating to a Jewish tradition of moderation, limiting conspicuous consumption and forbidding wanton vandalism to ensure a healthy and productive environment (God's original intent, His gift). This is a restraint distinguishing between human needs and wants (highlighting the limits of human wisdom, for example, Job): humanity can use nature, they have complementary roles, but not abuse it (something extended to human abilities, the need not to waste talents but to use them to enhance life, fulfilling God's pattern). It is meant to teach humanity to love the good (in creation, as does God, His regard for creation being a model for human action) not rejoice in destruction (a sin that will lead to human destruction: 'rejoice in that which benefits people . . . never destroy even a grain of mustard . . . [be] upset at any destruction . . . save anything from being spoilt (Rabbi Aaron Halevi)';[12] 'with the kind of measure a man measures, so shall he be measured (Mishnah Sotah 1:7)'[13] (Goodman 2002; Jacobs 2002; Katz 1994; Palmer and Finlay 2003; Regenstein 1991; Rose 1992b; Solomon 1992; Swartz 1996; Tirosh-Samuelson 2001).

The human position with respect to nature, in this sense, is as part of it: it is of the earth (the second creation narrative, Adam/human coming from *adamah/ humus* meaning earth) and will return to it at death, emphasizing their created relationship (something seen as highlighted in death rituals where the needs of the dead involve returning to earth, suffering if not, witnessed by the decay of flesh). Furthermore, not only did God create humans from the earth but all other life as well, highlighting that life is intended for it and that humanity is part of a reciprocal organic whole, the same substance as other life-forms, their needs being one. Despite this, humanity is also seen as the crowning achievement of creation, made in God's image to have 'dominion' over and 'subdue' it (i.e. *imago Dei*). However, this is not seen as a permit for domination or destruction. Although it accords humanity a privileged position as the 'honoured guest' of creation, it also conveys a 'stewardship' (*paqid*, tradition-ally an official with responsibility for a specific task), the responsibility to 'till and tend' nature (and 'name', or in other words, 'understand', animals). This is something intrinsic to creation: the earth is a garden to be cared for and humanity made to do this (fulfilling God's mandate of imposing order over chaos, virtue of a covenant with Him, represented by circumcision, something seen as being in tension with human fallibility, hence God's biblical blessings, obligations and rituals). Thus there is seen to be no wilderness tradition in Judaism as this implies a landscape without people and an escape from his-tory. Rather the cultivated field is the ideal with Eden not pristine emptiness but including humanity (Fink 2004; Goodman 2002; Hutterman 2002; Jacobs 2002; Katz 1994; Kraemer 2002; Maguire 2000; Schwartz 2002; Solomon 1992; Swartz 1996; Tirosh-Samuelson 2001, 2005a; Waskow 2002).

> There can be no doubt to any enlightened or thoughtful person, that the 'dominion' mentioned in the Bible . . . is not the dominion of a tyrant who deals harshly . . . in order to achieve his own personal desires and whims. It would be unthinkable to legislate so repugnant a subjugation and have it forever engraved upon the world of God, who is good to all and whose mercy extends to all. (Palmer and Finlay 2003:112)[14]

Such ideas are seen as stressing that humanity shares the burden of God's creative work, His sustaining of nature, needing to be a 'worthy' steward with 'proper' caring dominion (*avad*, to serve or participate in worship of the div-ine, based on a unique human combination of freedom to choose and intelli-gence to judge, guided by the Torah, exemplified by Noah rescuing and caring for all animal life). Such ideas are related to a marriage partnership where a man has to treat (subdue) his wife (nature) in such a way as to allow her (it) to fully develop, not hinder this. They are also related to the concept of 'kingship', a sacred mandate based on the condition of worthiness, suggesting humanity is only pre-eminent when acting with the highest responsibility, and if not, if abusing nature (a sign of debasement), it may decline, losing its spe-cial position, becoming dominated by beasts (something seen as suggested by the Hebrew word for 'take dominion' (*v'yirdu*) which is from the same root as 'to descend' (*yarad*)) (Fink 2004; Hutterman 2002; Katz 1994; Solomon 1992; Swartz 1996). In line with such ideas, Maguire (2000) highlights the theme of 'exile', seeing humanity alienated from its intended state, that of being in har-mony with nature, its egoism exiling it from its destiny of a harmonic Eden, which is a vision of the future, a 'promised land' not yet reached. Humanity (mirroring Adamic exile and Judaism's historical escape from destruction) is thus in a lost, desert existence at present, easily seduced by idols (consumer-ism), wandering naked in a desert of its own making: 'We have all become like one who is unclean, and all our righteous deeds are like a filthy cloth'

(Isa. 64.6). It thus bears only the 'scent of paradise', the hint of the possibility of a healed world, a return to an authentic creation and human self. Along these lines, Jacobs (2002) emphasizes (the need for) *teshuva*, repentance or return, a 'beginning again', rectifying and compensating (individual or collective) wrongs, arguing for an 'ecological *teshuva*' addressing pollution and restoring harmonious ecological balance (something also related to *tikkun olam*, or 'repair of the world', a restoration of the world to original harmony) (see Foltz 2002b; Green 2002; Tirosh-Samuelson 2001).

Such repentance and repair involves, for Maguire (2000), *sedaqah*, a compassionate, just, responsible, obligation to the stranger at ones side, biased towards the poor and suspicious of the rich (the community being more important than the individual, related to a desert experience where people need to work together to survive). In a similar way, Swartz (1996:100) highlights (the need for) *tzedek*, or justice for all, so that no one thing suffers disproportionately ('justice, justice shall you pursue', Deut. 16.20), while Palmer and Finlay (2003) argue that all creation (being meaningful and sacred) deserves mercy (e.g. 'the world is built on tender mercy', Ps. 89.3[15]).

> One's mercy must extend to all the oppressed. One must not embarrass or destroy them, for the higher wisdom is spread over all that was created: inanimate, vegetable, animal, and human. For this reason were we warned against desecrating foodstuffs . . . and in the same way, one must not desecrate anything, for all was created by His wisdom – nor should one uproot a plant, unless there is a need, or kill an animal unless there is a need.[16]

Humanity, therefore, is restricted in its use of nature, forbidden to show cruelty or take excess, encouraged to be sensitive and show kindness to animals, recognizing their ontological (suffering) being (e.g. comparing the worry of human and animal mothers for their offspring), what Regenstein (1991) sees as a Jewish tradition of compassion (the Jews being a 'merciful people'), the Talmud (Yebamot, 79a) seen as highlighting this as their first quality (exemplified by the Hebrew proverb 'the kind man first feeds his beasts before sitting down to his table' and the rabbinical law 'a good man does not sell his beast to a cruel person'). This is related to the Hebrew concept *tsa'ar ba'alei hayim*, the commandment and tradition to prevent the sorrow or suffering of living creatures ('to relieve an animal of pain or danger is a biblical law, superseding a Rabbinic ordinance'[17]), something that is part and parcel of righteousness and piety, summed up in the saying 'the principle of kindness to animals . . . is as though God's treatment of man will be according to (man's) treatment of animals'[18] (Goodman 2002; Solomon 1992; Tirosh-Samuelson 2001).

> [Judaism] stresses the obligations humans have to animals . . . Jewish law is remarkably strict in its requirement that animals be treated properly . . .

[reflecting] the traditional Jewish attitude of humane regard and compassion for animals . . . to treat animals kindly . . . [providing] homeless animals with food and shelter . . . [not] overloading beasts of burden . . . [helping] animals in distress . . . [disapproving] of blood sports [discouraging] hunting . . . [requiring] that [animals] be allowed to rest . . . [forbidding] the raising of animals under inhumane conditions. (Regenstein 1991:184, 190–4)

Along these lines *kashrut*, or the kosher code, restricted production and consumption and rules of cleanliness and purity of food (e.g. only eating meat of non-predatory animals, slaughtered in a painless way, not mixing milk/meat) is seen as stressing and balancing a crucial (sacred) connection between humanity and nature, something that is seen as needing to be ecologically applied to modernity in an eco-*kashrut*, extending obligations and restrictions more widely (e.g. tempering greed/possessiveness, rejecting biotechnology/pesticides/nuclear power, protecting nature). In line with such ideas, Green (1996) proposes vegetarianism as a '*kashrut* for our age', arguing that in Eden humans and animals eat only plants, only later (sin, exile) eating flesh, something Regenstein (1991) extends to the flood after which plant life was destroyed (seeing a special blessing before consuming fruits, vegetables and wine, but not meat), while he and Solomon (1992) also highlight the teaching of a return to an ideal vegetarian state when the Messiah comes, *kashrut* being a compromise until then (e.g. Isa. 11.69). Waskow (1996, 2002) relates such eco-*kashrut* ideas to humanity's consumption of coal, oil, plutonium and wood (extending obligations from Jewish individuals to human society), seeing humanity addicted to these, practising a form of idolatry, needing to consume them in a more sacred (less polluting) way. In line with this rituals and prayers, expressing gratitude for (and consecrating) nature, recognizing its life-giving importance, its bearing witness to God's benevolence and power, are seen as something that Judaism can give to environmentalism. Rose (1992a, 1992b, 1992c) argues that such blessings (*beracha*) pervade Judaism, asking permission and being thankful to God for being able to live in and use His creation (water, in particular, being blessed as availability and cleanliness of irrigation, reservoirs and wells, are seen as vital to *mayim chayim*, or 'living waters' of creation, while Rabbis are seen as stressing that anyone who eats without saying the proper blessing of thanksgiving is like a thief stealing from the creator) (see Fink 2004; Foltz 2002b; Katz 1994; Regenstein 1991; Swartz 1996; Tirosh-Samuelson 2001).

Our prayers are full of blessings, including those in relation to the environment. We have a blessing over the fruit of the vine, over bringing forth bread from the earth, a blessing on grapes and figs and dates, a blessing on vegetables . . . a blessing on smelling fragrant bark of a tree or sweet smelling plants. We even have special blessings to be said on the happening of natural events, lightning, thunder, on seeing the sea or beautiful trees or animals, on seeing a rainbow, on seeing the first blossom on a tree. And these blessings hallow nature, and respect the environment. (Rose 1992b:16–17)

Blessings . . . are . . . evocative of Judaism's sense of awe and thankfulness in the face of the wonders of God and nature . . . [For example] 'Blessed is the Eternal our God . . . who makes the wonders of creation . . . whose power and might pervade the world . . . who has fashioned goodly creatures and lovely trees that enchant the heart . . . who remembers the covenant with Noah and keeps its promise faithfully with all creation.' (Rose 1992c:2–3)

Such a sacred connection to nature is also seen highlighted in the Jewish calendar, rooted in and celebrating its rhythms and seasonal cycles. Prayers of reverence for nature in *Rosh Hashanah* and *Yom Kippur* are highlighted, as are *Sukkot's* act of living in temporary booths for seven days, this being seen as a way to experience and rejoice in (sacred) nature more directly as well as reminding of the desert experience, teaching that humans are wanderers, transient parts of creation. For Waskow (2002:310–11) *Hoshanah Rabbah*, the seventh day of *Sukkot*, is also an earth ritual, keyed to the seven days of creation, meaning (*Hosha na*) 'Please save us . . . Save the earth', asking God to save it from disaster, while *Pesach* is seen as a week of simple living eliminating the swollen 'leavening' or greed of modern 'pharaonic' life (calling on 'corporate pharoahs' to open their hearts and save the land they are destroying). And another such nature festival especially highlighted is *Tu B'shvat*, or New Year for Trees, where trees are planted, celebrating the Tree of Life and highlighting trees as a paradigm of God's blessing (humanity's story beginning with the trees of life and knowledge of good and evil). Also highlighted are biblical injunctions to avoid cutting fruit bearing trees, seeing them as symbolic cynosure of human responsibility to nature, following God, the 'first agriculturalist', occupied with planting at the beginning of creation, establishing the primacy of agriculture, the ideal state, putting down roots and being productive (not destructive), a tenure for fulfilled life and hope for the future: as Palmer and Finlay (2003:119) argue 'When people cut down the wood of a tree that yields fruit, its cry goes from one end of the world to the other' (comparing this to the departure of the soul from the body)[19] (Goodman 2002; Jacobs 2002; Pick 1992; Regenstein 1991; Rose 1992a, 1992b; Tirosh-Samuelson 2001).

As Rose (1992b:13, 17) argues 'Never in [Jewish] . . . festivals are we far away from nature . . . [they] are celebrations of nature, all of them. They teach concern for nature and love of nature'. And these ideas are seen as highlighting that religio-moral purity is necessary for residence in God's land, to ensure it flourishes, humanity needing to observe God's commands, bodily (food regulations), socially (justice), spatially (land obligations) and temporally (annual festivals). And an important element to this is seen to be *Shabbat*, the Sabbath, the seventh rest day, a retreat from production/consumption, allowing time for communion with nature (and God), argued as the last thing God created but the first in intention. This is seen as a mnemonic of humanity's ties to nature (refreshing them), a tangible reminder that it is worth more than monetary considerations, providing humility and restraint. It is seen as a sanctification of space and time (being eternity within human space/time), being, for Kaplan (2002:417), 'the answer to the problem of civilization . . . to work with things of space but be in love with eternity. Things are our tools; eternity, the Sabbath, is our mate'.[20] This is seen as transforming ideas of boundary and property, advancing the fellowship of creation, limiting human activity (creating awareness that what it 'owns' is temporary, mere projections of personal identity, that all ultimately belongs to God), slowing down human use of nature in a 'restful spirit', what is seen as possibly a last, best, hope for modern humanity, a spiritual vision of peace in a profane consumerist age (Fink 2004; Jacobs 2002; Kaplan 2002; Katz 1994; Maguire 2000; Palmer and Finlay 2003; Riskin 1992; Tirosh-Samuelson 2001; Waskow 1996).

> The idea of conservation may be found in the biblical institution of the sabbatical year (Lev. 25:1–5): 'Six years shall you sow your field, and six years shall you prune your vineyard, and gather in the produce thereof. But in the seventh year shall be a Sabbath of solemn rest for the land . . . you shall neither sow your field nor prune your vineyard' . . . [such] ceasing [of] all agricultural activity is to improve and strengthen the land . . . [and] to declare all produce ownerless . . . [a] restoration of the proper balance among man, God, and nature . . . 'man returns to the freshness of his nature, to the point where there is no need to heal his illnesses, most of which result from destruction of the balance of life as it departs even further from the purity of the spiritual and material nature.' (Introduction to Shabbat haAretz, 8–9)[21]

> '[W]e create nothing, we destroy nothing, and we enjoy the bounty of the Earth' . . . [the first] serves to remind us that we are not as supreme as God . . . [the second] that the world does not belong to us, but to God . . . [the third] that God is the source of nature's goodness.[22] Thus the concept of the Sabbath itself – the absence of work and the appreciation of God – imposes a strict limitation on human activity. (Katz 1994:59)

Schorsch (1992) sees such ideas relating to a strain of self-denial running through Judaism, imposing limits on human possibilities to enable spiritual renewal, freedom needing to be harnessed and channelled to be beneficent (yoked to a wider vision). Swartz (1996), in this sense, argues that the Sabbath is the first step to *shalom* or peace, being a pause to allow humanity to become 're-ensouled' (*va-yinafash*, thus modern humanity not only damages nature but also its soul, what Foltz (2002b:280) sees as ' "(catching) our breath", that is the breath of life we all breathe' (i.e. appreciating God/nature). Waskow (1996, 2002), similarly, argues the Sabbath is for a reason, creation needs rest and if humanity does not let it, it will get it anyway, at humanity's expense, the only choice being whether the earth's rest occurs with joy or disaster, whether humanity rests with it, reconsidering the modern project of unconstrained development (what he sees as a Sabbath denied), or becomes 'expelled in painful exile'. The flourishing of the land and the quality of people's lives, are, then, in this sense, causally linked: what humanity sows it reaps; if it follows Gods ordinances, such as the Sabbath and, especially, the Torah (God's revealed will, a sacred communication with humanity), it will prosper, if not it will suffer – 'If the Israelites accept the Torah, then you (creation) will flourish, if not, I will turn you back into desert and emptiness'[23] (Hutterman 2002; Tirosh-Samuelson 2001). As Waskow (2002:310, quoting the *Sh'ma*), relating such ideas to present eco-problems, states:

And if you act on Torah then rain will fall, the rivers will run and the earth will be fruitful and you will live well. And if you don't act on Torah, if you reject it, if you cut yourself off from this great harmony of the earth, then the great harmony will cease to be harmony and will cut itself off from you, and the rains won't fall (or, I would say, they will turn to acid) and the rivers won't run (or they and the oceans will flood), and the sky itself will become your enemy (as in the shattering of the ozone layer or the fouling of the atmosphere with too much carbon dioxide) and you will perish.

The Torah is thus seen as not merely giving instruction about human relationships, or the relationship between humanity and God, but also the human (and God's) relationship to creation, something seen as highlighted by the fact that creation was only completed (morally perfected) when the Torah was given to humanity and that it can only survive if it learns from and keeps to Torah ordinances (Hutterman 2002). The Torah is thus the guide to the complete and perfect created world and to study it is a portal to this; learning and knowledge are seen as vital elements in Judaism (relating to its very essence) and supreme religious values, enabling moral/spiritual cultivation, countering the strains and seductions of prosperity or oppression of an imperfect world, allowing revitalization/fulfilment of humanity/creation – as Riskin (1992:72) argues 'Just as the land [is] allowed to absorb sun, rain and dew [on the Sabbath] . . . [humanity should] absorb the sun, rain and dew of Torah study'.

Studying the Torah is thus devoting time to (worshipping) God and creation, a partnership between the time-bound and the timeless, consecrating their relationships and fulfilling them. It is seen as stimulating a withdrawing concentration or restraining inwardness lifting humanity above the materialism of outward concerns (following the idea that before God created the world He contracted Himself into a small corner of the existing cosmos, this ability to contract being a way to show Himself, to create) (Schorsch 1992;

Tirosh-Samuelson 2001). In this light, Fishbane (2002) also sees an 'Oral Torah' (*Torah She-be'al Peh*, the 'deep Torah of creation'), a primordial vitalization of God's wisdom in nature, His speaking 'I shall be what I shall be' being the infinite revelation at the heart of creation, embodied in all levels of organic coherence (unifying spirit/matter). Humanity distorts this, perceiving it through forms imprinted on the senses, the written Torah (*Torah She-bi-Khtav*) being humanity's conversion of it via a 'natural eye' of cognition, language and experience. Fishbane argues for the need to cultivate a 'spiritual eye', transcending worldly distinctions, a level of consciousness resonant with the concealed Oral Torah within nature, enabling it to be fully perceived. Similar ideas are seen in the Jewish mystical tradition, for example, Kabbalism that is seen envisaging God revealed in nature, a unifying reality behind the diverse corporeal world. Such a view (the 'holy sparks model') sees the expansion of the divine into nature drawing all diverse parts of it into a whole pattern (*sefirot*). Diverse nature thus contains the essence of original unified creation with this able to be uncovered via meditative ritual stimulating intuitive decoding of the underlying divine 'grammar', the 'divine sparks', ensouling corporeal entities (and returning creation to its original, non-corporeal, spiritual state). In this scheme, everything has its place in the harmonic, willed creation of God, at the heart of which is the revelation 'I am' (or 'to be'), the primordial/ eternal Torah, Y-H-W-H, the unified wisdom of God that is transformed into H-W-Y-H or diverse being (Y emanating, H creating, W shaping, H acting; the structure of *sefirot*) (Green 2002; Katz 1994; Schwartz 2002; Seidenberg D. M. 2005; Tirosh-Samuelson 2001, 2005a; Waskow 2002).

> What is the world? The world is God, wrapped in robes of God so as to appear material. And who are we? We are God wrapped in the robes of God and our task is to un-wrap the robes and to dis-cover, uncover, that we are God. (Waskow 2002:311)[24]

In this sense, the purpose of wisdom is to recognize and re-establish the divine pattern of holistic unity, humanity having the task, virtue of *imago Dei*, of restoring nature to primordial harmony (*tiqqun olam*, repair of the world), reversing God's journey from One to many, restoring multiple existence to the harmony of One (creation and revelation are thus parallel manifestations of the primordial Torah, showing the holiness of existence and how to live with that fact). This is seen as involving becoming self-conscious of the roots of (humanity's roots in) God, the One, seeing evolution as a movement towards care and harmony rather than competition and separation, recognizing humanity's created being as communal and relational (Green 2002; Katz 1994; Seidenberg D. M. 2005; Tirosh-Samuelson 2001, 2005a; Waskow 2002). In this light, Gellman (2002) highlights (Martin Buber's) ideas of the 'I-Thou' relationship which stress that God is hidden in things (animals, nature) and the way to experience this (the aim of existence) is through a direct, unconditional, 'I-Thou' encounter with them, whole being to whole being (not seeing the other indirectly and conditionally, as a partial objective 'It', but as a whole subjective 'Thou'). Such a view sees reality based on reciprocity, a mutual acceptance, interaction and understanding: nature is a 'waiting Thou', God is hidden within it, and, therefore, an 'I-Thou' encounter with it is an encounter with Him, the 'eternal Thou'. Furthermore, this relational behaviour is argued as redeeming creation, which began with a relationship. Thus Waskow (2002:307–9, 315) argues for an 'I-Thou' spiral of growth (via 'eco-kosher' practice, prayer, ritual) connecting to and caring for nature, reining in the 'I-It' tendencies of modernity: 'In one spiral, my I eyes what I have just done, to do it more effectively. In the other spiral, my I eyes the face of the Other and sees within it my own face, sees within its different-ness my own uniqueness, and so can love my neighbour as deeply as myself.'

I can contemplate a tree . . . I can assign it to a species and observe it as an instance, with an eye to its construction and its way of life . . . I can dissolve it into a number, into a pure relation between numbers and externalize this. Throughout all this the tree remains my object . . . But it can also happen, if will and grace are joined, that as I contemplate the tree I am drawn into a relation and the tree ceases to be an It . . . What I encounter is . . . the tree itself. (Gellman 2002:371)[25]

To our knowledge the world and the 'I' are two, an object and a subject; but *within* our wonder the world and the 'I' are one in being, in eternity. We become alive to our living in the great fellowship of all beings, we cease to regard things as opportunities to exploit. Conformity to the ego is no longer our exclusive concern, and our right to harness reality in the service of so called practical ends becomes a problem. (Kaplan 2002:411)[26]

Thus, Palmer and Finlay (2003:125), see a Jewish human-(God)-nature 'harmony in four parts'[27] (something that, in Gellman's (2002) terms, stresses a prophetic ethics and responsibility, judging and alleviating discord and fulfilling the divine vision of unity and peace):

One man sings the song of his own soul, for it is there that his satisfaction is complete. Another sings the song of his people, transcending the bounds of his own individual soul . . . A third man's soul expands beyond the Jewish people to sing the song of man, his spirit embraces all humanity, majestic reflection of God . . . And a fourth is transported still higher, uniting with the entire universe, with all creatures, and all worlds, with all of these does he sing.

Conclusions

Ecological interpretations of Judaism (stressing concrete obligations as well as a 'Jewish theology of nature') see it intimately tied to nature, integrating people, land and God, stressing nature as meaningful and humanity in a sacred relationship to it, seeing humanity's God-given Edenic self as relational, in tune with nature, although through self-absorption being rejected, resulting in alienation and suffering, the flourishing of nature and the quality of humanity's moral/spiritual behaviour being causally linked. Humanity is thus seen as intended to be in a symbiotic relationship with nature (*shlemut*, original creation) but failing in this, something exemplified by the Jewish people and Israel: the Jewish Diaspora is seen as an alienation from promised nature, the result of humanity rejecting its true harmonic self, creating an exiled 'non-people', while Zionism is a return to nature/harmonic self (and an ecological statement, a template for humanity as a whole). Humanity, therefore, is seen as needing to steward nature, not abuse it, to fulfil both: by observing God's commandments and practising rituals that sanctify it's ties to nature and being compassionate and just, recognizing and engaging nature's subjectivity, its God-given intrinsically valuable being, preventing its suffering, humanity may thus unite with it (and God) and reach (create) 'Eden' (and meet God's intent, its destiny).

Judaism is thus stressed as emphasizing a theocentric view where nature is divinely created and owned, God's gift, with a loving integrity, intrinsically 'good', an original blessing. It is an illusion to God, meeting His intents, independent of human cause and effect, and should be of concern to humanity, who was created last, behind it (humanity does not own nature but is a tenant requiring God's permission to use it, hence biblical restrictions on how to relate to it). All creatures are their own projects, created 'according to kind', for their own sake and due just deserts. Nature (biodiversity) should thus be cherished as part of God's purpose, conserved, lived in, not wasted (*bal taschit*, 'do not destroy'). Humanity is to complement nature, loving the good not rejoicing in destruction (recognizing that it is of the earth and will return to it and will suffer if separated from it). Although creation's crowning achievement, made in God's image, it is bound by a covenantal trust to care for it as God's steward ('subduing' nature to allow it to develop, like a marriage or kingship, a mandate based on worthiness). It has to tend it, discerning and fulfilling (serving) God's order (if not done humanity declines, becomes debased/exiled). In this sense, Eden is not wilderness but includes humanity, being a vision of a future, an ideal promised land not yet reached, nature needing constant human vigilance and care to achieve it (*teshuva*, repentance or return, rectifying mistakes, and *tikkum olam*, repair of the world, stressing the restoring of nature (and humanity) to original harmony (restoring ecological balance), a compassionate, merciful, responsibility (*tzedek* or justice for all), restraining ego, putting others first, preventing the suffering of creatures (*tsa'ar ba'alei hayim*)).

Such ideas are related to *kashrut*, the kosher code, restricted consumption and rules of cleanliness connecting humanity and nature and celebrating God (His purposeful creation) with an eco-*kashrut* seen as needed, extending these obligations to modern society, consuming nature in a more respectful and sacred, less arrogant and idolatrous, way. In a similar way, blessings, prayers and rituals, are seen to consecrate humanity and nature's sacred relationship, highlighting a more ecological understanding and lifestyle: for example, *Sukkot*, teaching that humanity is temporary, wandering in nature, and asking to save it, stressing eliminating 'swollen' (greedy) life and 'pharanoic' (destructive) institutions; *Tu B'shvat*, celebrating trees as paradigms of God's blessing; *Shabbat*, restraining from consumption/production, allowing nature rest, refreshing communion with it (with eternity, remembering God's harmonic creation). Humanity, in this sense, needs to follow God's ordinances with respect to nature, especially the Torah, which reveals how to relate to it, being a guide to the perfect world, with nature seen as an 'Oral Torah', a vital expression of God's being, His compassion and wisdom being embodied in all levels of organic life. Thus what is needed is cultivation of an intuitive 'spiritual eye' to be able to discern this, attending to natural rhythms (communion with nature in this sense being communion with God). Such natural revelation of God is also seen in Jewish mysticism stressing diverse nature as divine sparks of God's unified creation, God's creative wisdom (Y-H-W-H) transforming into diverse materiality (H-W-Y-H), with humanity's purpose to wisely reconnect with nature and establish divine unity, via a relational, unifying, 'I-Thou' encounter (with its subjective being rather than objective form).

Notes

[1] Referenced to Albert Vorspan, *The Crisis of Ecology: Judaism and the Environment* (New York: Union of American Hebrew Congregations, 1970).
[2] Tirosh-Samuelson (2005a, 2005b) analyses historical Jewish understandings of nature, from early esoteric cosmology, through the influence of Hellenistic philosophy and the scientific revolution, to the challenges of secularization. She highlights descriptions of nature in Jewish texts, seeing the Hebrew Bible as the foundational text, highlighting divine creation and stewardship (the paradigm being the people of Israel) and sees reverence for nature in early Jewish scholars and Rabbinic literature, as well as medieval and Enlightenment sources (descriptions of it being used as lessons, pointing to God). From such sources she sees the beginnings of Jewish environmentalism occurring in North America around 1970, responding to the charge of Judeo-Christianity being the cause of the environmental crisis, and highlights legal/ethical positions and rituals/symbols promoting modern Jewish ecological thinking (highlighting Martin Buber, Aharon David Gordon, Abraham Joshua Heschel, Samson Raphael Hirsch, Yosef Dov Soloveitchik, Arthur Waskow and Arthur Green). Hahne (2005) sees Intertestamental literature referring to a

good creation, God sustaining it, and the effect/redemption of sin. Lerner (2005) concentrates on Jewish law (*halakhah*) and environmental protection, what he sees as a living tradition, constantly being shaped by new issues. Gerstenfeld (2005) highlights texts stressing Judaism and sustainability, dangers of consumerism, and the need for rest for the land to maintain biodiversity, highlighting the need to follow commandments within Judaism's theocentric world-view. In this light, Seidenberg, D. (2005) sees environmental issues having deep roots in Jewish civilization (while noting that consciousness of this is new).

3   Vogel (analysing 'environmentally friendly' biblical/rabbinical themes) argues that Judaism has a complex relationship to nature with both green and non-green elements, the preservation of nature not being seen as the most important societal value, human life being more important, and nature being threatening as well as benevolent, needing to be used and enjoyed as well as protected, seeing the key point being to obey God's ordinances and balance human values and needs with those of nature. Tirosh-Samuelson (2005a) sees a conceptual gap between Jewish tradition and the secular outlook of environmentalism, seeing ecology as a minor agenda for Jewish leadership.

4   From Solomon (1992:48).

5   From Katz (1994:58).

6   Referenced to Allen, E. L., The Hebrew View of Nature, *Journal of Jewish Studies* 2, no. 2 (1951):103.

7   Referenced to Rabbi Barry Fruendel, Kesher Israel Congregation, Washington, DC, 'The Earth is the Lord's: How Jewish Tradition Views Our Relationship and Our Responsibility to the Environment', *Jewish Action*, Summer, 1990.

8   Referenced to Aryeh Levine, R., in *A Tzadik in Our Times*, Simcha Raz, ed. (Jerusalem, 1976), pp. 108–9.

9   From Goodman (2002:228).

10   Referenced to Abraham Joshua Heschel, *God in Search of Man: A Philosophy of Judaism* (Philadelphia: Jewish Publication Society of America, 1956), pp. 43–51.

11   From Goodman (2002:252).

12   From Solomon (1992:49).

13   From Palmer and Finlay (2003:118), referenced to Sefer haHinnukah.

14   Referenced to Rav Kook, 'Hazon ha Tzimhonut vehaShalom, Afikim baNegev II', in *Lahai Ro'i*, ed. Yohanan Fried and Avraham Riger (Jerusalem, 1961), p. 207.

15   From Solomon (1992:26).

16   Downloaded from www.arcworld.org/faiths.asp?pageID=81, 15 Sept. 2006; Referenced to Moshe Cordovero, R., Tomer Devorah 3 (de-italicized).

17   Referenced to Hertz, J. H., ed., *The Pentateuch and Haftorahs* (London: Soncino Press, 1958).

18   Referenced to Animals, Cruelty to, *Encyclopedia Judaica* (Jerusalem: Keter, 1974), pp. 6–7.

19   Referenced to Pirtkei Rabbi Eliezer 34.

20   Referenced to Abraham Joshua Heschel, *The Sabbath* (New York: Farrar, Straus and Young, 1951), p. 48.

21   Downloaded from www.arcworld.org/faiths.asp?pageID=81, 15 Sept. 2006 (de-italicized).

22 Referenced to David Ehrenfeld and Phillip J. Bentley, 'Judaism and the Practice of Stewardship', *Judaism* 34 (1985):310.

23 bShabb. 88a, from Hutterman (2002:286).

24 Referenced to Rebbe of Chernobyl.

25 Referenced to Martin Buber, *I and Thou*, trans. Walter Kaufman (New York: Scribner's, 1970), pp. 57–9.

26 Referenced to Abraham Joshua Heschel, *Man is Not Alone* (New York: Farrar, Strauss and Young, 1951), p. 39.

27 Referenced to Rabbi Avraham Yitzak haKohen Kook, Orot haKodesh II, 444.

Chapter 7

Christian Visions

God . . . created nothing unnecessarily and has omitted nothing that is necessary . . . [thus] man's dominion cannot be understood as license to abuse . . . dominion cannot be anything other than a stewardship in symbiosis with all creatures . . . [manifesting] the Lord's exclusive . . . dominion . . . man may not reduce to chaos or disorder, or, worse still, destroy, God's bountiful treasures . . . for St Francis, work was a God-given grace to be exercised in that spirit of faith and devotion to which every temporal consideration must be subordinate. All human effort in the world must therefore lead to a mutual enrichment of man and creatures . . . Therefore, in the name of Christ who will come to Judge the living and the dead, Christians repudiate . . . forms of human activity . . . [not] in accordance with God's will and design [for] . . . nature which threatens to destroy it and, in turn, to make man the victim of degradation.

(Father Lanfranco Serrini, The Christian Declaration on Nature, WWF 1986:11–13)

God envisioned a world of beauty and harmony, and He created it, making every part an expression of His freedom, wisdom and love . . . At the centre . . . He placed us human beings . . . [giving] us an immortal soul, the source of self-awareness . . . in His image . . . in order to co-operate with Him in realizing . . . the divine purpose for creation . . . [but we] sinned . . . rejecting [this] . . . Among the results of this first sin was the destruction of the original harmony of creation. If we examine carefully the . . . environmental crisis . . . we must conclude that we are still betraying the mandate God has given us: to be stewards . . . in watching over creation in holiness and wisdom. God has not abandoned the world. It is His will that His design and our hope for it will be realized through our cooperation . . . What is required is an act of repentance on our part and a renewed attempt to view ourselves . . . and the world around us within the perspective of the divine design for creation.

(Makrides 2005:339–40)[1]

Ecological interpretations of Christianity revolve around a groundwork of themes (Old and New Testament, following God's ordinances but through the lens of Jesus), providing the basis for what is seen as an 'ecological reformation' to a 'creation-centred' spirituality that values and cares for

nature:[2] God wisely created the world from nothing (emphasizing its dependence on Him, His ownership), seeing it as 'good', and still sustains it, being
immanent (conferring intrinsic value on it); God created humanity in his
image (*imago Dei*) from the world (adam = *adamah* = earth), to have a relationship with and care for it (and God); humanity sins against this, seeking
self-awareness, failing in its care, and becomes alienated from nature (and
God, causing suffering); God provided the means to overcome this in a 'new
creation', the loving incarnation of Jesus (God dwelling/suffering in nature)
and passing on of the Holy Spirit (to humanity and wider creation). To these
can be added Jesus' commandments to 'love God' (to which can be added the
Old Testament statement that the 'fear of God' is the beginning of wisdom)
and 'love thy neighbour' (which may be extended to nature). Within such
themes, then, Christianity is seen as rediscovering nature as valuable, reorienting to its revelatory power and communal being, highlighting (the hope/
promise of) a 'sacrificial' humanity overcoming selfishness and fulfilling its
God-given relational role in creation (redeeming itself *and* nature, fulfilling
that latter as the dwelling place of God's relationship), stressing repentance
of wrongs and preaching a prophetic vision of what should and could be (see
Blackwelder 2005; ELC 1996; Haught 1996; McDaniel 1994; McFarland-Taylor
2005; McGrath 2003; Marshall 2000; Nash 2005; Page 1992; Rand 2000; Reid
2001; Wensveen 2005).

> [I]t is the destiny of humanity to restore the proper relationship between God
> and the world as it was in Eden. Through repentance, two landscapes ... human
> [and] natural . . . can become the objects of a caring and creative effort . . .
> 'We must attempt to return to a proper relationship with the Creator AND
> creation . . . just as a shepherd will in times of greatest hazard, lay down his
> life for his flock, so human beings may need to forgo part of their wants and
> needs in order that the survival of the natural world can be assured' . . . The
> challenge to all Christians is to discover anew the truth that God's love and
> liberation is for all creation, not just humanity.[3]

In line with such ideas several authors stress themes that may enable
'Christian eco-literacy', reacquainting humanity with nature. DeWitt
(1997:91–2) and McGrath (2003:29) suggest fundamental ecological principles within Christianity: *earth-keeping*, where just as God sustains humanity,
so humanity must sustain nature; *Sabbath*, where nature must be allowed rest
and recover from human use; *fruitfulness*, where the fecundity of nature is
to be enjoyed rather than destroyed; and *fulfilment and limits*, where humanity needs to accept a limited role within nature to ensure fulfilment. Hessel
(2004:1–2) sees 'biblically-informed imperatives' enabling an 'ecologically-
alert' Christianity: nature being a community valuable to God, embodying His
love and wisdom; a covenantal commitment, prophetic tradition, sacramental

sensibility and Trinitarian iconography, stressing (ecological) community; a recognition of sin and the need for redemption (e.g. from ecological destruction); and a virtue ethics or 'bio-responsibility' of frugality, humility and justice, grounding human morality in the earth household (*oikos*) based on ecological stewardship (*oikonomos*). McFague (2000:29–40), similarly, sees 'ecological Christologies' showing 'ecological potential': *prophetic or covenantal*, stressing a cruciform justice for oppressed nature; *wisdom*, seeing Jesus as the (earthly) embodiment of God's redeeming energy; *sacramental*, seeing divine immanence affirming/sanctifying nature; and *eschatological*, seeing God working to transform nature towards peace and reconciliation. Such Christian 'ecological revisioning', for Wensveen (2005), is grounded in teachings that affirm the creative and relational aspects of the Trinity in nature, stressing its intrinsic value, its reflection of divine goodness, seeing the Fall as the source of environmental problems, distorting nature's original goodness, with God promising that it will be liberated from this suffering, Jesus symbolizing an environmental life to come.

In line with such views the 'integrity of creation' is stressed, nature being valuable through being harmoniously created and sustained by the loving action of God (His 'breath', *ruah*; and as He is just and righteous so is nature, reflecting His perfect intent). Nature is God's gift, made via His grace, to reveal His creativity, bearing witness to His beneficence and power: ' "The heavens declare the glory of God, and the firmament showeth God's handiwork" (Psalm 19:1) . . . "The Earth is the Lord's and all it contains" (Psalm 24:1)'.[4] Nature matters to God; He loves it and its creatures, caring for their well-being (seeing them as 'good', rejoicing in them). Thus they have intrinsic value, fitting God's intended function, having divine purpose (even predatory or wild elements, and nature as a whole is good as an ordered interdependent community): 'with my wisdom I (God) have organized and I govern all the world with such order that nothing is lacking and nothing could be added to it. Everything is provided for . . . made with the greatest order and providence' (Catherine of Siena).[5] To love and care for nature and its creatures, then, is to love and care for God, to abuse them is to abuse God (hence to 'love' or 'fear' God is the basis of respect and care for nature, something to which it will witness, administering discipline or retributive justice if not done) (Basset et al. 2000; Berry 2000; Blackwelder 2005; Callicott 1997; DeWitt 1997; ELC 1996; Hessel 2004; Kalapurachal 2003; Page 1992; Palmer and Finlay 2003; Rand 2000; Regenstein 1991; Wielenga 2003).

> Creation came into being by the will and love of . . . God, and as such it possesses an inner cohesion and goodness. Though human eyes may not always discern it, every creature and the whole creation in chorus bears witness to the glorious . . . harmony with which creation is endowed. (World Council of Churches, Palmer and Finlay 2003:83–4)

You (God) set the earth on its foundations . . . giving drink to every wild animal . . . the birds of the air have their habitation . . . You cause the grass to grow
for the cattle, and the plants for people to use . . . O lord how manifold are your
works! In wisdom you have made them all (Psalm 104) . . . Let them praise the
name of the Lord, for he commanded and they were created. He established
them . . . he fixed their bounds, which cannot be passed. (Psalm 148)[6]

Nature is thus seen as a sign of God, reflecting the divine attribute of goodness, everything within it having a unique God-given place and role. It conveys knowledge about, is a powerful testimony to, God, praising Him in its
very being (irrespective of utilitarian purpose): as McGrath (2003:35) states:
'There is no life in the sea, No creature in the river, Nothing in the heavens . . .
no bird on the wing, No star in the sky, Nothing beneath the sun, That does
not proclaim God's goodness'[7] (see Bauckham 2000; Blackwelder 2005; ELC
1996; DeWitt 1997; Page 1992; Palmer and Finlay 2003; Rajotte and Breuilly
1992; Wensveen 2005). In this sense, Chryssavgis (2000, 2005) sees nature as
an 'icon' of God, reflecting Him, being part of the 'liturgy of heaven', able to
disclose the true reality of experience. Contemplating nature thus involves
recognition of God's presence, each place and moment being a window to
eternity, an epiphany of God in the world and the existence of the world in
God. Nature is thus a point of entry to a new reality, revealing the eternal
dimension behind material reality, its form and function representing God's
vision of a perfect world to come, being an image eternally engraved by Him,
sealed with the gift of the Holy Spirit. It is, then, a bearer of God, of truth, a
tangible connection between spirit and matter, created and uncreated (this
stressing its sacramentality, all things being signs of the transcendent, and its
apophatic dimension, its aesthetics reflecting divine grace, with this not being
idolatry, for Chryssavgis, as creation is not worshipped in place of God but God
worshipped through creation).

[N]ature is all good and fair in itself, and grace was sent out to save nature
and destroy sin, and bring fair nature back again to the blessed place from
which it came, which is God . . . nature has been tried in the fire of tribula-
tion, and that no lack or defect is found in it. So nature and grace are of one
accord; for grace is God, as uncreated nature is God. (Julian of Norwich)[8]

Nature in this respect is also seen as God's 'Book of Works', the eternal Word
of God (*logos*, primordial creative voice[9]) reflected in (speaking through) every
plant and animal (these being teachers, hence living close to and studying
nature is a way to sense the presence of God, hence monasteries in remote settings). In this sense, humanity needs to learn nature's divine lessons of organic
wholeness, justice and reconciliation, a learning that is subjective as much as
objective, accepting that life-forms have experiences and phenomenological

consciousness and engaging these directly, being to being not being to thing. And by accepting nature as sharing God's being, God is also experienced in this, humanity discovering the extraordinary in the ordinary. In this sense, nature can assist humanity to worship God, to share His concerns which it highlights, that of sustaining an interdependent creation and assisting its fruitfulness and peace (being a fellow created worshipper, seeing other creatures as family and becoming a (caring) participant in this, that is, 'love thy neighbour') (Bauckham 2000; Berry 2000; Blackwelder 2005; Deane-Drummond 2004; DeWitt 1997, 2005; Hessel 2004; Kalapurachal 2003; Lodhal 2005; McGrath 2003; Palmer and Finlay 2003; Rand 2000; Wallace 2000).

> We know Him by . . . the creation, preservation, and government of the universe; which is before our eyes as a most elegant book, wherein all creatures, great and small, are so many characters leading us to see clearly the invisible things of God, even his everlasting power and divinity. (Belgic Confession, DeWitt 1997:85)[10]

> But ask the animals, and they will teach you, the birds of the air, and they will tell you. Ask the plants of the earth, and they will teach you, and the fish of the sea will declare to you. Who among these does not know that the hand of the Lord has done this? In his hand is the life of every living thing (Job 12:7–10). (Blackwelder 2005:308)

In line with such ideas biblical rules on the treatment of nature are stressed, in particular, the 'Sabbath' principle, God's commandment to let the earth rest and recover (seen as arguably the most important commandment and an ecological blessing and wisdom): 'For six years you shall sow your land and gather in its yield; but the seventh year you shall let it rest . . . that the poor . . . and wild beasts may eat' (Exod. 23.10–11).[11] This is seen as a recognition and reflection of creation's divine balance and a desire to liberate it from relentless exploitation, protecting and nurturing it and its relationships, rectifying inequality and restoring equilibrium: God is seen as having 'finished' creation by celebrating the first Sabbath, thus it is seen as sealing its divine pattern (thus the human Sabbath is a celebration of creation). The Sabbath is thus seen as an expression of gratitude for God's gift of creation as well as a pointer to a future yet to come, of harmony and rest, and the human action (harmonious, loving, respectful) needed to fulfil this: 'six days you shall labour . . . but the seventh day is a Sabbath to . . . God' (Exod. 20.9–10).[12] And if this is not done it is stressed that humanity (creation/God) will suffer, highlighting connection between correct human practice and creation's health (its ecological/moral/spiritual interrelation), the need to wisely cultivate God's wisely created creation (combining honour to God with sensitivity to the land) (Deane-Drummond 2000, 2004; DeWitt 1997; McGrath 2003; Mische 2000; Moltmann 2000; Northcott 2000; Page 1992; Regenstein 1991; Ruether 1992; 2000a; Wielenga 2003).

In a similar light, the importance of animals is stressed (e.g. 'Are not five sparrows sold for two pennies? And no one of them is forgotten before God', Lk. 12.6[13]). Regenstein (1991) sees them created as companions for humanity (on the same day, from the same substance, possibly with 'souls'), seeing the Bible stressing their faithfulness and wisdom, Mosaic law teaching kindness to them and Revelation prophesizing punishment for abusing them, with Jesus teaching appreciation for and mercy towards them (using them in parables, for example, the good shepherd, or being represented by them, for example, dove, fish, lamb). Animals, in this sense, are seen as subject to God's protection with a future of peace, knowing their created roles better than humanity: 'Psalm 145:9: . . . "The Lord is good to all, and his tender mercies are over all his works" . . . Jeremiah (8:7–8): . . . the stork . . . swallow . . . crane . . . Observe the time of their coming; But my people know not . . . Isaiah 1:3: . . . The ox knoweth his owner . . . But Israel doth not'.[14] In line with such ideas, Edwards (2006) sees God incarnated in the whole biotic community of life, His Spirit creatively present within each creature as a faithful companion (a 'deep incarnation', binding them all in communion). God thus knows them personally, delighting in their beauty and fecundity and suffering with them. For DeWitt (2000) God thus cares for them in the context of their particular identities (predator or prey, scaly or furry). He thus argues for encountering them via a 'human-creature-Creator' relationship where humanity and animals are coordinated by God, His relationship with them being primary, humanity's secondary. Animals, in this sense, are humanity's neighbours, with a purpose known to God but not humanity, requiring neighbourly treatment. God's love extends to them, their suffering matters to Him (all being redeemed, able to have a 'pelican (sheep, sparrow) heaven') and humanity needs to reflect this, re-creating the loving relationship to animals fractured by the fall (e.g. 'Proverbs 12:10 . . . A righteous man has regard for the life of his beast, but the tender mercies of the wicked are cruel'[15]) (Blackwelder 2005; ELC 1996; Lodhal 2005; Palmer and Finlay 2003; Randolph 2005).

In this sense, the human role in creation is seen to be one of value but also responsibility. It is seen as having a special relationship to God virtue of *imago Dei*: 'Let us make man in our image and let them have dominion over the earth . . . Fill the earth and subdue it' (Gen. 1.26–8).[16] However, this is interpreted not as giving it mastery over nature, a right to exploit it without moral restraint, but rather responsibility for it, a 'righteous' rule (Hebrew kingship on which it is based is seen as authorizing rule answerable to God for the well-being of the realm, thus tyranny over nature (argued as not being suggested anywhere in the Bible) is seen as distorting humanity's intended purpose of nourishing creation and a forfeit of its right to rule). Nature, in this sense, was not created exclusively for humanity, as a setting for its glory or redemption, but for God. Humanity, although special, is still an earthly creature and its role lies within nature: *imago Dei* does not involve taking the place of God but representing Him in a 'right dominion', humbly exercising power for the whole of nature's benefit, emphasizing its 'givenness' not imposing on it, maximizing not diminishing the quality of life (a delegation of responsibility as much as a privilege, the 'dignity' of *imago Dei* being to honour God and creation; degrading nature thus comes from human arrogance/sin and is a violation of God's trust and loss of dignity). God's intention for humanity, then, in this sense, is a stewardship (*oikonomos*) of nature, a 'cooperative dominion', being a neighbour of the household of creation, with the task of tending it, being a channel for God's grace, exercising power with humility and praise: '[humanity] is placed by God in the fruitful garden and instructed to serve . . . and keep [it]' (e.g. Gen. 2.15; similar to serving and guarding the temple)[17] (Bakken 2005; Bassett et al. 2000; Bauckham 2000; Callicott 1997; DeWitt 2000; ELC 1996; Hessel 2004; Kalapurachal 2003; Kinsley 1994; McDaniel 1994; McGrath 2003; Page 1992).[18]

> Stewardship is the traditional Christian expression of the role of people in relation to creation. Stewards, as caretakers for the things of God, are called to use wisely and distribute justly the goods of God's earth . . . They are to care for the earth as their home, and as a beautiful revelation of the creativity, goodness and love of God . . . out of respect for the Creator who loves all creatures, and out of a charity that calls us to love our neighbor. (McGrath 2003:41)[19]

Humanity thus needs to recognize its place as an interdependent part of nature and join the 'hymn of creation', something that, for Bauckham (2000), involves a 'horizontal' sibling relationship, alongside fellow creatures in a shared home, rather than a 'vertical' dominating one, above them looking down on them.[20] For DeWitt (2000) this involves 'con-service', reciprocally 'serving with' other creatures and nature as a whole, supporting its life-sustaining diversity and fruitfulness, maintaining its God-given integrity, something involving knowing and enhancing its relationality, enabling it to serve God in its myriad ways, fulfilling its purpose. As God keeps humanity, then, so humanity should keep nature (imaging His sustaining love and praising Him in the process). In this respect, for Chryssavgis (2000), humanity, like nature, has to be an 'icon' of God, a living image of Him, existing on both the spiritual and material levels, being creative as well as created, working in nature via the light of the Creator, being the meeting point of creation, of its union (receiving the gift of creation and offering it back to God via a reciprocal relationship with nature (and thus God)) (see Hiebert 2000; Kinsley 1994).

> Just as the priest at the Eucharist offers the fullness of creation and receives it back as the blessing of Grace in the form of the consecrated bread and wine, to share with others, so we must be the channel through which God's grace and deliverance is shared with all creation. The human being is simply

yet gloriously means for the expression of creation in its fullness and the coming of God's deliverance for all creation.[21]

Such human action in nature is seen as 'covenantal', based on God's covenant with the people of Israel (and all living creatures) that re-established creation after the flood, with Abraham, gifting Israel to them, and with Moses, stressing it conditioned by human action, whereby God promises that creation will be a 'promised land' liberated from suffering. This is God's pledge of intention, faithfulness and grace, to bring about peace, something promised for all nature not just humanity, although it occurs via humanity, which is expected to uphold covenantal obligations of relational peace in response: 'I will betroth you to me in righteousness . . . justice . . . love . . . mercy . . . faithfulness' (Hosea 2.18–23).[22] In this sense, before God, humanity and nature are living partners in the same covenant and to disobey this creates imbalance, causing (personal, social, ecological) problems. Thus all actions have moral meaning and either divine judgement or blessing: 'He turns . . . a fruitful land into a salty waste, because of the wickedness of its inhabitants . . . He turns a desert into pools of water . . . And there he lets the hungry live' (Ps. 107.33–6).[23] In this sense, also, God is seen as giving humanity choice, endowing it with free will and reason, able to understand correct covenantal behaviour and realize it, with the admonition to 'choose life', to act in fellowship with nature, upholding the covenant, this enabling a life lived safely in a safe land (as opposed to breaking it causing unsafe life in an unsafe land) (Bassett et al. 2000; DeWitt 1997; Granberg-Michaelson 2006; Kalapurachal 2003; McFague 2000; Moltmann 2000; Page 1992; Regenstein 1991; Ruether 1992, 2000a; Wensveen 2005).

In light of these ideas, the effects of sin are stressed, with humanity seen as fallen, rejecting God's authority and failing in its created role, not caring for creation as God intended but idolatrously loving self and being covetous, seeking to be the arbiter of divine knowledge, understanding nature anthropocentrically, being uncaring and unjust towards it, rejecting or losing sight of its creaturely place and calling, living a 'perverted' stewardship, harming creation and ultimately itself: 'all of creation, God gives humankind to use. If this privilege is misused, God's justice permits creation to punish humanity' (Hildegard of Bingen).[24] Humanity, through sin, thus causes disruption and deterioration in the human-creation-God covenantal relationship and is, correspondingly, expulsed from the 'garden', becoming alienated from creation (and God). In response it becomes hostile to humanity: it partakes of and witnesses God's covenant and its rejection and reacts to it, 'crying out', replacing blessing with curses; 'The earth lies polluted under its inhabitants; for they have transgressed the laws, violated the statutes, broken the everlasting covenant. Therefore a curse devours the earth, and its inhabitants suffer their guilt' (Isa. 24.4–13).[25] In this sense, to overcome sin, to repent and sacrifice autonomous human self, recapturing a biblical sense of nature and humanity within it as Gods harmonious creation, is to recover a right relationship with God and creation, reversing the idolatry, alienation and enmity, of anthropocentrism, enabling a new unpolluted, world (a 'saving ark' for the righteous; by redeeming themselves humans redeem creation): 'If my people . . . will humble themselves and pray and seek my face . . . I will forgive their sins and heal their land' (2 Chron. 7.14)[26] (Bassett et al. 2000; Bauckham 2000; Callicott 1997; ELC 1996; Kinsley 1994; McDaniel 1994; McGrath 2003; Northcott 2000; Page 1992; Regenstein 1991; Roskos 2005; Wensveen 2005; Wielenga 2003).[27]

Human self-consciousness (*imago Dei*) is thus both a blessing and a curse as it can lead either to peace and fulfilment or violence and suffering.[28] To enable the former, for humanity to be able to choose the right path and overcome sin, it is stressed that God became incarnated in Jesus, becoming an embodied, 'enfleshed', suffering part of nature (and in human form, in particular, stressing humanity as responsible for the care of creation), highlighting its specialness and His relationship to it and pointing to its redemption (from within, showing the salvic power of matter, being the prime example of self-sacrifice for the whole, of the intended solidarity of creation, enabling holistic relational harmony). Jesus is thus seen as God participating in creation's struggles, showing the way to repair it (via self-sacrificial love), also being an 'icon' allowing the divine light behind creation to become a shared reality, demonstrating that resurrection and redemption is communion with nature. Thus humanity, by accepting Jesus, embodying his example, can be an immanent channel for God's healing grace, fulfilling itself as 'priests of creation' (the true *imago Dei*). Such ideas are seen as revaluing nature, reintegrating it with spirit, envisaging it as part of God's body, God investing Himself in matter, being eternally present in all things (addressing what makes these flourish or suffer, stressing nature not merely as a stage for salvation but as integral to it). In a similar way, ideas of 'cosmic Christ' stress that Jesus came to redeem not only humanity but all of nature, pervading and connecting the cosmos with sacredness (being present in and redeeming all creative reality, a saviour for the flourishing of creation). Jesus is thus constantly available everywhere, mediated through matter, and constantly suffers (is recrucified) via human sin (God thus makes Himself dependent and vulnerable, demonstrating a willingness to suffer for and with nature, hoping for and relying on a renewing of the ideal harmonic relationship between it and humanity to be healed) (Chryssavgis 2000; Edwards 2006; Kalapurachal 2003; Kinsley 1994; McDaniel 1994; McFague 1987, 1996, 2000; McFarland-Taylor 2005; McGrath 2003; Reid 2001; Wensveen 2005).

For God so loved the world that he gave his only Son . . . [not] to condemn the world, but in order that the world might be saved through him. (John 3.16–17) . . . He (Jesus) is the image of the invisible God, the firstborn of all creation; for in him all things in heaven and on earth were created, things visible and invisible . . . in him all things hold together. (Collossians 1.15–17)[29]

Nature, therefore, in this sense, is a sacrament of God, charged with His grandeur, manifesting His glory: it is also *imago Dei*. It is thus the primary subject and revelation, a way to know God. Thus a 'sacramental' (creation-centred) approach to it is seen as necessary, appreciating it as a valuable community and the site of revelation, mediating the sacred, and being more holistic and subjective in relating to it, interacting with it directly, in a relational, Trinitarian, way ('I' to 'Thou', following God, the most relational 'Thou', in a relationship with all things; nature is not 'other', then, but rather being part of God is a subject to be engaged; humanity thus needs to be a partner with fellow creaturely worshippers inhabited by Christ). The Trinity, the communion of Father, Son and Holy Spirit, in this sense, is seen as stressing communion or relationship as the core of reality, and by recognizing God as inhabiting nature, this means that nature is essentially, at its core, Trinitarian, a communion (*koinonia*). Thus to be alive, to be human, is to be relational not autonomous and salvation is the realization and experience of this. Such an approach, then, affirms that God is creator of the world and a creative presence within it, binding transcendence and immanence, stressing that nature, the place of divine habitation, must be treated with care, respect and worship (Chryssavgis 2000; Fox 2001; Haught 1996; Kinsley 1994; McFague 1987, 1996, 2000; McGrath 2003; Palmer and Finlay 2003; Ruether 1992; 2000a).

In line with this, the third person of the Trinity, the Holy Spirit, is seen as providing a useful approach to caring for nature. It is seen as a healing and life-giving force, the principle of being, present at creation and dwelling in nature (the power of God at work in it), in all creatures and natural processes, binding and sustaining the community of life and enabling its communication with God (a gift via the grace of Jesus, so again as humans abuse nature they abuse God, 'wounding' the Spirit). It is thus the animating principle of nature, a reciprocal indwelling of divine and earthly action, a divine companionship uniting all in redemptive love. In this sense, it is seen as the source of the new, the becoming of creation, being empowering and relating and thus able to provide the 'power of becoming', the hope and possibility of redemption and capability to attain the perfection of a new creation, guiding humanity in discerning the appropriate (harmonious, loving, relational) way of interacting with nature (in this sense being the 'healing Spirit'). Thus humanity needs to listen to the Spirit within it (the source of knowledge and the gift of reason) to become a 'cruciform (ecological) midwife' to a new (repaired) creation (Deane-Drummond 2000, 2004; Edwards 2001, 2006; Field 2005; Hessel 2004; McFague 1996; Moltmann 2000; Wallace 2000).

[I]t is the spirit who, everywhere diffused, sustains all things, causes them to grow, and quickens them in heaven and on earth . . . transfusing into all things his energy, and breathing into them essence, life and movement. (Field 2005:344)[30]

Spirit calls us to ecological consciousness. We are dependent on nature and belong to the natural order. It is not simply an object for domination and exploitation, but the Spirit's project, to be redeemed along with us. Nature is our home, blessed by God who took flesh, and it is destined for renewal. (McGrath 2003:31)[31]

Such ideas highlight the redeeming and restoration of creation in an ecological sense, the protection of nature being an eschatological vision, a hopeful, prophetic, ecological 'good news' of a world salved. In this sense, the 'world is groaning in travail as it awaits its liberation from . . . suffering' (Rom. 8.22),[32] waiting to be 'set free from its bondage to decay' (Rom. 8.19–23),[33] a 'general deliverance' freeing from humanity's sin. Creation (the environmental crisis), is not a lost cause, then, rather it is the embodiment of hope and promise (God's gift, Jesus, pre-exists it). In Christ, God saves both humanity and nature, giving a vision of earthly communion perfected, a restoration of creation, a 'new heaven and a new earth' (Rev. 21.1) where 'The wolf and lamb shall feed together' (Isa. 65.25),[34] restoring what has been distorted, delivering from evil, a healing that can begin here and now via (more environmentally friendly, stewardly) human action (combining the human 'is' (present) with a Christian 'ought' (future)): 'the invitation to come and receive the water . . . [and] the tree of life to everyone who is faithful' (e.g. Rev. 2.7, 21.6, 22.17)[35] (Berry 2000; Chryssavgis 2000; DeWitt 2005; Edwards 2006; ELC 1996; Haught 1996; Hessel 2004; Lodhal 2005; McFague 2000; McGrath 2003; Rossing 2000; Wensveen 2005).[36]

Such redemptive healing is seen to occur through God's Wisdom, a concept which is also seen as able to inspire environmentally friendly behaviour. Wisdom, in this sense, personifies the Trinity, being inherent in creation (the secondary manifestation of God) and embodied in Jesus (Wisdom Incarnate) and the Holy Spirit, being God's immanent agent in creating and sustaining the world (incarnating the cosmogonic principle of creation/redemption, thus creation has 'nature wisdom'). It is thus seen as able to direct right living in creation, integrating being and becoming, nature being created in Wisdom and Wisdom emerging from it. Humanity, in this sense, is seen as needing to discern, experience and assist, the underlying Wisdom in nature via its God-given intelligence, creating a 'wise' knowledge and interaction beyond limited rational knowledge and dominating behaviour (the language of Wisdom being seen as non-human and experiential/spiritual), a dynamic, prophetic process with the goal of the redemption of creation, oriented on Christ's sacrificial suffering (the 'wisdom of the cross', learning to reconsider environmental issues via suffering, replacing worldly human understanding with redemptive knowledge). Such a new human wisdom is seen as a virtue ethic of fortitude, justice, prudence and temperance, a natural law in dialogue with human inclinations (restraining economic or technological actions). The concept of Wisdom, in this sense, then, is seen as expressing an ontological state of being and an ethical directive, highlighting an internalization and expression of God within nature's being and a natural spiritual knowledge reminding humanity that it cannot live apart from it (Deane-Drummond 2000, 2004; McFague 2000; Moltmann 2000; Page 1992; Rae 2000; Ruether 2000a, 2000b, 2001).

> Wisdom . . . pervades and permeates all things . . . She arises from the . . . active power of God . . . and the image of his goodness. She is one but can do all things, herself unchanging, she makes all things new . . . she enters into holy souls and makes them Gods friends and prophets . . . She spans the world in power from end to end and orders all things benignly (Wisdom of Solomon 8). (Ruether 2000a:611)

Wisdom is seen as female ('Mother *Sophia*') and Christian 'eco-feminism' promotes such feminine spirituality ecologically, critiquing what it sees as 'male' (modern) ideas that alienate, dominate and damage, nature and stressing 'female' ones that unite, respect and care, for it. In this scheme, modern views are seen as stressing patriarchal themes (e.g. God as Father/King/Lord), highlighting transcendence and judgement, seeing humanity (mind, spirit) as separate from and higher than (female) nature (body, matter), a logic of domination seen as causing environmental problems. Thus eco-feminism stresses new female themes (e.g. God as Mother/friend/lover), highlighting immanence and love, seeing humanity and nature as interdependent and mutually supporting, a logic of equality seen as able to inspire care for nature. Such ideas are seen as revaluing body/matter (seeing their sacrificial capacity to nurture life), reintegrating them with mind/spirit, creating an ethic of 'partnership' (rather than 'ownership') leading to mutual flourishing (not exploitation). They stress a conception of *imago Dei* based on human kinship and responsibility with nature not alienation and domination of it, something seen as able to create a 'healing relationality', the ability to identify and communicate with nature, learning from and sharing with it, making whole what has been separated, encouraging the flourishing of what has been degraded (Beattie 2005; Deane-Drummond 2004; Fox 2001; Hobgood-Oster 2005; Kinsley 1994; Larkin 2001; McFague 1987; Ruether 1992, 2000b, 2001).[37]

Such a caring approach to nature is seen exemplified by St Francis of Assisi, who is seen as renouncing self, treating animals as siblings and living a simple lifestyle, in solidarity with nature. He is seen as valuing nature's being, its meekness and ability to respond (praising God), showing kindness and respect to it, establishing friendship with it, perceiving the spirit of God and the transforming power of Christ in it (God's creative power and forgiveness). Also stressed in this way, as representatives of an 'ecological motif' in Christianity, are Christian saints such as Augustine, Basil, Columba, Cuthbert and Patrick (and later Luther and Calvin), who are seen as appreciative of nature's blessing, demonstrating concern for it, seeing it as tangibly good and significant, God being invested in and nourishing it, grace flowing through it and lying in friendship with and care of it. More recently, Albert Schweitzer is seen as an example of respect, reverence and sensitivity, to nature, avoiding harming it. And, in a similar way to such ideas, a monastic lifestyle (which many saints practised) is argued as an example of an environmentally friendly lifestyle, providing humility, praise and stewardship, seeing selfishness and accumulation as weaknesses, stressing asceticism, self-restraint and intimate connection to nature. Such a lifestyle is seen as a priestly vocation of self-sacrifice, freeing from attitudes that abuse nature, limiting exploitation (with such ideas, especially fasting or vegetarianism, reminding that humanity does not live by 'bread', that is, material goods, alone). Such monasticism is seen as countercultural, critiquing and rejecting materialism and stressing different lifestyle possibilities for humanity beyond the modern Western model (Bauckham 2000; Carroll et al. 1997; Chillister 1992; Chryssavgis 2005; Hooper and Palmer 1992; Kinsley 1994; McDaniel 1994; McGrath 2003; Regenstein 1991; Reid 2001; Sotitiu 2005).

In this sense, for Lodhal (2005), there is a need to become 'evangelists of shalom', making Jesus' ways a model of action in nature, becoming defenders of it, what Wensveen (2000) sees as an 'ecological virtue ethics' (with new eco-theological concepts of virtue, for example, selflessness and sustainability, and vice, for example, arrogance and destruction). McDaniel (1997) sees such ideas as opportunities to create 'green grace', accepting humanity's imperfections and overcoming them through creating an empathic relationship with nature, sharing its suffering as well as its joy, creating a 'sense of place' and 'reverence for life', realizing bodies as incarnations of its energies, united in divine life. In this light, DeWitt (1997, 2000) sees a hopeful Christian 'good news' enabling a harmonious 'good life' in relation to nature, a mindful society where contentment not maximization is the goal: repenting of its destruction (rethinking crimes and rights in relation to it), recognizing it belonging to God, fulfilling His intent, and that humans are part of this, needing to humbly image God's justice and love for all things, observing Sabbath rests and communing with nature (celebrating its value in ritual) (see Rajotte and Breuilly 1992). For Fritsch (1997) such 'good life' is an 'eco-pilgrimage' to 'eco-justice', seeing nature as a blessing, being instructed by its (fecund) presence, acting upon it compassionately (confessing to and overcoming human insensitivity and greed, mourning creation's suffering).

In this light, the American Baptist Churches and the Evangelical Declaration on the Care of Creation, for McGrath (2003) and the World Council of Churches, for Palmer and Finlay (2003), stress a calling to respond to the environmental crisis, repenting of human abuse of nature and affirming human responsibility for it:

Affirm the goodness and beauty of God's creation . . . Acknowledge our responsibility for stewardship . . . Pursue a lifestyle that is [ecologically] wise and responsible . . . Demonstrate concern with 'the hope that is within us', as despair and apathy surround us in the world. (McGrath 2003:36–7)

[W]e have failed in our stewardship . . . Therefore we repent of the way we have polluted, distorted, or destroyed . . . [twisting or ignoring] biblical revelation to support our misuse of [creation] . . . [seeking] to learn all that the Bible tells us about the Creator, creation, and the human task . . . to understand what creation reveals about God's divinity, sustaining presence and everlasting power. (McGrath 2003:45)

We affirm the creation as beloved of God . . . 'good' in God's sight . . . We . . . resist the claim that anything in creation is merely a resource for human exploitation . . . [and] commit ourselves to be . . . co-workers with God, with moral responsibility to . . . conserve . . . the integrity of creation both for its inherent value to God and in order that justice may be achieved. (Palmer and Finlay 2003:85)

Conclusions

Christianity, interpreted ecologically, is stressed as highlighting a harmonic creation, sustained by a loving wise God, humanity as an integral but destructively rebellious part, and the means to heal such rebellion and destruction via the incarnation of God (Jesus, Holy Spirit, Wisdom) in nature, emphasizing its suffering and stressing a new harmonic way of being for humanity. This, then, emphasizes the revelatory power of nature and its relational being, while also recognizing humanity's fallibility, its egoist tendencies, as well as its (and creation's) redemption, providing a prophetic, sacramental, vision of covenantal stewardship (stressing humanitys ability to adopt a more limited, selfless and less destructive, lifestyle, allowing nature rest, fulfilling its fecundity, rediscovering it as enlivened by God's love, spirit and wisdom).

Integrity of creation ideas stress nature as 'good', with meaning and value, through being harmoniously created and sustained by God . It is thus (originally) a perfect community, valuable to God, depending on His judgement, being His possession, fitting and reflecting His (loving, wise) intended function and purpose. To 'love' or 'fear' God thus means loving nature (while abusing it is abusing God, something it will bear witness to and possibly administer retributive justice). Nature is thus an 'icon' of God, conveying knowledge of Him, revealing the eternal dimension behind materiality, an epiphany connecting spirit and matter. It is God's 'Book of Works', a means to know Him. Humanity thus needs to be a student of nature, engaging it subjectively, being sensitive to and caring for it (knowing, worshipping and thereby assisting, God's creativity). In this sense, the 'Sabbath', the commandment to let the earth rest and recover and enjoy its fruitfulness is seen as a way to care for nature, expressing gratitude and respect for it (finishing creation, fulfilling it, connecting right worship with health; if not done humanity will suffer). Similarly, animals are intrinsically 'good', possessing God's blessing and wisdom (God being creatively within each creature, knowing and caring for them intimately), and thus require care, a calling to 'love thy (animal) neighbour' and be a 'good (ecological) shepherd'.

In this scheme, humanity, virtue of *imago Dei*, is seen as God's representative on earth, but this is not seen legitimating domination and abuse but rather duty and responsibility, the requirement to lovingly fulfil creation as God intended. Humanity's role is a covenantal stewardship of nature (God entrusting nature to it), maximizing not diminishing the quality of life, humbly exercising power (righteous rule, being a channel for God's grace, a vocation of imaging God, His loving compassion, celebrating and honouring nature not exploiting and degrading it). Ideas of sin, however, stress humanity failing in its role, not caring for nature as God intended, living in false relations to it, loving/worshipping self or material goods, seeking to be the arbiter of divine knowledge, being hostile to nature (which in response becomes hostile to humanity). However, also stressed is the possibility (hope) of overcoming sin and re-creating a harmonious relationship to nature (and God), by repenting of wrongs and sacrificing autonomous self, embracing selflessness, reversing alienation. To this end God became en-fleshed in the prime example of self-sacrifice and solidarity, Jesus (sharing creation's suffering, highlighting care). Humanity thus needs to follow Jesus' self-sacrificial care, acting as 'priests of creation', properly fulfilling *imago Dei* (and, in this sense, Jesus is also seen as redeeming all creation, not just humanity, inhabiting nature and affirming it, being eternally present in it, a 'deep incarnation' revaluing matter, imbuing it with spirit: it is part of His/God's body).

Humanity thus needs to accept nature as evoking the sacred and interact with it in a relational 'I-Thou' way, subjectively knowing it, not objectively knowing about it, a Trinitarian approach based on the essence of God and creation (and humanity) being fellowship. To enable this God's Holy Spirit, present at creation and dwelling in nature as a dynamic presence in life, holding it in redemptive love, is seen as providing a 'power of becoming', the possibility of attaining a new harmonic creation, guiding humanity in discerning the appropriate (caring, relational, sacrificial) way of interacting with nature. Similarly, Wisdom (the secondary manifestation of God, embodied in Jesus, present in the Holy Spirit, in nature), is seen as able to direct 'right living' in creation, being an underlying creative, ordering energy, integrating being and becoming, with humanity needing to discern this and live in a 'wise' (caring, relational, sacrificial) way ecologically (an 'eco-feminist' critique of 'male' domination, stressing 'female' relationality, Wisdom being female). Such ideas (exemplified by St Francis) are seen as stressing a countercultural, ascetic, self-renunciation and simple lifestyle, revering and affirming (kinship with) nature, limiting production/consumption, something seen as enabling 'green grace', an ecological virtue ethics subordinating human ego to God's created community (an eco-pilgrimage to a 'good life' of eco-justice).

Notes

1 Referenced to *Common Declaration by John Paul II and the Ecumenical Patriarch Bartholomew I, Sourozh* 90 (November 2002), pp. 19–21.

2 Hessel and Ruether (2000) argue that although Christianity's multiple traditions may take competing or cooperative, constricting or liberating, forms, the aim should be to explore environmentally friendly elements in them. McDaniel (1994), similarly, sees a need to accentuate positive Christian ecological contributions and critique negative ones, opening Christianity to new insights, seeing it as an ongoing tradition capable of self-criticism and improvement. He thus sees various Christian creation-centred theologies being developed, biblical, cosmological, feminist, mystical, First World/Third World, while others highlight ecologically influential spiritualities of Eastern Orthodoxy, Protestantism (Liberal/Evangelical/Reformed) and Roman Catholicism (Carroll et al. 1997; Hessel 2004; Taylor and Kaplan 2005; Foltz 2002b; Kinsley 1994; Nash 2005; Regenstein 1991).

3 Downloaded from www.arcworld.org/faiths.asp?pageID=69, 15 Sept. 2006; quote referenced to the Orthodox Churches document 'Orthodoxy and the Ecological Crisis', 10–11 (de-italicized).

4 From DeWitt (1997:93).

5 Downloaded from www.environment.harvard.edu/religion/religion/christianity/texts.index.html, 15 Sept. 2006; referenced to *The Dialogue*.

6 Downloaded from www.environment.harvard.edu/religion/religion/christianity/texts.index.html, 15 Sept. 2006.

7 Referenced to Celtic Christianity (de-italicized).

8 Downloaded from www.environment.harvard.edu/religion/religion/christianity/texts.index.html, 15 Sept. 2006; referenced to *Showings*.

9 For a detailed examination of this in relation to ecology see Burton-Christie, D., Words beneath the Water: Logos, Cosmos, and the Spirit of Place, in *Christianity and Ecology: Seeking the Well-Being of Earth and Humans*, Hessel, D., and Ruether, R. R., eds. (Cambridge, MA: Harvard University Press, 2000), pp. 315–26.

10 Referenced to Phillip Schaff, *The Creeds of Christendom, with a History and Critical Notes*, vol. 3, *The Evangelical Prtoestant Creeds with Translations* (Grand Rapids: Baker Book house, 1966), p. 384.

11 From Wielenga (2003:137).

12 From Northcott (2000:169).

13 From Blackwelder 2005:308).

14 From Regenstein (1991:22, 35, 37). Regenstein (1991) stresses animal sacrifices being condemned in Isaiah, Samuel, Micah, Psalms, Amos, Jeremiah and Proverbs, and sees vegetarianism suggested in Genesis, Leviticus, Isaiah, Amos, Jeremiah, Psalms and Proverbs, and practiced by early church leaders.

[15] From Regenstein (1991:22).

[16] From Kalapurachal (2003:113).

[17] From ELC (1996:247–8).

[18] In some lines of thinking stewardship is still seen as anthropocentric, not counter-cultural enough, asserting human superiority and 'management' of nature (i.e. reform environmentalism) (Bakken 2005; Bauckham 2000; Deane-Drummond 2004; Kinsley 1994).

[19] Referenced to 'The Columbia River Watershed: Caring for Creation and the Common Good' (February 2001).

[20] Hiebert (2000) sees different creation narratives leading to different images of the human vocation in creation: 'priest' (Gen. 1.1–2.4), implying potent authority, overseeing and supervising nature; and 'farmer' (Gen. 2.4–3.24), implying earthly toiling, participating within nature (he seems to favour the latter as more environmentally friendly although also seeing their harmonization, stressing humanity within yet tending nature).

[21] Downloaded from www.arcworld.org/faiths.asp?pageID=69; referenced to the Orthodox Churches document 'Orthodoxy and the Ecological Crisis', p. 8 (de-italicized).

[22] From Granberg-Michaelson (2006:5).

[23] From Ruether (1992:210).

[24] From Bassett et al. (2000:51), referenced to *Ordo Virtutum*, Vision Thirteen:1.

[25] From Wielenga (2003:135–6).

[26] From McGrath (2003:38).

[27] Sin/environmental damage may also be seen as a failure of Christianity through acquiescing to or legitimating human domination in the modern industrialized way of life (hence Lynn White's (1967) critique), although the latter is also seen as not specifically Christian but based on Enlightenment ideas of nature as profane (see Deane-Drummond 2004; Hessel 2004; Kinsley 1994; Nash 1989).

[28] For Rossing (2000) this is eschatologically stressed in two contrasting cities described in Rev. 17: 'Babylon', an unjust place of commerce and violence, and 'New Jerusalem', a just place of equality and peace, the formers ruin seen as an allegory of environmental catastrophe, the latter as promising environmental harmony, with the message being to come out of Babylon and enter New Jerusalem.

[29] Downloaded from www.environment.harvard.edu/religion/religion/christianity/texts.index.html, 15 Sept. 2006.

[30] Referenced to John Calvin, *The Institutes of Christian Religion*, McNiell, J. Y., ed. (Philadelphia: Westminster, 1960), p. 138.

[31] Referenced to Pinnock, C. H., *Flame of Love: A Theology of the Holy Spirit* (Downers Grove: Inter-Varsity Press, 1996).

[32] From Wensveen (2005:355).

[33] From McGrath (2003:50).

[34] Quotes from McGrath (2003:49–50).

[35] From Rossing (2000:216, 218).

[36] For Brett (2001) such ecological eschatology is not simply futurology as it also relates to past and present, being action in anticipation and remembrance (future creation via past events in present action), and is not prediction but symbolism,

not aiming for human control but to create awareness and hope, being grounded in the 'Christ-event', the future's culminating point occurring in the historical incarnation.

37 Such ideas link social justice to environmental justice, seeing nature as the 'new poor' and environmental degradation occurring in 'sacrifice zones' with environmentally friendly living requiring social inclusion and fair consumption, a call to sustainability and preferential option for the poor, this correcting the destructive option for the rich, supporting visions of diverse, harmonious, self-sustaining, communities (see Deane-Drummond 2004; Hessel 2004; Ruether 1992, 2000b; Scharper 2002; Wallace 2000).

Chapter 8

Islamic Visions

Muhammad [said] . . . 'The world is green and beautiful and God has appointed you his stewards over it' . . . Muslims need to return to . . . this way of understanding themselves and their environment . . . We often say that Islam is a complete way of life, by which it is meant that our ethical systems provide the bearings for all our actions. Yet our actions often undermine the very values we cherish . . . We must judge our actions by them. They furnish us with a worldview which enables us to ask environmentally appropriate questions . . . weigh the environmental costs and benefits of what we want, what we can do within the ethical boundaries established by God, without violating the rights of His other creations. If we use the same values . . . as scientist or technologist, economist or politician as we do to know ourselves as Muslims – those who submit themselves to the Will of God . . . we will create a true Islamic alternative, a caring and practical way of being . . . to the environmentally destructive thought and action which dominates the world today.

(Dr Abdullah Omar Nasseef, *The Muslim Declaration on Nature*, WWF 1986:24–5)

Muslim contemplatives and mystics have loved nature . . . because they have been able to hear the prayer of all creatures . . . to God . . . Fallen man, who has forgotten God, has become deaf to this . . . Islamic society has always been noted for its harmonious relation with the natural environment . . . preserving to this day a sapiential knowledge combined with love of [nature] . . . a metaphysics . . . which unveils her role as the grand book in which the symbols . . . of Divine majesty and beauty are engraved. It also possesses an ethics, rooted in revelation and bound to Divine Law, which concerns the responsibilities and duties of humanity toward the nonhuman realms of the created order.

(Nasr 1992:90–1, 104–5)

Ecological interpretations of Islam[1] stress it as being a religion of the book and thus stress the importance of the Qur'an in valuing nature (in itself, as a creation of God, and as a way to know God), as well as delineating humanity's role in caring for and fulfilling it. In this light, the Qur'an is stressed as the revealed word of God (set down by Muhammad), a comprehensive illuminating

and guiding text, containing whatever pertains to the human and natural condition: a divine genre, filled with semantic depth, a source of inspiration and
stimulus to imagination, connecting God, nature and humanity, with nature
metaphysically anchored in the divine and morally connected to humanity
(participating in revelation, there being no demarcation between natural and
supernatural). It is thus seen as addressing the primordial nature of reality
(hence Islam is called the 'primordial religion', *al-din-al-hanif*), explaining
the meaning of nature and humanity within it (Maguire 2000; Nasr 1992;
Nomanul Haq 2001; Ozdemir 2003, 2005).

> The Qur'an lays down the foundations for the conduct of our affairs in cre-
> ation. At one level it is about conserving the body and the soul and the
> marking out of our relationships with the natural order; at another level it is
> about the communities of beings that fly and crawl and lope and swim; and
> at yet another level it is about the cosmos, the elements, forests, mountains
> and rivers. The body of teaching in the Qur'an that deals with these matters
> may be described as 'Ilm ul Khalq (Knowledge of Creation) which predates
> the science of Ecology by fourteen centuries. (Bassett et al. 2000:56)[2]

The purpose of the Qur'an, in this sense, is seen as being to awaken humanity to holistic understanding of its relationships with God and nature, mandat-
ing knowledge of the latter as a form of worship, a way to know God (or lack of
it as dissociation from God). A Qur'anic approach to nature is thus not seen
as anthropocentric nor necessarily biocentric but theocentric: '(God) is the
creator of everything (6:102) . . . God holds Earth and heaven from collapsing
(35:41)'.[3] Ozdemir (2003:6–9), in this sense, highlights Muhammad's revela-
tions, in particular, the command from God to ' "Read" . . . in the name of your
Lord and Sustainer' (96:1), seeing the meaning of this involving a way of looking at the world: 'reading' (looking with an 'observant eye' at) nature in the
name of God, with Him in mind, this being an invitation to investigate nature
and everything in it. The Qur'an is thus seen as emphasizing (the need to
understand) the ultimate principle beyond nature, the reason why it exists and
what it means, stressing that it is not there by accident, by chaos or meaningless evolution, but rather through the existence of a Creator. Thus it is seen as
stressing its beauty, harmony and value, seeing no demarcation between what
God reveals and what nature manifests but rather seeing the very meaning of
reality, of God, manifested and clarified by nature (it being the cosmological
evidence of God's existence) (see Basset et al. 2000; Maguire 2000; Ozdemir
2005; Parvaiz 2005; Saritoprak 2005).

> The Qur'an rejects the argument that nature is meaningless . . . God does
> not create . . . without a serious purpose . . . 'In the creation of the heavens
> and the earth, and the alternation of night and day, there are indeed Signs

for men of understanding . . . "Our Lord! not for nothing have you created (all) this!" ' (Qur'an 3:190–1) . . . One immediate conclusion, from an
environmentalist perspective, is that every individual creature or being has
its own ontological existence as a sign of God, and by its very being manifests and reveals His majesty and mercy. Therefore, every creature deserves
attention and consideration . . . A sincere follower of the Qur'an is always
aware of the fact that 'Our Lord is He who gave to each (created) thing its
form and nature, and further gave (it) guidance' (Qur'an 20:50). (Ozdemir
2003:10–11)

Islamic views on ecology, therefore, are centred around the Qur'an, seen
as replete with references to the status and meaning of nature, to 'precious'
resources of air, livestock, plants and water (seen speaking of trees, gardens
and orchards, frequently) and to their sustainable use (in agriculture and
building), proscribing wastefulness, with numerous injunctions to respect animals and nature: Ahmad (2003) and Masri (1997) note 500 verses referring
to nature, its balance, diversity, fecundity and value, giving guidance on its
appreciation and use (see Foltz 2003a, 2005b).

No kind of beast is there in earth, nor fowl that flieth with its wings, but
is folk like you (Qur'an Majeed, Sura VI)[4] . . . There is no moving creature
on earth but God provides for its sustenance (Qur'an Majeed 11:6) . . . And
the earth – He has spread it out for all living beings, with its fruits, blossom-
bearing palms, husk-coated grains, and fragrant plants (Qur'an Majeed
55:10–12) . . . in the creation of all the animals pervading the earth, there
are portents for those who believe (Qur'an Majeed 45:4) . . . Everything we
have created is in due measure and proportion (Qur'an Majeed 54:49) . . .
we have spread out its expanse and cast on it mountains in stable equilibrium, and caused life of every kind to grow . . . justly weighed (Qur'an
Majeed 15:19) . . . Do not spread corruption on earth, after it has been put
in order (Qur'an Majeed 7:56).[5] (Regenstein 1991:249–50)

Saritoprak (2005:1322–3) sees the Qur'an stressing the importance of
respecting nature as God's creation, mentioning the earth on nearly every
page, and the moon, sky, stars, sun and water, frequently, having chapters
named after nature ('Thunder' (chapter 13), 'Date Trees' (chapter 16), 'Cave'
(chapter 18), 'Moon' (chapter 54), 'Iron' (chapter 57)) and verses after animals
('The Cow (chapter 2), 'The Cattle' (chapter 6), 'The Bee' (chapter 16), 'The
Ant' (chapter 27), 'The Spider' (chapter 29)). Similarly, the earth is seen as
stressed as the cradle of humanity and a glorification of God (and at times a
living creature), with examples of the bounties of God in it stressed, such as
mountains as protections, night a covering garment, the sun a lamp providing
daylight, or clouds laden with rain a form of God's mercy (and stressing the

earth suffering when inappropriately treated and being a tool of punishment swallowing non-believers). Water, similarly, is seen as the source of life, a gift from God, a helper sent from the sky to help fruits grow for sustenance (as well as a tool of punishment and destruction, pure water being a gift to those in paradise, contaminated water a punishment for non-believers). And other aspects of nature also are seen as valued for providing nourishment and sustenance, as sources of life-giving vitality.

> Have they not seen how We have created for them of Our handiwork the cattle . . . Benefits and diverse drinks have they from them. Will they not then give thanks? (36:71–3) . . . Let man consider his food. How we pour water in shower. Then split the earth in clefts. And cause the grain to grow therein. And grapes and green fodder and olive-trees . . . fruits and grasses. Provision for you and your cattle (80:24–32) . . . He it is who sends the winds as tidings heralding His mercy, till when they bear a cloud heavy with rain . . . to a dead land, and cause water to descend thereon and thereby bring forth fruits of every kind (7:5). (Saritoprak 2005:1323)

Nature (especially water), is also seen as being referred to as a tool for cleanliness (*tahaarat*, considered one of the fundamentals of Islamic belief), enabling understanding of God who values purity: 'God loves those who are clean' (200:22, 9:106).[6] The Qur'an is thus seen as teaching humanity to reflect on and be thankful for nature's (God's) bounties, being responsible and utilizing them carefully, without abuse or waste (water, for example, must not be wasted even by those living next to the ocean): 'God does not like the wasteful (10:83) . . . the wasteful are the friends of Satan (17:27)'.[7] Such ideas, then, are seen as prohibiting pollution, stressing a clean environment (e.g. God sends rainwater to clean the earth, so humanity must preserve its cleanliness, and this also involves cleanliness of, not polluting, the body). Also stressed, in this sense, are the words and deeds of Muhammad in the *Hadith* literature seen as stressing protection of natural resources and their equitable availability to all: 'If you have a sapling if you have the time, be certain to plant it, even if Doomsday starts to break forth' (*Musnad* 183–4, 191, III).[8] Muhammad is seen as the archetypal responsible and trustworthy (clean) man, an example to all, conscious of his environment and who developed a spirit of love and care towards it (and a desert dweller, sensitive to the delicate natural balance needed for survival, aware of the integrity of ecosystems and the importance of water and forests). He is seen as organizing tree planting and creating conservation areas, where vegetation could live unmolested, as well as showing kindness and protection towards animals, admonishing mistreatment of them (e.g. banning killing, except for food, which is to be swift, conscientious slaughter): 'The Most Merciful One is merciful towards those who are merciful. Act kindly to those on the earth so that those in the heavens . . . will be merciful to you'

(Tirmizi, *Birr* 16)[9] (Ahmad 2003; Foltz 2003a, 2005a, 2005b; Ozdemir 2005; Saritoprak 2005; Wescoat 2005b).

The Qur'an and *Hadiths* are also seen to influence *Sharia*, or divine law, the absolute standard of performance for the Islamic way of life, of how to relate to, and live in God's creation properly.[10] This suggests, for Chisthi (2003), that Islamic scriptures, the statements they make about nature and the human role in it, are meant to be a concrete guide for living: asceticism is not encouraged rather there is an imperative for a productive life, an ethical engagement and spiritual journey between humanity and nature. Important to this is the engendering of consciousness about nature's harmony, a fundamental concept being, for Ahmad (2005), that every organism partakes in God's creation and thus deserves respect (all are united under one source of order, God, and so harm to one affects all, humanity is thus regulated via a concern for preventing harm to the wider community). Islamic scripture, law and custom, are thus seen to provide a foundation for opening human awareness towards the valuableness of nature: Foltz (2005a) sees legal obligations extended to animals, including the 'right of thirst' (access to water), and an 'animal bill of rights' ensuring proper care, for example, being allowed to mate, given clean shelter, kept safe from harm, not overburdened (Chishti 2003; Izzi Dien 1997; Nasr 1992; Nomanul Haq 2001; Ozdemir 2003). Parvaiz (2005:876) also highlights such ideas:

> Muslim legal scholars have ruled that Allah's creatures possess inviolability . . . In Islamic Law all animals have certain legal rights . . . One of the fundamental principles of Islamic Law is the Prophetic declaration: 'There shall be no damage and no infliction of damage.' This 'No Damage Law' is of immense significance in the human-nature relationship. Another relevant *Shari'a* rule is: 'The averting of harm takes precedence over the acquisition of benefits'. It aims at achieving good . . . without causing significant damage . . . 'A private (smaller scale) injury or damage is accepted to avert a general (larger) injury' . . . the larger community takes precedence over [the] smaller.

Ahmad (2005) sees such Islamic sources providing guidance to the 'right path', a particular 'Islamic' way of acting of harmony and justice. In line with this, the term 'Islam' is seen as deriving from *salam-silm*, meaning peace and wholeness. Unity is thus seen as an essence and impetus within Islam, based on the 'oneness' of God, the 'All-encompassing' (*al-Muhit*), who peacefully sustains life (*al-salam*). God, in this sense, has sole ownership of nature, being almighty, indivisible and universal (although also beneficent and merciful: 'when God completed the creation He wrote . . . "My mercy has taken precedence over my anger"'[11]). God is thus concrete not abstract, a beneficent power in ongoing creation ('God originates creation then repeats it', 10:4[12]) as well as its end process ('to God is the final goal', 24:42[13]). He is 'the One', the 'Everlasting Refuge for all Creation', from which everything else stems, a monotheistic principle that is seen as fundamental to Islam (unity being seen as the truth (*haqq*) of it, every Muslim needing to believe that 'there is no God but God', with idolatry a sin). Everything, including humanity, thus defers to God (thus humanity does not 'own' things, for the real owner is God, it only enjoys the 'usufruct' of things, subject to divine law, hence excess or waste is frowned upon, with the merit of civilization lying in the merit it yields, in proportion to its harm).[14] Humanity is thus immersed in the divine *Muhit* and is only unaware of it because of its forgetfulness and negligence. To remember God is thus to see Him everywhere, to experience nature as *al-Muhit* (God is also seen as *al-Hasib*, or 'One Who Takes Perfect Account' the knowledge of which is seen as driving a desire to seek out understanding of the holistic consequences of actions and take a long-term view: thus *al-Muhit* and *al-Hasib* are seen as possibly able to stimulate environmentally friendly behaviour through the pursuit of the divine) (Ahmad 2003; Chishti 2003; Khalid 2005; Masri 1997; Nasr 1992; Palmer and Finlay 2003; Said and Funk 2003; Timm 1994).

Say: He is Allah the One and Only; Allah the Eternal Absolute; He begetteth not nor is He begotten; And there is none like unto Him (112.001–4) . . . Say: Allah's guidance is the (only) guidance . . . for it is to Him that we shall be gathered together. It is He Who created the heavens and the earth in true (proportions): the day He saith 'Be' Behold! it is. His Word is the truth. His will be the dominion . . . He knoweth the Unseen as well as that which is open. For He is the Wise well acquainted (with all things). 006.071–3 . . . Who is there can intercede in his presence except as He permitteth? . . . Nor shall they compass aught of His knowledge except as He willeth. 002.255 . . . To Him belongs what is in the heavens and on earth and all between them and all beneath the soil. 020.006 . . . To Allah we belong and to Him is our return. 002.155–6.[15]

In this sense, *tawhid*, or 'unity', is seen as important, being a primordial testimony, the foundation of *Din al Islam*, 'The Way of Islam', with all aspects of Islamic belief seen as rooted in its integrating vision. In this scheme, creation is part of the Oneness of God (who knows, measures and judges, it) and is an interdependent (harmonic, peaceful) pattern of just relationships (purposefully ordered, made to obey, reflect and worship God). This totality is seen as defining humanity's relationship to nature (and God), the basis of Islam being to establish *tawhid* (interpreted dynamically as 'unifying', not only belief in God but conduct demanded by this), creating a 'right' relationship of harmony, peace and justice: as Ammar (2005:863), states (quoting Muhammad), 'all creatures are God's dependents and the most beloved among them is the one that does good to God's dependents'. Humanity and nature are thus at one and at peace in the consciousness of *tawhid*. To approach truth (the ultimate reality,

God) they must harmonize, developing a *tawhidic* frame of mind, establishing just relationships. In this sense, there needs to be a vigilant restraint on the part of humanity with respect to nature. It cannot 'possess' it, any ownership is temporary, a trust and a test (selfishly pursuing goals, unbalancing unity, is seen as anti-Islamic). Such a *tawhidic* restraint involves a surrender to the whole (submitting to God, His meaning and purpose, being 'Muslim'), rejecting a vision of reality rooted in exclusiveness and searching for unified peace (doing what is beautiful, *ishan*), an impulse which is the innermost state of creation (reflecting higher realities – the *umma* or community of God). Thus, for Said and Funk (2003:161), Islamic ecological sensibility is *tawhidic* (Afzaal 2005; Ammar 2005; Foltz 2003b; Khalid 2005; Palmer and Finlay 2003; Said and Funk 2003).

This sense of unity, of the oneness of God, means that divine and nature are ontologically united: there is divine transcendence from and incomparability with creation (*tanzih*) but also divine immanence in and similarity to it (*tashbih*) – God is both far and near. Nature is, then, a sign (*aya*) of God, a divine work of art and medium of remembrance (a 'natural book' of God – 'The seven heavens and the earth, and all the beings therein, Declare His glory' (17:46)[16] – thus to defile it is blasphemy). It provides lessons for humanity, witnessing God in the same way that phrase-units of the Qur'an do (these also being seen as *aya* or signs). In this sense, for Nasr (1992), there is a cosmic Qur'an (*al-Qur'an al-takwini*) complementing the written one (*al-Qur'an al-tadwini*) through which God's meaning can be read (by the sage with the 'inner-eye', veiled to the ego-obsessed). Nature is meaningful, enabling awareness of and creating obligation towards God, being His prime miracle (greater than humanity). Thus, for Nasr, nature is *ayat Allah*, *vestigial Dei*, and, for Saritoprak (2005), *Sunnat-Allah*, the 'Way of God', and to protect it is to protect God. It is also seen as 'Muslim': it (instinctively) submits to (works in accordance with) God's will, not being able to disobey His natural laws. Islamic faith, in this sense, is not seen as a distraction from the world but an all-encompassing awareness of it (Islamic prayer is seen as a synthesis of the prayers of all creatures enabling Muslims to participate in the call of creation, realizing their integration with nature before God) (Afzaal 2005; Ammar 2005; Chishti 2003; Denny 2004; Khalid 2005; Nomanul Haq 2001; Ozdemir 2003, 2005; Said and Funk 2003; Timm 1994).[17]

Seest thou not that it is God whose praises are celebrated by all beings in heaven and on earth . . . Each one knows its prayer and psalm. And God is aware of what they do (Qur'an Majeed 24:41) . . . Seest thou not that unto God pay adoration all things . . . the sun, the moon, the stars, the mountains, the trees, the animals (Qur'an Majeed 22:18). (Regenstein 1991:250)[18]

Since God has made Man from dust, it behooves thee to recognize the real nature of every particle of the universe, That while from this aspect they are

dead, from that aspect they are living; silent here but speaking Yonder . . .
The mountains sing with David . . . The wind [carries] . . . for Solomon . . .
the sea understands [God] . . . The moon obeys [Muhammad] . . . They all
cry, 'we are hearing and seeing and responsive' . . . Ascend from materiality
into the world of spirit, hearken to the loud voice of the universe. (Ozdemir
2003:18)[19]

Nature, for Nomanul Haq (2001), thus works according to God's *amr*, or
commands, everything being 'measured out', given its natural principle of
being and its place in the larger cosmos: each thing has a particular *amr*, its
own unique command and role from God, within the unity of nature, something that cannot be violated (nature's intelligibility flowing from this). And
this denotes not only a system of self-sustaining laws of nature (e.g. the *amr* of a
mango is to grow into a mango tree, that of an egg to hatch into a bird, a sperm
to develop into an embryo), but also a universal operative principle, all things
playing an assigned role in the larger whole, *amr* being the specific principle
of each thing but only in relation to those of all others in the whole of nature.
Thus nature is made up of interdependent *amrs* that together make up its *amr*,
which is to exist in and glorify the unity of God. It works purposefully and relationally, being an embodiment of God's deliberation and mercy. In everything
that lives, therefore, there is a reward, all exist to support and nourish the
process of life. Thus animals, although intended to benefit humanity, are valuable (thoughtfully created by and obeying God) and need to be respected and
cared for (if killed there should be as little suffering as possible, something
relating to *halal* (lawful) slaughter; this being a way of receiving God's bounty,
to not do so impious) (Bassett et al. 2000; Regenstein 1991; Saritoprak 2005).

There is a meritorious reward . . . for every act of charity and kindness to every
living creature (*Hadith Awn*, 7, 222:2533) . . . A good deed done to an animal is
as meritorious as a good deed done to a human being, while an act of cruelty
to an animal is as bad as an act of cruelty to a human being (*Hadith Mishkat*, bk
6, ch 7, 8:178) . . . He who takes pity on a sparrow and spares its life, God will be
merciful to Him (*Al-Tabarani*) . . . There is no man who kills . . . anything . . .
without a justifiable cause, but God will question him about it (*Hadith Al-Nasai*,
7, 206). (Regenstein 1991:251)[20]

Animals are seen as symbols of Gods power, living in communities and
having skills, being able to communicate via sophisticated language (which
humanity can understand, for example, Solomon being taught the language
of birds, this seen as a blessing and sign of favour (27:16)). Animals praise
God in their own ways (via their own *amr's*, fulfilling God's design). Hence
they are worthy of respect and need understanding and communicating with
(their *amr's* need to be understood and appropriately interacted with). There

is, then, in this sense, no clear-cut distinction between animals and humanity, both have their roles within creation which is seen as an interdependent family (*ayal*) of God. Humanity is part of nature, a natural entity, participating in its unity, so to offend or damage it is to offend or damage oneself (if one part of nature suffers all suffer), what is termed *ulm-al-nafs*, or self-injury. Damaging the balance of nature is thus thought to damage humanity while being kind to it creates kindness to humanity (bringing it closer to God) (Callicott 1997; Foltz 2002a, 2005c; Izzi Deen 1996; Izzi Dien 1997; Masri 1997; Nomanul Haq 2001; Ozdemir 2003; Regenstein 1991).[21]

The earth, in this sense, is also seen as a mosque, a means of purification and fit place for humanity's *amr* of exercising its intellect and morality to fulfil God's unifying plan in creation, understanding and submitting to guiding signs (in nature and the Qur'an). It is thus a way for humanity to reach paradise (via caring for it; degrading it prevents this): paradise is seen as a harmonious garden (*jannah*, containing the righteous) and life on earth a preparation for this, so humanity needs to make a harmonious garden of the earth (being righteous, cultivating an 'inner-garden' of harmonious thought). Petruccioli (2003) and Wescoat (2003, 2005a), in particular, highlight this, concentrating on the sanctity of 'man-made nature' (cultivated, as opposed to hostile desert) seeing a fertile earth covered with greenery having value (green also being the 'blessed colour'). Cultivation is thus a sign of God's life-giving creativity, something linked to *haram*, sacred precincts or protected inviolable zones (Mecca is a *haram*), and *hima*, fertile sanctuaries or land set aside for the common good, these seen as providing promise for environmental conservation through 'bringing to life' (*ihya*) 'dead' land (*mawat*), cultivating 'alive' land (*amir*; thus there is no concept of untouched wilderness or pristine, non-cultivating, human relationship to nature, in Islam). Such ideas relate to the requirement to be a benefactor and cultivator not a corruptor or destroyer, allowing all created beings to benefit from the harmonious 'just' use of natural resources (Chishti 2003; Izzi Deen 1996; Denny 2004; Dutton 1992; Foltz 2005b; Llewellyn 1992, 2003; Milani 2003; Nomanul Haq 2001; Saritoprak 2005).

In line with such ideas humanity is stressed as having the role of *khalifa*, or 'vice-regent', a covenant with God to guard creation, offered to and rejected by the heavens, earth and mountains, but accepted by humanity, which subsequently bears God's *amana*, or trust (thus abusing nature is betraying this trust). This is seen as a sacred duty of being responsible for creation, a 'benign domination', using but not abusing it as it was not created solely for humanity's benefit but for the benefit of all. And it is a task that will be judged, how humanity relates to nature, good or bad, will ultimately be assessed by God (it is accountable for its actions: '006.165 . . . He hath raised you in ranks some above others: that he may try you in the gifts He hath given you'[22]). *Khalifa* does not warrant tyranny over an enslaved world but selfless 'servantship' (*al-ubu-diyyah*) in submission to God, following His role for humanity, (and creation) what is seen as *tawakkul* or trust in God. It is a privilege, allowing utilization of nature to fulfil humanity's interests, but also a duty and responsibility, humanity needing to maintain nature's holistic integrity. Creation is a gift for humanity but with the conditions of it upholding what is right, in sight of God, His harmonic intent, from which it has no independent rights (Callicott 1997; Chishti 2003; Denny 2004; Foltz 2002a, 2003b, 2005a; Izzi Dien 1997; Khalid 2005; Nasr 1992; Nomanul Haq 2001; Ozdemir 2003; Palmer and Finlay 2003; Parvaiz 2005; Timm 1994).

> We are God's stewards . . . on earth . . . not masters . . . it does not belong to us to do what we wish. It belongs to God and He has entrusted us with its safekeeping . . . The *khalifa* is answerable for his/her actions, for the way in which he/she uses or abuses the trust of God. (Dr Abdullah Omar Nasseef, The Muslim Declaration on Nature, WWF 1986:23)

> Islam is not an ecstatic religion commanding detachment from worldly goods. Muslims are left with the duty to enjoy and use the bounties of the Earth . . . [but this] is always attached to a moral dimension of obedience and the fulfilment of the covenant to God. (Ammar 2005:864)

Khalifa is a moral duty to better nature not degrade it, to be a creature of God as well as the earth, an invitation to do good (*al-maruf*) and prohibit evil (*al-munkar*). It a measure of humanity's *ehsan*, or acts of worship, living in a way pleasing to God: 'You who have *iman* (faith), Do not make *haram* (unlawful), The good things Allah has made *halal* (lawful) for you, And do not overstep the limits' (5:87).[23] It is a test of faith in God's harmonic design for creation. Thus the appropriate response to the honour of managing it is one of gratitude and loyalty, being the channel of God's grace, at one with His purpose. Humanity has to bear witness to God in creation, submitting to His will and purpose – it has to be 'Muslim'. However, unlike other creatures which do this by instinct, according to the laws of nature (their *amr's*), humanity *ought* to do so, having free will and the faculty of reasoning, and bringing this 'ought' and the 'is' of action together is the privilege and risk of being human (its *amr*). Humanity has been given the choice either to act according to divine guidance or to follow its own desires, this 'gift of mind', being part of the responsibility of seeking knowledge (the foundation for belief: *Iman*, reasoned conviction). Any human 'superiority' thus lies not in dominating power but in the fact that it is morally accountable before God as no other creature is. It comes at a price, the requirement of enabling 'due balance' (*mizan*) of the 'due measure' (*qadir*) of things (balancing its needs with the needs of nature, protecting not disturbing the natural balance) (Afrasiabi 2003; Ammar 2002, 2005; Chishti 2003; Dutton 2003; Khalid 2005; Masri 1997;

Nasr 1992; Nomanul Haq 2001; Ozdemir 2003; Palmer and Finlay 2003; Parvaiz 2005; Timm 1994).[24]

(Allah) Most Gracious . . . He has created man: He has taught him speech (and Intelligence). The sun and the moon follow courses (exactly) computed . . . And the firmament has He raised high and He has set up the balance (of justice) In order that ye may not transgress (due) balance. So establish weight with justice and fall not short in the balance. It is He Who has spread out the earth . . . which of the favors of your Lord will ye deny? (055.001–013)[25]

The Islamic cosmos thus exists according to a purposeful, balanced and just, pattern. There is nothing that is not fully measured out. Everything is in a knowable measure. And humanity, virtue of its intelligence, can and should comprehend this and conduct a balanced and just life. This is seen as a 'cosmology of justice', the need to combat injustice and establish justice, within society and nature, 'wealth' being seen as a trust given by God, to be used gently and generously to advance His creative purposes. In this sense, Islam is seen as countercultural (in relation to Western ideas), stressing a social contract binding individual to community, *jamat* or congregation being central, where equality and generosity are valued not dominance and accumulation, and issues of social justice, tending the vulnerable and critiquing the powerful, have broader relevance, embracing concern for nature (Ammar 2002, 2005; Dockrat 2003; Dutton 2003; Foltz 2002a; Khalid 2005; Maguire 2000; Nomanul Haq 2001; Ozdemir 2003; Palmer and Finlay 2003; Parvaiz 2005).

O ye who believe! Stand out firmly for justice as witnesses to Allah even as against yourselves or your parents or your kin and whether it be (against) rich or poor . . . Follow not the lusts (of your hearts) lest ye swerve and if ye distort (justice) or decline to do justice verily Allah is well acquainted with all that ye do. 004.135 . . . Whoever recommends and helps a good cause becomes a partner therein: and whoever recommends and helps an evil cause shares in its burden. 004.085. Allah doth command you to render back your trusts to those to whom they are due; and when ye judge . . . judge with justice. 004.058 . . . stand out firmly for Allah as witnesses to fair dealing . . . Be just: that is next to Piety. 005.009.[26]

Humans, then, have to be *musleheen*, correctors or reformers, rather than *mufsideen*, corruptors or spoilers. Such human realization of vice-regency, relates to *fitra*, the natural, primordial (balanced, just, peaceful, unified) state for creation and humanity's natural, primordial (balanced, just, peaceful, unified) place in it. In this scheme, humanity is an integral part of nature, not separate from it, originating within it and sharing its purpose, being part of its unfolding pattern, needing to use its talents to assist this (its *amr*, something that, for Callicott (1997), means humanity is the *telos* of creation; for Foltz (2002a, 2003b) a 'theanthropocentric' view): 'Set yourself firmly towards the Deen (the way, the life transaction), As a pure believer, Allah's natural pattern on which he made humankind' (30:29).[27] In this sense, there is seen as being no original sin in Islam but rather a hopeful conception of humanity, its natural response to nature being a relationship of utilization for the purpose of enabling God's balance. In the very principle of its being humanity is committed to following God: human nature is theomorphic, to recognize and emulate God is to be in a naturally human state (natural and moral law are linked). Thus dominating and abusing nature is an aberration, going against human nature, a symptom of unbelief, anti-Muslim (a loss of relationship to God). And such human disassociation from its true primordial being needs to be reversed and its instinctive balanced and just nature realized (Chishti 2003; Foltz 2005b; Izzi Deen 1996; Khalid 2005; Nomanul Haq 2001; Palmer and Finlay 2003; Parvaiz 2005; Said and Funk 2003).

'True' humanity, in this sense, submits to and serves God, acting with *haya*, a respectful deference or grateful tolerance, with concern for the other (for nature and thus for God's plan/glory). It is an attitude of appreciation, respect and reverence for the gift of existence (the opposite of hubris; connected to the requirement to pray, to remember how blessed creation is). To do otherwise is to be an unbeliever (it is the absence of *haya* that is seen as causing social and environmental problems). The aim is to practise *hisba*, the application of good and removal of evil, not only a 'no-harm' principle but also a positive empowering action, an obligation to influence the behaviour of individuals and society at large. It is an individual and social conscience, warding off complacency or evil, replacing a predatory society with a disciplined community of (environmentally) sociable human beings: 'Let there be of you a society that calls to goodness, establishes right and eradicates wrong. Sure are they who shall prosper' (3:104).[28] Important to this is that humanity is not seen as able to give itself totally to that which is evil but is able to give itself totally to that which is good (virtue of *fitra*) (Afrasiabi 2003; Ammar 2002; Dockrat 2003; Izzi Dien 1997; Khalid 2005; Llewellyn 2003; Maguire 2000; Parvaiz 2005).[29]

Such thought and action is seen as the 'striving', or *jihad*, of humanity, the inner struggle to purify self and behave correctly, in a manner which furthers rather than disrupts the divine harmony (a spiritual journey of increasing servantship, of perception of the 'Light of God' and commitment to creation). And it is argued that what may be needed is a more recognizable 'green *jihad*', purifying the personal, social and spiritual, roots of the environmental crisis. Such is seen as being a necessary reform/rediscovery (*islah*) and renewal (*tajid*) of Islam, a true fulfilment of it as *din al-fitra*, religion true to the primordial nature, and *din al-sahl*, religion fostering a way of ease. In this sense, Islam is seen to be inherently environmentally friendly, having deep-ecological principles, expressing a fundamental reality of balance, justice, peace and unity.[30] Thus it is seen as able to address the environmental crisis at its roots, widening the Islamic *din*, or way of life, to include ecological sensitivity, fulfilling Islam as a religion of divine majesty (*jalal*) and divine beauty (*jamal*), a concrete living experience of God (Chishti 2003; Denny 2004; Foltz 2002a, 2005a; Nasr 1992; Nomanul Haq 2001; Said and Funk 2003). For Palmer and Finlay (2003:105–6), Islam thus affirms the conclusion that humanity needs to abandon mammon and listen to the prescriptions of God on the conservation of nature:

> Qur'anic principles . . . state in clear terms that Allah, the One True God, is the . . . Creator . . . and . . . Owner of the Universe. To Him belong all the animate and inanimate objects, all of whom should or do submit themselves to Him. Allah, in His Wisdom, appointed us, the creatures that He has conferred with the faculty of reason and with free will, to be His vice-regents on earth. And while Allah has invited us to partake of the fruits of the earth for our rightful nourishment and enjoyment, He has also directed us not to waste that which Allah has provided for us – for He loveth not wasters. Furthermore, Allah has also ordered us to administer his responsibilities with justice. Above all, humanity should conserve the balance of Allah's creation on Earth. By virtue of our intelligence, we (when we believe in the One Universal Allah, the Creator of the Universe) are the only creation of Allah to be entrusted with the overall responsibility of maintaining planet Earth in the overall balanced ecology that we found.

Conclusions

Ecological interpretations of Islam stress it as addressing the primordial nature of reality, the relationships between God, humanity and nature (based on the Qur'an, God's revealed word). Nature, in this scheme, is a balanced, just, peaceful, unified pattern, created by and functioning according to Gods design, each part having its own purpose, its role within the interlocking whole. It is thus sacred and valuable in of itself: it reveals God, being a cosmic Qur'an (and is thus a way to cleanliness, not to be wasted). Within this humanity has the role of stewarding nature, facilitating its balance, being just and peaceful towards it, encouraging its thriving, unifying and fulfilling it (and itself) according to God's intent (bearing His trust for it; knowledge of nature is thus a form of worship, what God reveals and nature manifests are essentially the same). Thus Islam is seen as tempering human arrogance, placing it within the bounds of God's ownership and purpose, stressing the need to abandon selfish ideas and to submit to God, understanding and following His balanced, peaceful and just, prescriptions, uniting with Him via uniting with nature (humanity is meant to live in nature, not apart, but as a harmonic not dominant part, and it will be judged in this, being accountable and punishable for its ecological actions).

The Qur'an (Muhammad, *Sharia*) is seen as a way to awaken a higher consciousness in humanity, one unified with nature and God, stressing nature as God's gift, imbued with His purity and sacredness, and prescribing injunctions on how humanity is to interact with it (in a similarly pure, sacred, thankful and unwasteful way, aware of its balance, justice, peace and unity). Islam is thus seen as stressing the unity or 'Oneness' God (*al-Muhit*), encompassing nature and humanity (which is not independent, not owning things, but subject to divine law, to God's ownership), with unity of creation (*tawhid*) the foundation of the 'Way of Islam': to establish unity is to create a right relationship with nature and God, one that is harmonic, just and peaceful (Islam coming from *salam-silm*, peace, security and wholeness). This is seen as a surrender to the whole (to God), enjoying, remembering and witnessing God's perfection, creating community (*umma*), following nature which is a sign of God, a meaningful medium of revelation, providing lessons in divine unity. Nature, in this sense, is Muslim, submitting to God instinctively, each part of it working according to His *amr*, or commands, interdependently making up the wider cosmic *amr* of unity. All nature's creatures are thus important, pointing to and being loved by God, living in communities, able to communicate, having beauty and skills. They thus have intrinsic value and must not be abused but protected, treated compassionately with understanding (humanity is part of a larger whole thus to injure nature is to suffer self-injury).

The human role in this Islamic cosmology is as a vice-regent (*khalifa*, its *amr*), responsibly guarding nature in a servantship to God, bearing His trust for it (*amana*). The aim in this is to make a garden of nature as this corresponds to God design and purpose for it (paradise being a garden; nature is thus is a testing ground for humanity's worship of God). Humanity needs to enhance (God's) creativity within nature, bringing to life dead lands (as God does), being a beneficent cultivator not corrupt destroyer. To be Muslim humanity needs to use its God-given intellectual capacities and free will to assess and implement the due-balance of nature (*mizan*), moderating its own needs with that of the wider created community. This is seen as a cosmology of justice, all things having their designated just role in the whole, with humanity called to combat injustice and establish justice, a contract binding (human) individual to (environmental) community (*jamat*, the more obedient and accountable to this the better, for nature and humanity, the less the worse). Humans need to be correctors or reformers (*musleheen*) not corruptors or spoilers (*mufsideen*), this relating to the primordial state of creation and humanity's (proper) place in it (*fitra*): Islam is the primordial religion, fostering a way of balance, justice, peace and unity (creation's natural state), and humanity, as the *telos* of this, has a primordial place, bringing it to this ultimate state (natural and moral law being linked, separating from and abusing nature thus goes against true harmonic human nature). Humanity achieves this through acting respectfully, with gratitude for the gift of existence and with concern for others (*haya*), applying good and removing evil (*hisba*), a striving to purify self and create a concrete living experience of God (*jihad*, which needs to be more recognizably linked to environmental issues in a 'green *jihad*').

Notes

1   Foltz (2003a, 2003b) sees Islam concerned with social justice and humanity's relationship to God rather than environmental issues, per se (seeing the (Muslim) poor suffering from environmental degradation more than the (Western) rich), although he does see Islamic environmentalism, from canonical sources, and Muslim environmentalism, from cultural practices. Others see Islamic eco-ideas hidden by Greek, Judeo-Christian or Western views, with the environmental crisis occurring due to the Islamic world not being properly Islamic but aping Western ideas (Nasr 1992; Nomanul Haq 2001; Ozdemir 2003; Timm 1994).

2   Referenced to Fazlun Khalid, Introduction, *Qur'an: Creation and Conservation* (Birmingham, UK: Islamic Foundation for Ecology and Environmental Sciences (IFEES), 1999).

3   From Saritopak (2005:1321).

4   Referenced to Guy Delon, in report distributed by the Animal Welfare Institute, Washington, DC.

5   Referenced to Al-Hafiz B. A. Masri, 'Synopsis of Islamic Teachings on Animal Rights', distributed by International Network for Religion and Animals, Silver Spring, MD.

6   From Saritopak (2005:1323).

7   From Saritopak (2005:1323).

8   From Ozdemir (2005:1124).

9   From Ozdemir (2005:1125).

10 Foltz (2005b) and Wescoat (2005b) also stress analogical reasoning (*qiyas*) of the classical jurists, the consensus (*ijma*) of the community of believers (*ummah*; authoritative through the saying 'my community will not agree on error'), and codified sources of custom (*urf*), conduct (*adab*), and individual discernment (*ijtihad*). Foltz (2005a) and Nasr (1992) see Islamic philosophy as influential, coining the term *tabi'a* to represent nature (similar to Latin/Greek *natura/physis*), possibly as a first principle.

11 From Timm (1994:85), referenced to Al-Bukhari, vol. 4, bk 54, ch. 1, p. 279.

12 Also 29:19–20, 30:11, 27, 85:13, from Timm (1994:85).

13 From Timm (1994:86).

14 For Nasr (1992) Islam opposes the absolutization of Promethean man, not glorifying humanity at the expense of God or creation. For Nasr, the traditional Muslim, *Homo Islamicus*, has always lived in awareness of the rights of others, including non-humans, being conscious of responsibility to God and nature.

15 Downloaded from www.arcworld.org/faiths.asp?pageID=75, 15 Sept. 2005 (de-italicized).

16 From Said and Funk (2003:165).

17 Said and Funk (2003) see complimentarily between ecology, the 'pattern of relations between organisms and their environment', and Islamic spirituality stressing an 'ecology of the spirit' and sacred 'pattern that connects'.

18 Referenced to Al-Hafiz B. A. Masri, 'Synopsis of Islamic Teachings'.

19 Referenced to Jalal al-Din Rumi in Reynold A. Nicholson, *Rumi, Poet and Mystic* (1207–1273) (London: George Allen and Unwin, 1950), p. 119.

20 Referenced to Al-Hafiz B. A. Masri, 'Synopsis of Islamic Teachings'.

21 Saritopak (2005:1324) sees the Qur'an stressing the end of nature as a punishment for human corruption: 'the earth will be shaken' (100:1); 'the sky will be torn away and mountains will become like discarded wool' (81:11); 'seas will be poured forth and will rise' (81:6; 82:3). Thus by polluting nature humanity hastens its own end while protecting it ensures that life continues (something the destruction of pre-Islamic civilizations is seen as testifying to). Thus present earthly life is a test for the future to be judged: 'And the garden (*Jannah*) will be brought nigh to the righteous and hell (*al-Jaheem*) will appear plainly to the erring' (26:90–1).

22 From Palmer and Finlay (2003:102).

23 From Khalid (2005:882).

24 For Nasr (1992) there is nothing more dangerous for nature than a *khalifat Allah*, or vice-regent, rejecting the role of *abd Allah*, or God's servant, as this means dominion devoid of care. However, such a risk, arising because of human free-will (preferred to pre-programmed goodness by God), illustrates the dignity humanity possesses in managing vice-regency and independent choice (see Izzi Dien 1997).

25 Downloaded from www.arcworld.org/faiths.asp?pageID=75, 15 Sept. 2006 (de-italicized).

26 Downloaded from www.arcworld.org/faiths.asp?pageID=75, 15 Sept. 2006 (de-italicized).

27 From Khalid (2005:881).

28 From Llewellyn (2003:220).

29 Khalid (2005), Izzi Dien (1997) and Llewellyn (2003) cite the *muhtasib* or learned jurist heading a state agency (also termed *hisba*) promoting what is (ecologically) proper, forbidding improper. Dockrat (2003) sees a social contract within Islam, linking private and public *hisba*, within *jam'at*, or congregation (the five pillars of Islam, almsgiving, fasting, pilgrimage, ritual and testimony, linking *batin*, inner nature and *zahir*, outer nature, within *imara*, or divinely sanctioned governance, exemplified by Muhammad).

30 Several authors see Islamic eco-principles: God is the ultimate reality, creating the world in balance, and understanding is only possible via a relationship to Him; humanity is only entitled to use nature as God's trustee, with an eye to balance, rewarded or punished appropriately; animals should be treated as partners of humanity; everything has ecological value/rights and humanity is not empowered to disturb this; natural degradation results from greed or lust for power, punishable infringements of God's trust; prevention of harm takes preference

over achievement; consumerism, creating false needs, is discouraged, waste not permitted (Ahmad 2003; Ammar 2001, 2002; Kumar 2003; Siddiq 2003). Such ideas for Afrasiabi (2005) involve a 'post-anthropocentric' interpretation of Islam (beyond 'soft-anthropocentrism' that he sees in most Islamic eco-theology), centring on a divinely valued creation with humanity God's noblest creature but with moral obligations to nature.

Chapter 9

Conclusion

The world's religions view the environment in different ways . . . but all are paying increasing attention to the natural world, as evidence of widespread degradation continues to pour forth. The planetary scale of the crisis has awakened a process [of] . . . retrieval, re-evaluation, and reconstruction of religious wisdom regarding human interaction with the natural world. In other words, religious traditions are finding in their own codex of wisdom ancient teachings that have been overlooked, or that are understood more profoundly in the light of the global environmental crisis.

(Gardner 2006:69)

The environmental crisis is more than physical effects: it has a moral and spiritual dimension, the physical degradation of nature being underpinned by a particular vision of it, the dominant modern Western world-view, a mechanical imagination, creating a view of nature as separate from, and lower than, humanity (separating mind/body, spirit/matter), disenchanting, devaluing, dominating and degrading it. Counter imaginations of nature (and humanity) are, therefore, seen as needed to redress this, ones seeing it as meaningful, subjective and spiritual (uniting mind/body, spirit/matter), inspiring environmentally benign behaviour (such ideas being highlighted by a developing ecological model arising from within the environmental movement seeing humanity and nature (and the sacred) in an interdependent partnership). Religious traditions, also seen as challenged, devalued and disempowered, by the (secularizing) modern world-view, seen as theo/eco-centric, holistic and organic, ethically and spiritually based, with personal and social influence and moral authority, are seen as possible sources of such ecological reimagination. They are seen as able to, and are encouraged to, engage the environmental problems created by modernity, creating new imaginations of nature and stimulating new environmentally friendly actions. And by doing this they are seen as thereby able to become revitalized and re-empowered, undertaking an important role in the world, acting as channels for humanity to re-experience (intimate, moral, spiritual) connection to nature and articulate environmental concern (although in this they are also challenged to adapt or extend their views, to ecologically reassess traditions, going beyond anthropocentric or dogmatic attitudes). In particular, the field of religion and ecology seeks to locate, promote and encompass, such religious-ecological engagement and imagination, providing common purpose and shared commitment, encouraging, stimulating, comparing and combining, environmental concern among religious traditions and channelling their diverse views into a mutually enriching dialogue, ethics and action, stimulating a religious (and ideally wider) reimagining of nature and humanity's relationship to and place within it.

In this book I have analysed such engagement and reimagining and explored some ecologically based religious views – different religious ecotopias, idealized visions of nature and humanity's place in it – stressed in the field, and in this conclusion I further explore and analyse such ideas by reviewing the metaphors and myths stressed in the religious ecotopian visions and exploring commonalities or convergences that may be developing, analysing what they may mean for environmentalism and religion in the modern world.

Religious-ecotopian visions

In the following sections I draw out and review main themes from Chapters 3 to 8, the main metaphors and myths expressed in each of the religious imaginations that together make up their different religious-ecotopian visions. They are the central elements of the visions, consistently stressed and used, providing their (evocative, powerful) narrative coherence and meaning (seen as significant within the field of religion and ecology and within each tradition, seen as containing some of their profoundest views concerning the order of nature and the human place in it, standing in contrast to the modern view). They are also, as I will show below, compared and contrasted in the field as a way of further developing the ideas. Again, I stress that the visions are new creations, new ecologically based imaginations, adapting, combining, extending or reappropriating, traditional themes, coalescing into, or being used to create, new religious-ecotopian forms, what are seen as more environmentally friendly definitions of nature and humanity.

Indian (Hindu and Jain) visions

Indian traditions are seen as deifying and revering nature, stressing organic visions seeing the universe as a dynamic, balanced/ordered, organism made of interconnected parts, each part embodying an underlying spiritual reality. Hinduism is seen as stressing a sacred topography, seeing the divine manifested in all forces, objects and processes, revering rivers and trees. Jainism is seen as stressing no God or first cause but rather seeing the universe as uncreated and eternal, seeing a livingness to nature, all things possessing a soul and having inherent value. Humanity in these visions is seen as needing to recognize such ideas, connecting to a wider reality and supporting all life via non-violence and self-restraint:

Hinduism

- Rivers/trees symbolize humanity's reciprocal relationship to nature and the divine: rivers have life-giving potential, being moral purifiers/sources of spirituality; trees are symbols of fecundity, generous/tolerant, with the forest, diverse yet harmonic, a model for (Indian) civilization.
- Nature contains divine consciousness/power, *prakriti/shakti*, producing/ nourishing life (the body of god/goddesses). Life is one-in-many/many-in-one; *atman*, inner-self, being (able to be) connected to the ultimate, underlying reality *Brahman* (life is the distilled essence of the divine).
- Humanity's role is to uncover ultimate reality/maintain cosmic order, via *dharma*, righteousness/moral law, a state of eternal balance/peace (*sanatana*) and corresponding model of social/cosmic performance (if transgressed, *adharma*, all suffer).
- Humanity achieves *dharma* via *ahimsa*, non-violence, restraining limited ego-self in favour of wider self, serving the common good, seeing nature as kin. Relates to *karma* (effects of action) and *samsara* (rebirth) where the moral quality of actions affects the whole/determines fate (liberating from material self or binding to the earthly life cycle).
- Gandhi is the exemplar of *ahimsa*: anti-materialistic/non-exploitative, acting communally/simply, practice related to asceticism/*karma-yoga*, desireless action, abandoning egoism/desire, and rituals participating in nature's reciprocity.

Jainism

- Stresses a living cosmos, extending the concept of life (beyond Western definitions) based on number of senses (including non-living/sentient), having a deep appreciation of biodiversity and inherent worth/fragility of life, stressing its care.
- Sees life-forms possessing a *jiva*, or soul, differently reincarnated dependent on the accumulation of karma via acts of violence clouding true perception (of interdependence); the world exists in interdependent *karmic* moral web with the aim being to achieve liberation from this via caring/egofree, acts.
- Stresses 'many-sidedness' multiplicity and mutuality: no single (e.g. human) perspective has the truth only partial access to it; knowledge of it is intrinsic to the soul but veiled by ignorance (egoism; failure to respect others is thus mistaken and diversity of (interdependent) truths needs recognition).

- Humanity needs to recognize its intertwined place in nature, accepting that life-forms and the whole they support need care, practising *sarvodayavada*, the lifting up of souls (cultivating diverse contextual views within harmonious existence).
- Stresses codes of conduct/ethics: *ahimsa* (central aspect, moral core), kindness, non-acquisition/possession, self-restraint, simplicity, truthfulness, the aim being to avoid negligence/harm in thought/word/deed; a positive, context-sensitive, cycle of care (with asceticism the purest moral model).

Chinese (Confucian and Daoist) visions

Chinese traditions are seen as stressing holism, organicism and vitalism, seeing no creator or creation but rather stressing a complete, balanced, harmonious, interdependent, universe based on continuity, wholeness and dynamism, a constant generative, emergent, diverse yet complete process. This is seen as unifying spirit and matter with the aim of existence not being to return to an otherworldly pristine state but to exist in worldly balance and harmony. Humanity is thus seen as needing to cultivate social and natural balance and/or follow nature's balance, curbing selfishness:

- 'Continuity of being' stresses organic holism/dynamic vitalism, seeing the universe as creative harmonious activity (*sheng-sheng*, production/reproduction), a fluid integrated whole, with the human quest to realize this.
- Nature is coordinated and enlivened via the *Dao*, a primeval essence, a spontaneously, creative, transformative, emergent power and order, beyond form, both what and how there is, nowhere and everywhere, nothing and everything (self-so; *ziran*, naturalness).
- Life is connected in the *Dao* via *qi*, a vital force assuming tangible forms, providing natural process with motive power, the basis of change/order (related to *li*, natural patterns or principles), composed of interdependent energies, *yin/yang*, different combinations of which compose different things.
- The aim is to connect to the *Dao*, channel *qi*, and balance *yin/yang*: for example, via Chinese gardens, painting, *fengshui*, or medicine, which capture/direct the flow of *qi* and produce relational balance by arranging bodies/objects/landscape in response to natural rhythms, capturing nature's essence, evoking wider reality.

Confucianism

- Stresses Cosmic humanism: humanity has an active role in nature, forming a trinity with heaven/earth, creating one body with the cosmos via moral (spiritual) responsiveness and relational resonance in tune with cosmic resonance (respond to movements of *qi* in nature).

- Humanity has the responsibility of facilitating the balance of nature, through cultivating an innate human goodness, extending sincerity from the human heart to the cosmos (an anthropocosmic view, fruitful interaction between self/community).
- Stresses an appropriate response to nature in accordance with *li*, emergent patterns/principles giving structure to *qi*, these being natural foundations for a moral response to nature, exemplified by *jen*, or humaneness, a primordial concern for others, exemplified by the Sage: an integrative wisdom curbing selfish desires (merging with nature/*Dao*).

Daoism

- Follows the *Dao* via spontaneous, intuitive, harmonic interaction with nature, valuing it for its own sake: *wu-wei*, non-action, letting everything grow according to its course; yielding not imposing, acting indirectly yet with generative potentiality (like water), facilitating the emergence of novelty.
- Non-heroic/interventional: trusting natural processes to operate in harmony, stressing skilled/wise craftsmanship, facilitating nature's inner-form not technical imposition, going beyond reason, acting with spirit, reflecting the totality, facilitating the *Dao* and assisting *ziran*, latent naturalness.
- 'Knowing' is perceiving nature's underlying harmony via relevatory experience, stressing process over form, 'know how' over 'know what', dynamic way over static truth, this denying ontological privilege, stressing contingent, negotiated harmony (seeing selfish reason unbalancing nature).

Buddhist visions

Buddhism is seen as ecologically sensitive, highlighting eco-centrism, holism and interdependence, and stressing compassion, selflessness, non-violence, simplicity and spiritual development. Humanity is seen as prone to self-destructive desire, an illusory attachment to earthly existence, which is the cause of suffering. It thus needs to realize this, to recognize the interrelatedness of life, and connect with its underlying reality, acting in a cooperative, egalitarian and mindful, way. This is seen as leading to a balanced, mutually supporting, responsible human and environmental flourishing:

- Highlights Buddha's enlightenment: understanding life's transience/mutual arising; his Four Noble Truths of the reality of suffering, the cause of suffering through desire/ignorance, freedom from suffering via freedom from desire, and freedom occurring via a life of discipline/balance.

- Suffering occurs through *trishna*, a delusional selfish attachment to existence (I-self), this needing to be overcome via moral/spiritual learning realizing interdependent reality (we-self; related to *anatman*, 'non-(ego)-self' and *sunyata*, emptiness of independence).
- *Karma* (cause and effect) and *samsara* (rebirth) link life in an interrelated moral continuum where actions have consequences (moral behaviour meaning better rebirth, immoral worse), progress in the continuum (enlightenment) occurring through recognizing life's interdependence and acting communally, with care.
- *Dharma*, 'path to truth', sacred law, and things in nature, stresses interdependent reality (suchness; nature conveys spiritual insight), with life sharing *dharma*-nature, a universal essence (being embryonic Buddha's/companions in *samsara*), humanity needing to realize this (through acting compassionately).
- Life-forms 'co-originate', arising simultaneously and being mutually affecting, causing/conditioning each other (and the whole: 'Indra's Net' of jewels, reflecting the whole/each other; if one is abused the whole/all others are; nothing is self-existing).
- Non-dualism and 'relational holism' stress identity-in-difference, organisms needing the whole/others, which need them in turn; the whole is the interworking of the parts, there is relationality of life between parts and parts/whole.
- Human enlightenment involves a 'progress' from separateness to cooperation (via compassion, loving kindness, non-violence); 'development' is interdependence with nature, the existential experience of others suffering (exemplified by the *bodhisattva*, or enlightened one, serving others).
- Stresses 'precepts', such as, not creating evil, practising good, affirming life, avoiding anger/lying/selfishness, and experiencing intimacy, and the 'eightfold path' of self-transformation of 'right' understanding, thought, speech, action, livelihood, effort, mindfulness and concentration.
- Aims for a 'middle way' moderate lifestyle, avoiding self-indulgence/denial, a 'mindfulness' being aware of humanity's destructive tendencies and creating *sangha*, a community practising harmony with nature, emphasizing 'Zen' practice, meditation developing 'oneness' with nature, a deep sense of place.
- *Ecosattvas*/'engaged Buddhism': countercultural environmentalism stressing 'skilful living' avoiding waste/protecting nature, seeing 'true development' as humanity in tune with nature, stressing holistic knowledge, an ethic of harmony/simplicity, stressing quality not quantity of life.

Jewish visions

Judaism is seen as stressing God as the loving Creator, embodied in nature, which is meaningful and valuable. Humanity is seen as inherently relational, in an intimate sacred relationship to nature, but through egoism exiled from this. It, therefore, needs to return to its original relationship and steward nature, not abuse or waste it, leading to fulfilment of both. By preventing suffering, being compassionate, observing the Sabbath, practising rituals, obeying the Torah (written and in nature), humanity is thus seen as able to reach (create) Eden (and meet God's intent):

- Stresses theocentrism, seeing nature as valuable, for the benefit/glory of God; there is a loving integrity to creation and divine ownership and meaning by virtue of God's continuous creative activity – an 'original blessing'.
- Sees humanity in a sacred symbiotic relationship to nature (*shlemut*, exemplified by Israel), a reciprocity based on peace/wholeness, where the prosperity of the land depends on human morality, with the Jewish Diaspora/environmental crisis parallel alienations, needing a return to the land (to the true reciprocal human self).
- Creation is good in itself, nature has beauty and value. Creatures are their own projects and due just deserts, nothing is in vain. Nature is an illusion to God. It meets His intents (independent of human cause and effect) and should be of concern to humanity.
- Creation is to be respected, conserved and improved, lived in (moderately) not wasted, something stressed by *bal taschit*, 'do not destroy'; humanity is to guard and complement creation (as God's gift, not for the benefit of humanity), not abuse or destroy it.
- Humanity is of the (interdependent) earth (and will suffer if separated from it), made in God's image, but also a tenant; it does not have dominion but rather needs to exercise stewardship, seeing nature subjectively not objectively (to avoid decline/destruction/exile).
- Eden is a vision of a future not yet reached, nature needing constant human vigilance/care to achieve it, something related to *teshuva*, repentance or return, and *tikkum olam*, repair of world: humanity needs to address pollution/suffering and restore ecological balance/relationship (through being just/merciful).
- Stresses a tradition of compassion/kindness, related to *tsa'ar ba'alei hayim*, the commandment to prevent sorrow/suffering, and to *kashrut*, the kosher code, restricted consumption/rules of cleanliness serving as a connection between humanity/nature, and a way of celebrating the sacred within it.
- Blessings/rituals consecrate humanity/nature's relationship to God: *Sukkot*, experiencing nature, teaching that humanity is temporary; *Tu B'shvat*, celebrating trees; *Shabbat*, the Sabbath, voluntary restraint from consumption/production, allowing communion/rest.
- Humanity needs to follow God's ordinances, especially the Torah, which completes creation, showing how to relate to it, with nature an 'oral Torah', an expression of God's being needing to be read and understood.
- Stresses God (creative wisdom; Y-H-W-H) transforming into diverse materiality (H-W-Y-H), highlighting communion with nature as communion with

God, recognizing humanity/nature as one, stressing a relational 'I-Thou' interaction (not a selfish 'I-It' one).

Christian visions

Christianity is seen as stressing natures revelatory, sacramental, power, highlighting God's perfect intent, stressing humanity's fallibility and sin, its egoist and destructive tendencies, harming this (avoiding its intended God-given role), while also stressing its and nature's ultimate redemption (and perfection). Humanity is seen as needing to repent its egoism and rediscover nature as intrinsically valuable, created and enlivened by God's Spirit and Wisdom, and guard and protect it, such human (and natural) redemption occurring via Jesus (his love, sacrifice; properly imaging God), such ideas stressing a prophetic vision of covenantal, stewardly, responsibility within a relational, sacred, creation:

- Integrity of Creation stresses nature is 'good' created/sustained by a loving God in a harmonious, reciprocal relationship. It is valuable, fitting God's intended function (as God is just/righteous so is creation). To love/fear God is thus to care for/love creation, to abuse it is to abuse God.
- Nature is a sign/icon of God, a point of entry to a new reality, revealing the eternal dimension, an epiphany of (caring/relational/redeeming) God, expressing His love. It is God's 'Book of Works' a means to know Him. Humanity thus needs to be a student of nature, engaging it subjectively.
- Animals are valuable, possessing intelligence/God's blessing and humanity needs to 'love thy (animal) neighbour', being a (ecologically) 'good shepherd'. The Sabbath stresses the need to let nature rest and express gratitude/respect for creation (if not humanity (creation/God) suffers, this connecting morality with harmony of nature).
- Humanity's role is a stewardship, based on a covenant with God, who entrusts creation to it. *Imago Dei* confers privilege but also duty/responsibility, a benign dominion, representing God in creation, maximizing not diminishing life, imaging God.
- Humanity sins, failing in the care of creation as God intended, loving self/materiality, seeking to be the arbiter of divine knowledge (creation is hostile in response). Overcome such sin, and its resulting alienation from nature/God, via self-sacrifice, reorienting humanity from selfishness to selflessness.
- To overcome sin God is embodied in Jesus, the true/new creation and icon of God's love/communion (redemption occurring via (Jesus') self-sacrifice). God redeems creation, not just humanity (He pervades it, nature is His body, this revaluing matter; suffering of nature is God suffering).
- Nature is a sacrament of God/*imago Dei* and humanity needs a sacramental approach to it, accepting it as mediating the sacred and interacting with it

in a direct, subjective 'I-Thou' way of loving Trinitarian communion (the essence of God/nature/humanity is fellowship; nature is thus not 'other').

- The Holy Spirit is a dynamic presence in nature, holding life in redemptive love, providing the 'power of becoming', guiding humanity in discerning the appropriate (caring/relational) way of interacting, bringing creation to fulfilment.
- Wisdom is the underlying (female) creative/ordering energy, directing 'right' (caring/relational) human living in creation, integrating being/becoming: eco-feminism critiques 'male' dualism/domination/objectivity/transcendence, stressing 'female' holism/relationality/subjectivity/immanence.
- Correct human behaviour involves renouncing self/affirming nature, living respectfully/simply, a countercultural 'spirit of asceticism', creating intimacy with nature, limiting consumption; a 'green grace' subordinating human ego to a higher power/web of life.

Islamic visions

Islam is seen as stressing theocentric and holistic understandings, where nature is a unified, interlocking, pattern continuously created by and functioning according to Gods design and purpose (humanity included as a functioning part). It is peaceful, balanced and just, intrinsically valuable in its being, reflecting or being a sign of God (being Muslim in its being). Humanity is seen to have a special role in this (its way of being Muslim), with nature created in anticipation of this role, that of being (self-consciously) a vice-regent, fulfilling (the community of) nature according to God's design and purpose, creating a garden of it, via balanced, just, peaceful, unifying, action:

- The Qur'an/Muhammad/*Sharia* stress interdependence of God/humanity/ nature, aiming to awaken a higher consciousness in humanity, encouraging a peaceful 'reading' of nature (God's gift), prescribing how to interact with it (thankful, unwasteful, sensitive).
- Islam means/stresses peace and wholeness (*salam-silm*). Nature (humanity) is encompassed in God's all-encompassing 'Oneness' (*al-Muhit*). Peaceful unity is a truth/impetus, the aim is to establish harmony in nature, being vigilant to (witnessing) God's perfection in it.
- *Tawhid*, the unity of creation, the foundation of Islam, stresses a peaceful/ unified human relationship to nature, stressing surrendering to the whole, and creating *umma*, or community, allowing deeper realization of God (His unifying purpose).
- Nature is a sign of God, through which He communicates, providing lessons in divine unity, being a medium of revelation. It is Muslim, submitting to God

in its being, working according to His *amr*, or commands (there is no onto-logical separation between divine/nature, transcendence/immanence).

- All creatures are loved by (dependent on) God and are important, living in communities and able to communicate, having beauty/skills, praising and being close/obedient to God. They are intended to benefit humanity but must be treated compassionately, not abused.

- Humanity is part of a larger reciprocal whole (nature's injury is thus self-injury). Its *amr*/role is *khalifa*, or vice-regency, making a garden/paradise of nature, submitting to God's unified design/purpose for it, fulfilling its uni-fied *amr* (via free will: nature is a testing ground for humanity's faith).

- Humanity bears witness to God in nature via its knowledge/intellectual cap-acities by enabling *mizan*, or balance, implementing the peaceful/unified due measure of things, balancing its own needs with that of the wider community, taking a moderate/middle path.

- Stresses a cosmology of justice where all things have a designated place/role in the balanced whole, with humanity called to create a just society (an environ-mental/social/transcendent contract binding humanity to the wider commu-nity; poverty, overconsumption, environmental degradation, are failures).

- Humanity should be correctors (*musleheen*) not corruptors (*mufsideen*) (of society/nature), this relating to *fitra*, or humanity's primordial place in cre-ation: Islam is the primordial religion, fostering a way of peace/unity, and humanity, as its *telos*, has the primordial role of bringing creation to its ultimate peaceful/unified state.

- Humanity achieves this through acting with *haya*, dignified/respectful reserve, a gratitude for the gift of existence, and *hisba*, applying good/removing evil, this relating to *jihad*, the striving to cultivate self/society/nature to be the concrete living experience of God.

Such visions, then, in their different ways, with or without a personal dom-inant God, with more or less human importance, seeing nature as a holistic process or a purposeful creation, sacred in itself or mirroring the divine, needing to be tapped into or tended, proffer coherent, idealized views of nature, humanity and the human–nature relationship (and the human–divine, nature–divine, and human–nature–divine, relationships), narratively explaining nature's and humanity's origins, values and purposes, the ultim-ate nature and purpose of life. They are ecotopian images of futures differ-ent from modernity, imaginative expressions of different desires, visions of what could and should be, ideals to strive for, examples to be worked towards. They stress different (green) possibilities, different nature's and different humanity's, each with their own cosmogonic/cosmological realities defining the truth of existence, the common good, and the appropriate way to achieve fulfilment within this, acting as different (ecological, moral, spiritual) orien-tation points for humanity. Their metaphors, in of themselves and in their ecotopian coherence, intimately and powerfully evoke deeper and wider connections and stimulate deeper and wider thinking, suggesting and stimulating new personal, social and environmental, perceptions, identities, realities and values (new (compelling, entrancing, persuasive) ways of seeing nature and humanity).

Levitas (1990, 2000) sees the necessity of such imaginative thinking, in particular, the process of imagining as much as the imaginative forms themselves, the dynamic pursuit of better ways of being for humanity, seeing this stimulating critique, acting as a catalyst to change as much as creating set futures, what she sees as 'anticipatory thinking', creatively exploring sustainable and equitable alternatives, a 'counter-factual' critique, challenging dominant orthodoxies.[1] What is important, in this sense, then, is not just the ecotopia itself, which may often be idealistic, unrealistic or unreachable, albeit an evocative, stimulating and useful guide and exciting possibility, but the quest, the journey, the constant imaginative ecotopian process, beholding the world and thinking of better rather than attempting to impose orthodoxy or falling into apathy or despair. It is in this, for Marty (2003:53–4) too, that such visions have their value, expanding the imaginative horizons of human potentialities, if used in a humanely ironic way, that is, critically, dynamically, reflexively and responsibly, being aware of the different possibilities, good or bad, intended or unintended, successful or unsuccessful, they may engender (thus avoiding naïve idealism[2]).

The point of such ecotopias, then, in this sense, is the striving. Attaining them perfectly may be impossible, this being too static, but they are meant to be pursued: their aim is (constructive, hopeful) reinterpetation and renewal. Although they may ultimately result in different conditions to those imagined they are able to and meant to stimulate new possibilities and give new direction to progress (breaking with an undesirable trajectory of history or undesirable elements of it and stimulating new ones: for example, rejecting modernity's idea of humanity as privileged, nature meaningless, in favour of ideas stressing a dynamic, sacred, nature, with humanity an interdependent part). Ecotopian visions – the process of ecotopianism – in this sense, may serve as lenses for learning and change, bringing to light important or problematic individual, economic, environmental, moral, political, religious, scientific, social or technological, issues and creating a guide for a variety of responses (subverting the imaginative projection of (modern) continuity, affording an opportunity to come to terms with the new). They may thus have the capacity to reformulate human progress, to refigure the self and the world (and to gain some measure of positive control over risky events and times, being the opposite of negative risk calculations, of a risk society), something that is seen as being useful, even a necessity, considering the rapid progress of the environmental crisis (see Benstein 2002; Carey 1999; De Geus 1999; Gottlieb 2006a; Hervieu-Leger 2000; Rothstein 2003).

Religious-ecotopian commonalities and convergences

Such religious-ecotopian visions are thus emerging, being encouraged and developed, in light of environmental issues, most particularly in the field of religion and ecology. And these visions, as well-being encouraged among different religions, are also being compared and contrasted, explored for commonalities and convergences, or traditions are being encouraged to explore common themes and compare and combine them, thus possibly converging and syncretizing around the focus of environmental issues, possibly stimulating or creating, as Taylor (2004) suggests, a new global earth (eco) religion (e.g. Tucker (2003:35, 2006:401) and Tucker and Grim's (2001:19) ideas of common religious concerns of 'reverence', 'respect', 'restraint', 'redistribution' and 'responsibility'; such ideas possibly strengthening the overall vision of religion as important to the resolution of environmental issues and enabling concerted large-scale action). Nasr (1996), for example, sees (a need for recognition of) commonality among religious views of the 'order nature':

> The study of the order of nature as envisaged in various religions . . . reveals remarkable correspondences and similarities . . . All religions in their deepest teachings, and despite important formal differences, relate the order of nature to the order within human beings and envisage both orders as bearing the imprint of the Divine Reality which is the Origin of both man and nature. There are religions in which the Earth plays a more important role than in others . . . Still, the order of nature has recalled over the ages and across many religious frontiers the order both within and beyond us . . . It is this lesson that the religions have taught over the ages in a hundred languages and with many levels of profundity. (Nasr 1996:24–5)

Nasr (1996:275–7) sees such different religious views of nature going beyond the external world of forms and addressing inner meaning, revealing a common underlying (spiritual) reality, something he sees as concrete and tangible from the point of view of the different religious contexts (a reality he sees being denied to the sector of humanity affected by secularism, scientism and modernism, which denies religious knowledge any legitimacy). In this sense, different religious traditions, within their corpus of metaphors, myths and rituals (within their imaginations and experiences of nature), experience and manifest an underlying (concretely important, meaningful) reality (essentially, in its barest form, that of the interdependence of the divine, humanity and nature). Furthermore, for Nasr (1996:6–7), there is a need for a (global) nexus of such divergent yet common religious views, as emphasized in perennial philosophy, a mutual enrichment and cooperation to resolve the environmental crisis based on a shared perspective of the sacredness of nature – a *cosmologia perennis* – something that he sees as able to make possible serious implementation of ethical principles concerning nature, challenging modern Western views and influencing modern Western individuals and social structures. For Nasr (1996:274–5), such a 'transcendent unity' of religions or 'global theology' opens up a space to reassert and relegitimate a religious view of the order of nature, both within traditions and in a global religious perspective, enabling a united religious voice confronting and challenging those who deny any meaning, purpose or sacredness to nature.

In a similar way, Oelschlaeger (1994) sees a 'caring for creation' theme as a way of coordinating and inspiring different religious views of nature and providing a plausible environmental ethic and commitment through not privileging one master narrative as in the modern world-view, denying different accounts of nature, different claims to ultimate knowledge or truth, but rather accepting them, enabling a coordinated variety of stories about caring for creation to creatively and collectively move toward sustainability. The goal, in this sense, is to enable a variety of traditions across the religious spectrum, from conservative to moderate to liberal to radical to alternative, to creatively think about and discuss obligation towards nature. The aim is thus to use a mosaic of multiple religious orders of nature to reweave an environmentally friendly sacred canopy, refashioning human relations with nature. This is seen to have the power to unite traditions and address environmental issues as creation is seen as being a root metaphor and comprehensive conceptual system across the spectrum of belief, undergirding the meaning of life, allowing common agreement at a primordial level, beyond differences, carrying obligations for humanity towards nature. Such a scheme is thus seen to prescribe a continuum of eco-theologies with individual and public plausibility and influence, articulating and converging on a core of belief to care for a sacred nature.

In this light, Gardner (2006:70–1) stresses commonalities between religious traditions ecological views: Hindu and Buddhist emphasis on correct conduct, including environmental obligations, Hindu theology engaging the world as a creative manifestation of the divine and 'Buddhist environmentalists' stressing the interdependent nature of reality; Confucianism and Daoism linking the divine, human and natural, worlds, in an organic world-view centring on *qi*, the dynamic, material force infusing and unifying matter and spirit, with humanity needing to pay attention to this to live in harmony with nature; the Judaic concept of covenant between God and humanity as able to be extended to creation, the Christian foci on sacrament and incarnation as lenses through which to view the world as sacred, and the Islamic concept of vice-regency, seeing nature not owned by humanity but given to it in a trust, as encouraging responsibility to preserve its balance. Gardner (2006:124) also explicitly highlights and compares religious scriptures criticizing excessive exploitation and suggesting human self-sacrifice and moderation. For example (my order):

- Hinduism: 'That person who lives completely free from desires, without longing . . . attains peace' (Bhagavad Gita II.71).
- Confucianism: 'Excess and deficiency are equally at fault' (Confucius XI. 15).
- Daoism: 'He who knows he has enough is rich' (Dao De Jing).
- Buddhism: 'Whoever . . . overcomes his selfish cravings, his sorrows fall away from him, like drops of water from a lotus flower' (Dhammapada 336).
- Judaism: 'Give me neither poverty nor riches' (Prov. 30.8).
- Christianity: 'No-one can be the slave of two masters . . . You cannot be the slave both of God and money' (Mt. 6.24).
- Islam: 'Eat and drink, but waste not by excess: He loves not the excessive' (Qu'ran 7.31).

Gardner (2006:123–4) sees in these ideas the concept of *restraint*, something he sees at the core of religious teachings, embracing the 'suffering' of self-denial, a moral/spiritual growth opposite to that of modernity that promises happiness and fulfilment via unlimited indulgence: instead of 'I choose, therefore I am' (creating self-absorption and narcissism) there is 'I am chosen, and therefore I am' (creating saints and mystics).[3] Such ideas for Gardner (2006:145–7) suggest the possibility of developing an ethic of 'bounded creativity', creating a new vision of progress understanding the importance of limits, challenging open-ended economic and technological development: he cites the Hindu concept of *dharma* (right conduct), the *Dao* (underlying law of the universe) of Daoism, and *li* (social propriety) of Confucianism, as limiting human developments this way. Such bounded creativity, for Gardner, expands Enlightenment values to include stronger ecological dimensions, exploring and using spiritual resources to broaden its scope and deepen its moral sensitivity, stressing a view of individual well-being as part of wider communal well-being. Such an effort to 'reclaim community' he sees in Judaism's notion of covenant, and Christianity's emphasis on universal love, as well as Buddhism, Confucianism, Daoism, Hinduism, Islam and Jainism, offering understandings of more cooperative, community oriented, and less self-interested societies, stressing geographic rootedness, mutuality and reciprocity. Such ideas Gardner (2006:156–8) sees as part of a (religious influenced) 'reintroduction to nature', stimulating appreciation and love of it.

DeWitt (2002:35–6) also sees complimentarily within religious traditions with respect to environmental ethics, citing similarities and shared commitment in the Assisi Declarations and statements by the Alliance of Religions and Conservation.[4] Although seeing some encouraging withdrawal from society, a simple, even monastic life, less manipulative of nature, attempting to achieve a benign harmony with it, while others engage society, somewhat manipulating nature while encouraging constraint on destructive behaviour, he argues that all share in the human habitation of the planet and in the concern for environmental degradation, recognizing creation's order and integrity, being committed to addressing human arrogance, ignorance and greed, and to caring for creation. For example (my order):

- Hinduism: 'We should "halt the present slide towards destruction . . . rediscover the ancient tradition of reverence for all life"' (Assisi) . . . '"Conserve ecology or perish" is the Bhagavad Gita's injunction' (ARC);
- Jainism: 'Avoiding "violence towards all of nature" is a fundamental doctrine resulting in "reverence for all life in all forms" and leading to "compassion for all living beings"' (ARC);
- Buddhism: 'Destruction of the environment . . . is a result of ignorance, greed and disregard for the richness of all living things' (Assisi) . . . 'All life is inter-related' and believers 'are called to show compassion to every living thing' (ARC);
- Judaism: '[T]he environment is . . . being poisoned . . . species . . . becoming extinct, it is our . . . responsibility to put . . . nature at the . . . center of our concern' (Assisi) . . . '[Nature] belongs to God and humanity has a place as . . . custodian of [it] . . . responsible to God' (ARC);
- Christianity: We 'repudiate all ill-considered exploitation of nature which threatens to destroy it' (Assisi) . . . 'God's creation and sustenance of the earth motivates people "to properly care for the land"' (ARC);
- Islam: 'People . . . "are responsible for maintaining the unity of His creation, the integrity of the earth"' (Assisi) . . . '[Humanity] is "Trustee of God, on earth" . . . "entrusted by God with its safekeeping"' (ARC).

Tucker (2002b:67, 78–9) similarly, sees religious views of nature based on an agreement that it has a sacred element and should be respected, seeing the heart of religious scriptures based on a profound sense of the dynamic flow of life, seeing convergence in four ways of seeing nature: as a reflection of the divine, a meeting place for the divine, a stepping stone to the divine, and a nurturing presence for the divine. In particular, she highlights and compares three religious perspectives: from 'Western biblical monotheistic tradition', envisaging an interactive cosmology of creator, creation and creature, she sees arising a stewardship ethic, humanity representing God in creation; from 'Hindu Vedic cosmology', based on the sacrifice of the divine, she sees an ethic of sacrifice, humanity giving back to the fecundity of nature, maintaining order; from the 'Chinese cosmological worldview', based on ongoing creativity, within the triad of heaven, earth and humanity, she sees a harmonic ethics of relational resonance between human self, society and nature. The point, for Tucker, is that although cosmologically different these visions all stress the sacredness of and need to care for nature, living in a dynamic, relational, spiritual, harmony with it, appreciating humanity's role in its continuing creativity. In line with such ideas, Basset et al. (2000:78) see 'Points of

Religious Agreement in Environmental Ethics'. For example:[5]

- The natural world has value in itself, not existing solely to serve humanity.
- There is a continuity of being between human and non-human beings that can be felt and experienced (although humans do have a distinctive role).
- Non-human beings are morally significant, having their own relations to God and/or their own places in the cosmic order.
- The dependence of humanity on nature can and should be acknowledged in ritual and expressions of appreciation/gratitude.
- Moral norms such as compassion and justice apply (in appropriate ways) both to human and non-human, the well-being of these being inseparably connected.
- There are legitimate and illegitimate uses of nature.
- Greed and destructiveness are condemned, restraint and protection are commended.
- Humanity is obliged to be aware/responsible in living with nature and should follow the practices for this prescribed by its traditions.

In similar way, Gottlieb (2006a:41–3) sees a variety of descriptions of nature's value and humanity's relationship to it within eco-theological writings possibly providing the foundation for a new moral code and world-view with different vocabularies but a common message, 'Seek out, recognize, and celebrate that which we have been ignoring, consuming, and destroying' (this inviting a personal transformation, realizing an 'ecological self' at the centre of spiritual lives, an intimate, experiential, connection with the 'more-than-human'). For example:

- Nature is a gift from God and should be treasured as such.
- Nature's majesty testifies to the grandeur of God, its behaviour is a celebration of God.
- Nature is permeated by a Divine Spirit.
- Because we have emerged from, depend on, and are like nature, we must extend moral value to it; we have responsibilities to it and must tend it; it is the stranger and the poor whom we are called on to care.
- Nature awes us with its scope and complexity; it is marvellous and calls forth a respect bordering on reverence.
- The interdependence and selflessness that mark the holistic character of ecosystems contain moral lessons.
- The environment has rights, deserves compassion and can suffer.
- Other animals have self-awareness, can communicate and have family structures, and, therefore, deserve moral concern.
- Distinguishing between ourselves and nature reflects a self-centred arrogance that will make spiritual growth impossible.

Running through such eco-theology, for Gottlieb (2006a:43, 190), is the sense that humanity can live communally with nature, that it can communicate with it, and that, therefore, communion with it is possible, something he sees ultimately permeated by two related and profound values: the reality of kinship with other members of the earth community and the importance of finding a way to balance human needs, desires and lives, and theirs. In a similar light, Kinsley (1994:227–32) stresses common recurrent religious-ecological themes among diverse cultures, individuals and traditions. For example:

- Holistic and organic reality, nature being a living spiritual being.
- The need to gain knowledge of and rapport with nature, humanity understanding itself only when it understands the land in which it lives.
- The human realm being directly related to the non-human realm.
- Reciprocity as the appropriate framework for relating to nature.
- Human embeddedness within nature (their dichotomy being illusory).
- A unity of existence.
- All aspects of reality being united in a shared moral system (extending moral obligations to nature).
- The need for human restraint in dealing with nature.
- Criticism of the view seeing humanity as primary and dominant and stress on seeing it as part of and obliged to care for nature.
- Recognition of the religious intensity and meaning of ecological concerns.

In line with the spirit of such ideas I have drawn out from my analysis of religious-ecotopian visions some common themes (in greatly simplified form) that I see as emerging and coalescing within religious environmentalism:

- Nature has intrinsic worth, virtue of (continuing) creation, independent of human values, being a balanced, dynamic, interdependent, unified, whole;
- Nature is a reciprocal web of life, connected to a wider underlying reality, infused with an energy/spirit, embodying, mirroring or worshipping, the divine;
- Humanity, virtue of self-consciousness, has a limited but special role; part of nature/the web of life, yet vital to enabling it to achieve its harmonious, integrated state;
- Anthropocentric human action upsets the web of life, the natural interdependent way of being, being addictive and (self) destructive, upsetting the ecological/spiritual balance;
- Humanity needs to experience energy/spirit and wider, interdependent being, and act with compassion, humility, justice and reverence, embracing selflessness (its natural state);
- The ideal (natural) human role is ascetic/relational; moderate, nonviolent, with minimal consumption, extravagance or waste, a simple life

of self-sacrifice (perhaps the central religious-ecotopian element, limiting humanity, facilitating the other/nature).

When considering such common themes it should be noted that they look decidedly similar to the ecological model analysed in Chapter 1. This, then, suggests a possible teleology: assessing religious traditions for ecological themes may be driven or influenced by the model (although, conversely, the model, or environmentalism itself, may be influenced by religious ideas, as mentioned in Chapters 1 and 2). There may be some circularity to the undertaking, then, in the utopian sense that it begins from some preconceived ideals of what it does not want, that is, the modern world-view/environmental destruction, and what it does want, that is, environmentally friendly/spiritual beliefs/actions. In terms of the expression and success of the ideas this may not be such a bad thing as it provides guidelines for interpretation, some baseline of what is and is not needed, at least so long as diversity, context, critique and change, are allowed for (which they are argued as being, i.e., the cross/multi-cultural orchestral approach, balancing mutually enhancing visions). Any common themes or convergences, then, in this sense, may need to be (and, according to the field of religion and ecology, are) open to contestation and negotiation (as may, and again, it is argued, are, the different religious-ecological visions themselves). In this sense, it may be best to view the undertaking in a dynamic way, a positive spiral of imaginative religious-ecological critique and construction, the ecological model, possibly influenced by religion, providing basic ideals which are then continually reconstructed, examined and refined (or deconstructed, challenged and opposed) in the exploration of religious traditions. Religious-ecotopian ideas, in this sense, individually or in common, are not necessarily set in stone but may rather be seen as fluid and adaptable seeking to provide creative inspiration for new identities (personally and socially, locally and globally).

Concluding remarks

Religious environmentalism is a growing phenomenon challenging modern secular assumptions about nature and humanity and exploring/promoting religious ones. Religion traditions are being used as or are realizing themselves as influential ways of evoking new understandings of and intimate connections with nature and stimulating environmentally friendly behaviour. They are, most especially in the field of religion and ecology, being encouraged to become centres of ecological thought, to reimagine nature (and humanity and themselves), being assessed for/providing different religious-ecotopian visions, ideals of a more environmentally (and spiritually) aware humanity in tune with nature. Such visions are also encouraged to interact within mutually enriching dialogue, no one tradition or vision being seen as enough (hegemony being seen as part of the problem), but rather a diversity of views (possibly within traditions in different local contexts) being seen as providing a variety of alternatives to the modern imagination of nature as well as creating a wider religious mosaic of it. In this way they are seen as able to provide a sense of moral urgency at environmental issues as well as explanations for them, offering different rationales for behaviour and vocabularies and communities to express them, challenging modern conceptions of self-identity as well as its environmental consequences. Such developments, then, highlight and demonstrate the powerful metaphoric resources and social avenues available to and being used by religious traditions to become relevant and influential in a dynamic and diverse dialogue about nature and humanity, engaging and highlighting the failings, the unresolved issues, of modern secular society.

Of course, this undertaking is not without its critics. Questions may be raised concerning whether it is legitimate to explore and adapt religions this way, especially out of context? Is this merely biased Western appropriation of traditions? Is it based on Western assumptions, of 'religion' as a unified concept and of an objective 'nature' needing protection, this overriding non-Western assumptions, imposing a universal 'religious' 'eco-ethic' on them? There are also questions concerning the human-centredness of many traditions, the lack of desire to embrace change (or slowness in doing so) and the ability to challenge dominant systems. Can religious-ecotopian visions actually become influential, enabling religious traditions move out of their privatized sphere? Will they merely provide resources for modern individualistic self-expression, tapped into as and when required, or can they provide more meaningful, communal, public identities? Will they become coopted, modified, diluted and simplified (deprived of deeper religious meaning), by modern secular society or can they reorient its basic assumptions (integrating religious meanings into it)? And there is the challenge of reconciling different religious traditions (or differences within them), of the orchestral approach, as well as questions of leadership and issues of power. Diverse, conservative and liberal, Western and non-Western, views may be allowed and encouraged but disputes between and within them may occur over authority on ecological metaphors and myths and use of tradition. Who decides on their use and interpretation? Is it inevitably a global 'academic' undertaking (as at present, although practice may be local and experiential)? Is it inevitably a 'liberal' undertaking, with overarching ecumenical concerns, and who decides on what the overarching concerns are? Conservative or more traditional views may be allowed and become influential but can they exist within the wider dialogue as in various councils of churches or would they (be allowed to) change the process, making it more activist or political, for example (or would this be too hegemonic)? Is an 'eco-religion', one based on ecological principles, possible?

Counter arguments to such points are that the field of religion and ecology's ideas and actions, although somewhat Western, liberal, based, at least in their inception and initial form (which may have been influenced by non-Western views), also encourage participation of non-Western traditions, albeit in a Western 'world religion' format, which may encourage the process to be less Western (in its views of religion or nature), possibly conservative or traditional, at least in certain contexts (something that may be useful for public influence, overcoming Western notions of privatized, non-political, religion). Furthermore, religious traditions are diverse and dynamic, able to adapt to or influence change, which means they are open to reinterpretation and adherents themselves interpret them in different, complex or simple, traditional or new ways, dependent on context (and in common, hence ecumenism; thus any anthropocentric or dogmatic views may be challenged and expanded, there may be no 'core' elements to traditions, in this sense, but a diversity, which needs to be recognized and embraced). New ecological interpretations of Hinduism, Jainism, Confucianism, Daoism, Buddhism, Judaism, Christianity and Islam, may thus not be the whole diverse story of these traditions or align with other (official or unofficial) interpretations but may be accepted. By accepting that religion cannot be conceptualized in a monolithic, static way, new ecological-based forms such as those expressed in the field of religion and ecology may be seen as legitimate.[6] Furthermore, they may influence other individuals or groups within the traditions or the traditions as a whole, realigning their foci, and in dialogue may lead to common orientations (distinct from or adapting/integrating secular approaches), enhancing their influence (and thus possibly reorienting modern society not capitulating to it). Context, diversity and change, are, perhaps, key. Religious environmentalism – 'eco-religion' – may be best viewed (and may need to be embraced) as a diverse process, a variety of actions, beliefs and dialogues, in different contextual settings in common (and continuous) assessment (a *movement* rather than a static singular form): there may be no definitive Hindu, Jain, Confucian, Daoist, Buddhist, Jewish, Christian or Islamic (or 'religious', in the universalizing Western sense of the term) perspective on nature, but rather a geographical, historical and social, diversity of perspectives (with many earth-centred ethics, spiritualities and theologies, developing, cosmological, existential and political, First World and Third World, from canonical sources and cultural practices) in mutual communication and action, providing a dynamic religious-environmentalist mosaic (with the key perhaps being to keep the diverse communication alive and coherent with common orientation and purpose).

In line with such ideas the field of religion and ecology seeks to and stresses the need to span a wide range of approaches and a variety of methodologies concerning religion and ecology and stimulate a 'creative adaptation' of them (what is seen as a fruitful tension between descriptive and critical, historical and prophetic, interpretative and engaged, perspectives). Such ideas are seen as acknowledging diversity, as well as possible uncritical appropriation of religious traditions, while also acknowledging their dynamism, seeing a (possibly uneasy but not without historical precedence) coexistence of traditional ideas with modern conditions, seeing religious traditions as living traditions, capable of self-criticism and renewal, accommodating heritage to new situations. Applying religious insights to ecology in this respect is seen as possibly representing the aim and meaning of the traditions accurately. The field's aim is thus to encourage and coordinate diverse religious-ecological views and offer *constructive insights* about the human–nature relationship, accentuating positive ecological contributions and critiquing negative ones. At present, where this involves different traditions being reinterpreted in parallel it seems to be working to inspire and stimulate them (or individuals/groups within them) to rethink their ecological attitudes, to deepen or extend themselves, recovering ecological elements that have been ignored or de-emphasized or reinterpreting themselves anew and creating new religious-ecological knowledge (providing different religious-ecological meanings, to be applied in different contexts). In doing this it encourages and coordinates a diversity of conservative and liberal views, official eco-theologies and popular eco-spiritualities, and thus also acts as a kind of 'council of ecological churches', a neutral arena for traditions, or environmentally inspired factions/representatives of them, to explore new issues and create common religious-ecological knowledge and experience (as well as allowing them an influential way, a new social/political arena, to voice their opinions, providing a common forum allowing them to work in parallel and/or union, with common purpose).

If environmentalism, per se (or other global religious forms) is anything to go by such religious environmentalism may have a future, although whether or not it becomes as inspiring and influential as it seeks to be, whether its religious ecotopias are lasting or transient, of major or minor relevance, is open to debate and may depend on context (possibly on an ability to balance macro and micro: it still works within the global modern context overall and although it may infuence this as a unified religious voice any concrete changes it could stimulate might need to be locally influential via a variety of religious voices). Neverthless what it shows is that religion is engaging modernity and its environmental crisis, being re-created and revitalized (albeit within teleological ecological aims), providing things which modernity does not (e.g. more communal and cooperative, moral and spiritual, hopeful and prophetic, values, and a wider reality in which to situate human action). In this respect, the real value and important role of religious environmentalism, of the field of religion and ecology, and of religious ecotopias, perhaps, as Gardner (2006:155, 166) notes, may be their prophetic intent, their ability to critically expose the limits of modern views (ecologically, morally, spiritually) and to imagine new futures, what he sees as 'theopolitical dynamite',[7] dynamic and powerful visions of what life can (should) be, this highlighting the need to be aware of and reassess what Benstein (2002:123–4) terms (from Aramaic) *alma de'atei*, 'the world that is coming', the world we create and perpetuate. As Gottlieb (2006a:13) argues: 'Religious environmentalism . . . offers . . . *alternative* [visions] to the ones that dominate society now . . . [setting] itself against the reigning social vision, putting forward values that will ultimately serve people and the earth far better than the ones currently in place.' It is in this prophetic imagination that religion is perhaps best able to engage modernity and the environmental crisis. As two of the field of religion and ecology's central figures, Mary Evelyn Tucker and John Grim (2005:2614), argue, religions can (and perhaps should) be liberating provocateurs of social change, both repositories of enduring values and motivators of moral transformation.

> It is the vocation of the prophet to keep alive the ministry of the imagination, to keep on conjuring and proposing futures alternative to the single one the king wants to urge as the only thinkable one. (Gardner 2006:155)[8]

Notes

1. Levitas (2000:199) cites Bloch, E., *The Principle of Hope* (Oxford: Basil Blackwell, 1986) as a source for such ideas.
2. In this light, Berry (1990:4) sees religious environmentalism needing a 'post-critical naivete' involving transcending modern understandings through reflexively uniting them with traditional mystique (rather than naively returning to a lost golden past).
3. Referenced to Richard Rohr, 'Giving Up Control in Life's Second Half' and 'We Should Ask Why So Few Transformations Happen in Church', *National Catholic Reporter*, 8 February 2002 and 28 March 2003.
4. Referenced to WWF (1986) and Alliance of Religions and Conservation, World Wildlife Fund 2000, www.panda.org/living planet/sacred_gifts/assis_2.html.
5. Referenced to Pedersen, K. P., Environmental Ethics in Inter-religious Perspective, *Explorations in Global Ethics: Comparative Religious Ethics and Inter-religious Dialogue*. Twiss, S. B., and Grelle, B., eds (Boulder, CO, and Oxford, UK: Westview Press, 1998).
6. Andre Droogers (As Close as a Scholar Can Get, in *Religion: Beyond a Concept*, de Vries, H., ed.:448–63, New York: Forham University Press, 2008) interestingly argues that religious scholars may be integrated within the religions they study, that their 'secular' 'academic' analyses may recreate 'religion', being part of the religious experience/process. In this sense, the field of religion and ecology's (or this book's) interpretations may be legitimate new religious forms, adding to religious knowledge and experience.

7 Referenced to Daniel C. Maguire, 'Poverty, Population, and Sustainable Development', in Center for Development and Population Activities, 'Interfaith Reflections on Women, Poverty, and Population' (Washington, DC, 1996), p. 49.

8 Referenced to Walter Brueggeman, *The Prophetic Imagination* (Minneapolis, MN: Fortress Press, 1978), p. 40 (de-italicized).

Bibliography

Abram, D., 1990. The Perceptual Implications of Gaia, in *Dharma Gaia: A Harvest of Essays on Buddhism and Ecology*, Badiner, A. H., ed.:75–92, Berkeley, CA: Parallax Press.

Adler, J. A., 1998. Response and Responsibility: Chou Tun-i and Confucian Resources for Environmental Ethics, in *Confucianism and Ecology: The Interrelation of Heaven, Earth and Humans*, Tucker, M. E., and Berthrong, J., eds:123–49, Cambridge, MA: Harvard University Press.

Afrasiabi, K. L., 2003. Toward an Islamic Ecotheology, in *Islam and Ecology: A Bestowed Trust*, Foltz, R. C., Denny, F. M., and Baharuddin, A., eds:281–96, Cambridge, MA: Harvard University Press.

Afrasiabi, K. L., 2005. Islam and Post-Anthropocentrism, in *The Encyclopedia of Religion and Nature*, Taylor, B., and Kaplan, J., eds:872–3, London and New York: Thoemmes Continuum.

Afzaal, A., 2005. Tawhid (Oneness of God), in *The Encyclopedia of Religion and Nature*, Taylor, B., and Kaplan, J., eds:1623–4, London and New York: Thoemmes Continuum.

Agarwal, A., 2000. Can Hindu Beliefs and Values Help India Meet Its Ecological Crisis? in *Hinduism and Ecology: The Intersection of Earth, Sky, and Water*, Chapple, C. K., and Tucker, M. E., eds:165–79, Cambridge, MA: Harvard University Press.

Aggarwal, S., 2005. India's Sacred Groves, in *The Encyclopedia of Religion and Nature*, Taylor, B. R., and Kaplan, J., eds:831–3, London and New York: Thoemmes Continuum.

Ahmad, A., 2005. Islamic Law, in *The Encyclopedia of Religion and Nature*, Taylor, B., and Kaplan, J., eds:885–7, London and New York: Thoemmes Continuum.

Ahmad, I., 2003. Islam and Ecology, in *Ecology and Religion: Ecological Concepts in Hinduism, Buddhism, Jainism, Islam, Christianity and Sikhism*, Narayan, R., and Kumar, J., eds:162–72, New Delhi: Deep & Deep Publications (P) Ltd.

Alley, K. D., 2005. Hinduism and Pollution, in *The Encyclopedia of Religion and Nature*, Taylor, B. R., and Kaplan, J., eds:777–9, London and New York: Thoemmes Continuum.

Ames, R. T., 2001. The Local and the Focal in Realizing a Daoist World, in *Daoism and Ecology: Ways within a Cosmic Landscape*, Giradot, N. J., Miller, J., and Xiaogan, L., eds:265–382, Cambridge, MA: Harvard University Press.

Ammar, Nawal, H., 2001. Islam and Deep Ecology, in *Deep Ecology and World Religions: New Essays on Sacred Ground*, Barnhill, D. L., and Gottlieb, R. S., eds:193–211, Albany: State University of New York Press.

Ammar, Nawal, H., 2002. An Islamic Response to the Manifest Ecological Crisis, in *Worldviews, Religion, and the Environment: A Global Anthology*, Foltz, R. C., ed.:376–84, Belmont, CA: Thompson/Wadsworth.

Ammar, Nawal, H., 2005. Islam and Eco-Justice, in *The Encyclopedia of Religion and Nature*, Taylor, B., and Kaplan, J., eds:862–6, London and New York: Thoemmes Continuum.

Apffel-Marglin, F., and Parajuli, P., 2000. 'Sacred Grove' and Ecology: Ritual and Science, in *Hinduism and Ecology: The Intersection of Earth, Sky, and Water*, Chapple, C. K., and Tucker, M. E., eds:291–316, Cambridge, MA: Harvard University Press.

Asad, T., 1993. *Genealogies of Religion: Discipline and Reasons for Power in Christianity and Islam*, Baltimore and London: Johns Hopkins University Press.

Badiner, A. H., 1990. Introduction, in *Dharma Gaia: A Harvest of Essays on Buddhism and Ecology*, Badiner, A. H., ed.:xiii–xviii, Berkeley, CA: Parallax Press.

Bakken, P. W., 2005. Stewardship, in *The Encyclopedia of Religion and Nature*, Taylor, B. R., and Kaplan, J., eds:1598–9, London and New York: Thoemmes Continuum.

Barlow, C., 1997. *Green Space, Green Time: The Way of Science*, New York: Copernicus.

Barnhill, D. L., 1997. Great Earth *Sangha*: Gary Snyder's View of Nature as Community, in *Buddhism and Ecology: The Interconnection of Dharma and Deeds*, Tucker, M. E., and Williams, D. R., eds:187–218, Cambridge, MA: Harvard University Press.

Barnhill, D. L., 2001. Relational Holism: Huayan Buddhism and Deep Ecology, in *Deep Ecology and World Religions: New Essays on Sacred Ground*, Barnhill, D. L., and Gottlieb, R. S., eds:77–106, Albany: State University of New York Press.

Barnhill, D. L., 2005a. Aesthetics of Nature in China and Japan, in *The Encyclopedia of Religion and Nature*, Taylor, B., and Kaplan, J., eds:16–18, London and New York: Thoemmes Continuum.

Barnhill, D. L., 2005b. Buddhism – East Asian, in *The Encyclopedia of Religion and Nature*, Taylor, B. R., and Kaplan, J., eds:236–9, London and New York: Thoemmes Continuum.

Bassett, L., Brinkman, J. T., and Pedersen, K. P., eds, 2000. *Earth and Faith: A Book of Reflection for Action*, New York: Interfaith Partnership for the Environment/United Nations Environment Programme.

Batchelor, M., 1994a. Even the Stones Smile: Selections from the Scriptures, in *Buddhism and Ecology*, Batchelor, M., and Brown, K., eds:2–17, Delhi: Motilal Barnarsidass Publishers.

Batchelor, M., 1994b. Look Deep and Smile: The Thoughts and Experiences of a Vietnamese Monk (Talks and Writings of Thich Nhat Hanh), in *Buddhism and Ecology*, Batchelor, M., and Brown, K., eds:100–9, Delhi: Motilal Barnarsidass Publishers.

Batchelor, S., 1994. The Sands of the Ganges: Notes towards a Buddhist Ecological Philosophy, in *Buddhism and Ecology*, Batchelor, M., and Brown, K., eds:31–40, Delhi: Motilal Barnarsidass Publishers.

Bauckham, R., 2000. Stewardship and Relationship, in *The Care of Creation: Focusing Concern and Action*, Berry, R. J., ed.:99–106, Leicester: Inter-Varsity Press.

Beattie, T., 2005. Feminist Theology: Christian Feminist Theology, in *The Encyclopedia of Religion*, Jones, L., ed.:3034–9, Farmington Hills, MI: Thomson Gale.

Benstein, J., 2002. *Alma De'atei*, 'The World That is Coming': Reflections on Power, Knowledge, Wisdom, and Progress, in *The Good in Nature and Humanity: Connecting Science, Religion, and Spirituality with the Natural World*, Kellert, S. R., and Farnham, T. J., eds:123–35, Washington, Covelo, London: Island Press.

Berman, M., 1982. *All That is Solid Melts into Air: The Experience of Modernity*, London and New York: Verso.

Berman, M., 1984. *The Re-Enchantment of the World*, Toronto, New York, London, Sydney: Bantam Books.

Berry, T., 1990. *The Dream of the Earth*, San Francisco: Sierra Book Clubs.

Berry, T., 1999. *The Great Work: Our Way into the Future*, New York: Bell Tower.

Berthrong, J., 1998. Motifs for a New Confucian Ecological Vision, in *Confucianism and Ecology: The Interrelation of Heaven, Earth and Humans*, Tucker, M. E., and Berthrong, J., eds:237–63, Cambridge, MA: Harvard University Press.

Beyer, P., 1990. Privatisation and the Public Influence of Religion in Global Society, *Theory, Culture, and Society*, 7 (2–3):373–95.

Beyer, P., 1992. The Global Environment as a Religious Issue: A Sociological Analysis, *Religion*, 22:1–19.

Beyer, P., 1994. *Religion and Globalization*, London, Thousand Oaks, New Delhi: Sage Publications.

Beyer, P., 2003. Social Forms of Religion and Religions in Contemporary Global Society, in *Handbook of the Sociology of Religion*, Dillon, M., ed.:45–60, Cambridge: Cambridge University Press.

Blackwelder, B., 2005. A Christian Friend of the Earth, in *The Encyclopedia of Religion and Nature*, Taylor, B. R., and Kaplan, J., eds:307–10, London and New York: Thoemmes Continuum.

Bolle, K. W., 2005a. Cosmology: An Overview, in *The Encyclopedia of Religion*, Jones, L., ed.:1991–8, Farmington Hills, MI: Thomson Gale.

Bolle, K. W., 2005b. Myth: An Overview, in *The Encyclopedia of Religion*, Jones, L., ed.:6359–71, Farmington Hills, MI: Thomson Gale.

Bourdieu, P., 1977. *Outline of a Theory of Practice*, Cambridge: Cambridge University Press.

Bowen, J. R., 1998. *Religions in Practice: An Approach to the Anthropology of Religion*, Boston, London: Allyn and Bacon.

Brett, G. C. M., 2001. A Timely Reminder: Humanity and Ecology in the Light of Christian Hope, in *Earth Revealing, Earth Healing: Ecology and Christian Theology*, Edwards, D., ed.:159–76, Collegeville, MN: The Liturgical Press.

Brockelman, P., 1997. With New Eyes: Seeing the Environment as a Spiritual Issue, in *The Greening of Faith: God, The Environment and the Good Life*, Carrol, J. E., Brockelman, P., and Westfall, M., eds:30–43, Hanover and London: University Press of New England.

Brockelman, P., 1999. *Cosmology and Creation: The Spiritual Significance of Contemporary Cosmology*, New York, Oxford: Oxford University Press.

Brown, B., 1994. Toward a Buddhist Ecological Cosmology, in *Worldviews and Ecology: Religion, Philosophy, and the Environment*, Tucker, M. E., and Grim, J. A., eds:124–37, Maryknoll, NY: Orbis Books.

Bruce, S., 1996. *Religion in the Modern World: From Cathedrals to Cults*, Oxford: Oxford University Press.

Bruun, O., 2002. *Fengshui* and the Chinese Perceptions of Nature, in *Worldviews, Religion and the Environment: A Global Anthology*, Foltz, R. C., ed.:236–45, Belmont, CA: Thomson/Wadsworth.

Burke, C. E., 2001. Globalization and Ecology, in *Earth Revealing, Earth Healing: Ecology and Christian Theology*, Edwards, D., ed.:21–44, Collegeville, MN: The Liturgical Press.

Cadman, D., 2002. With Our Thoughts We Make the World, in *A Sacred Trust: Ecology and Spiritual Vision*, Cadman, D., and Carey, J., eds:162–70, London: The Temenos Academy.

Callenbach, E., 2004. *Ecotopia*, Berkeley, CA: Banyan Tree Books in association with Heyday Books.

Callicott, J. B., 1997. *Earth's Insights: A Multicultural Survey of Ecological Ethics from the Mediterranean Basin to the Australian Outback*, Berkeley, Los Angeles, London: University of California Press.

Capra, F., 1982. *The Turning Point*, London: Wildwood House.

Carey, J., 1999. *The Faber Book of Utopias*, London: Faber and Faber.

Carroll, J. E., Brockelman, P., and Westfall, M., 1997. Introduction: Getting Our Bearings, in *The Greening of Faith: God, The Environment and the Good Life*, Carrol, J. E., Brockelman, P., and Westfall, M., eds:1–10, Hanover and London: University Press of New England.

Casanova, J., 1994. *Public Religions in the Modern World*, Chicago and London: University of Chicago Press.

Castree, N., and Braun, B., 1998. The Construction of Nature and the Nature of Construction: Analytical and Political Tools for Building Survivable Futures, in *Remaking Reality: Nature at the Millennium*, Braun, B., and Castree, N., eds:3–42, London and New York: Routledge.

Chapple. C. K., 1994. Hindu Environmentalism: Traditional and Contemporary Resources, in *Worldviews and Ecology: Religion, Philosophy, and the Environment*, Tucker, M. E., and Grim, J. A., eds:113–23, Maryknoll, NY: Orbis Books.

Chapple, C. K., 1997. Animals and Environment in the Buddhist Birth Stories, in *Buddhism and Ecology: The Interconnection of Dharma and Deeds*, Tucker, M. E., and Williams, D. R., eds:131–48, Cambridge, MA: Harvard University Press.

Chapple, C. K., 2000. Introduction, in *Hinduism and Ecology: The Intersection of Earth, Sky, and Water*, Chapple, C. K., and Tucker, M. E., eds:xxxiii–xliv, Cambridge, MA: Harvard University Press.

Chapple, C. K., 2001a. Hinduism and Deep Ecology, in *Deep Ecology and World Religions: New Essays on Sacred Ground*, Barnhill, D. L., and Gottlieb, R. S., eds:59–76, Albany: State University of New York Press.

Chapple, C. K., 2001b. The Living Cosmos of Jainism: A Traditional Science Grounded in Environmental Ethics, *Daedalus*, vol. 130, issue 4:207–24.

Chapple, C. K., 2002a. Contemporary Jaina and Hindu Responses to the Ecological Crisis, in *Worldviews, Religion and the Environment: A Global Anthology*, Foltz, R. C., ed.:113–18, Belmont, CA: Thompson/Wadsworth.

Chapple, C. K., 2002b. Introduction, in *Jainism and Ecology: Nonviolence in the Web of Life*, Chapple, C. K., ed.:xxi–xliii, Cambridge, MA: Harvard University Press.

Chapple, C. K., 2002c. Jainism and Ecology, in *When Worlds Converge: What Science and Religion Tell Us about the Story of the Universe and Our Place in It*,

Matthews, C. N., Tucker, M. E., and Hefner, P., eds:283–92, Chicago and La Salle: Open Court.

Chapple, C. K., 2004. Hinduism, Jainism, and Ecology, downloaded from www. environment.harvard.ecu/religion/religion/hinduism/index.html, 2 Feb. 2004; referenced to *Earth Ethics* 10, no. 1 (Fall 1998).

Chapple, C. K., 2005a. Buddha, in *The Encyclopedia of Religion and Nature*, Taylor, B. R., and Kaplan, J., eds:227–30, London and New York: Thoemmes Continuum.

Chapple, C. K., 2005b. Jainism, in *The Encyclopedia of Religion and Nature*, Taylor, B. R., and Kaplan, J., eds:893–5, London and New York: Thoemmes Continuum.

Chapple, C. K., 2005c. Yoga and Ecology, in *The Encyclopedia of Religion and Nature*, Taylor, B. R., and Kaplan, J., eds:1782–6, London and New York: Thoemmes Continuum.

Cheng, C. Y., 1998. The Trinity of Cosmology, Ecology and Ethics in the Confucian Personhood, in *Confucianism and Ecology: The Interrelation of Heaven, Earth and Humans*, Tucker, M. E., and Berthrong, J., eds:211–35, Cambridge, MA: Harvard University Press.

Cheng, C. Y., 2002. On the Environmental Ethics of the *Tao* and the *Ch'i*, in *Worldviews, Religion and the Environment: A Global Anthology*, Foltz, R. C., ed.:224–36, Belmont, CA: Thompson/Wadsworth.

Chillister, J., 1992. Monasticism: An Ancient Answer to Modern Problems, in *Christianity and Ecology*, Breuilly, E., and Palmer, M., eds:65–75, London and New York: Cassell.

Chishti, S. K. K., 2003. *Fitra*: An Islamic Model for Humans and the Environment, in *Islam and Ecology: A Bestowed Trust*, Foltz, R. C., Denny, F. M., and Baharuddin, A., eds:67–82, Cambridge, MA: Harvard University Press.

Chryssavgis, J., 2000. The World of Icon and Creation: An Orthodox Perspective on Ecology and Pneumatology, in *Christianity and Ecology: Seeking the Well-Being of Earth and Humans*, Hessel, D., and Ruether, R. R., eds:83–96, Cambridge, MA: Harvard University Press.

Chryssavgis, J., 2005. Christianity – Christian Orthodoxy, in *The Encyclopedia of Religion and Nature*, Taylor, B. R., and Kaplan, J., eds:333–7, London and New York: Thoemmes Continuum.

Clarke, P. B., and Byrne, P., 1998. *Religion Defined and Explained*, Basingstoke and London: Macmillan Press.

Codiga, D., 1990. Zen Practice and a Sense of Place, in *Dharma Gaia: A Harvest of Essays on Buddhism and Ecology*, Badiner, A. H., ed.:106–11, Berkeley, CA: Parallax Press.

Connolly, P., 1999. *Approaches to the Study of Religion*, London and New York: Cassell.

Cort, J. E., 2002. Green Jainism? Notes and Queries toward a Possible Jain Environmental Ethic, in *Jainism and Ecology: Nonviolence in the Web of Life*, Chapple, C. K., ed.:63–94, Cambridge, MA: Harvard University Press.

Craddock, E., 2005. Shakti, in *The Encyclopedia of Religion and Nature*, Taylor, B. R., and Kaplan, J., eds:1523–4, London and New York: Thoemmes Continuum.

Cronon, W., 1996a. Introduction: In Search of Nature, in *Uncommon Ground: Rethinking the Human Place in Nature*, Cronon, W., ed.:23–56, New York and London: W. W. Norton and Company.

Cronon, W., ed., 1996b. *Uncommon Ground: Rethinking the Human Place in Nature,* New York and London: W. W. Norton and Company.

Davie, G., 2000. *Religion in Modern Europe: A Memory Mutates,* Oxford: Oxford University Press.

Deane-Drummond, C. E., 2000. *Creation through Wisdom: Theology and the New Biology,* Edinburgh: T&T Clark.

Deane-Drummond, C. E., 2004. *The Ethics of Nature,* Oxford: Blackwell.

Deegan, C., 2000. The Narmada: Circumambulation of a Sacred Landscape, in *Hinduism and Ecology: The Intersection of Earth, Sky, and Water,* Chapple, C. K., and Tucker, M. E., eds:389–400, Cambridge, MA: Harvard University Press.

De Geus, M., 1999. *Ecological Utopias: Envisioning the Sustainable Society,* Utrecht: International Books.

Denny, F. M., 2004. Islam and Ecology: Abestowed Trust Inviting Balanced Stewardship, downloaded from www.environment.harvard.edu/religion/religion/islam/index.html, 2 Feb. 2004; referenced to *Earth Ethics* 10, no. 1 (Fall, 1998).

De Silva, L., 1994. The Hills Wherein My Soul Delights: Exploring the Stories and Teachings, in *Buddhism and Ecology,* Batchelor, M., and Brown, K., eds:18–30, Delhi: Motilal Barnarsidass Publishers.

Devall, B., 1990. Ecocentric Sangha, in *Dharma Gaia: A Harvest of Essays on Buddhism and Ecology,* Badiner, A. H., ed.:155–64, Berkeley, CA: Parallax Press.

Devall, B., and Sessions, G., 1985. *Deep Ecology: Living as if Nature Mattered,* Salt Lake City: Gibbs M. Smith, Inc/Peregrine Smith Books.

DeWitt, C. B., 1997. A Contemporary Evangelical Perspective, in *The Greening of Faith: God, the Environment, and the Good Life,* Carroll, J. E., Brockelman, P., and Westfall, M., eds:79–104, Hanover and London: University Press of New England.

DeWitt, C. B., 2000. Behemoth and Batrachians in the Eye of God: Responsibility to Other Kinds in Biblical Perspective, in *Christianity and Ecology: Seeking the Well-Being of Earth and Humans,* Hessel, D., and Ruether, R. R., eds:291–316, Cambridge, MA: Harvard University Press.

DeWitt, C. B., 2002. Spiritual and Religious Perspectives on Religion and Nature, in *The Good in Nature and Humanity: Connecting Science, Religion, and Spirituality with the Natural World,* Kellert, S. R., and Farnham, T. J., eds:29–64, Washington, Covelo, London: Island Press.

DeWitt, C. B., 2005. Christianity – An evangelical Perspective on Faith and Nature, in *The Encyclopedia of Religion and Nature,* Taylor, B. R., and Kaplan, J., eds:369–71, London and New York: Thoemmes Continuum.

Dobson, A., 2000. *Green Politicial Thought,* London and New York: Routledge.

Dockrat, H. I., 2003. Islam, Muslim Society, and Evironmental Concerns: A Development Model Based on Islam's Organic Society, in *Islam and Ecology: A Bestowed Trust,* Foltz, R. C., Denny, F. M., and Baharuddin, A., eds:341–76, Cambridge, MA: Harvard University Press.

Dryzek, J. S., 2005. *The Politics of the Earth: Environmental Discourses,* Oxford: Oxford University Press.

Dutton, Y., 1992. Natural Resources in Islam, in *Islam and Ecology,* Khalid, F., and O'Brien, J., eds:51–67, London and Herndon, VA: Cassell.

Dutton, Y., 2003. The Environmental Crisis of our Time: A Muslim Response, in *Islam and Ecology: A Bestowed Trust*, Foltz, R. C., Denny, F. M., and Baharuddin, A., eds:323–40, Cambridge, MA: Harvard University Press.

Dwivedi, O. P., 1996. *Satyagraha* for Conservation: Awakening the Spirit of Hinduism, in *This Sacred Earth: Religion, Nature, Environment*, Gottlieb, R. S., ed.:151–63, New York and London: Routledge.

Dwivedi, O. P., 2000. Dharmic Ecology, in *Hinduism and Ecology: The Intersection of Earth, Sky, and Water*, Chapple, C. K., and Tucker, M. E., eds:2–22, Cambridge, MA: Harvard University Press.

Eder, K., 1996. *The Social Construction of Nature: A Sociology of Ecological Enlightenment*, London, Thousand Oaks, New Delhi: Sage Publications.

Edwards, D., 2001. For Your Immortal Spirit is in All Things: The Role of the Spirit in Creation, in *Earth Revealing, Earth Healing:Ecology and Christian Theology*, Edwards, D., ed.:45–68, Collegeville, MN: The Liturgical Press.

Edwards, D., 2006. Every Sparrow that Falls to the Ground: The Cost of Evolution and the Christ Event, *Ecotheology: The Journal of Religion, Nature and the Environment*, 11, 1:103–23.

ELC (Evangelical Lutheran Church in America), 1996. Basis for Our Caring, in *This Sacred Earth: Religion, Nature, Environment*, Gottlieb, R., ed.:243–50, New York and London: Routledge.

Evernden, N., 1992. *The Social Creation of Nature*, Baltimore and London: Johns Hopkins University Press.

Field, D. N., 2005. The Reformed Tradition in Its Own Words, in *The Encyclopedia of Religion and Nature*, Taylor, B. R., and Kaplan, J., eds:344–6, London and New York: Thoemmes Continuum.

Field, S. L., 2001. In Search of Dragons: The Folk Ecology of Fengshui, in *Daoism and Ecology: Ways within a Cosmic Landscape*, Giradot, N. J., Miller, J., and Xiaogan, L., eds:185–200, Cambridge, MA: Harvard University Press.

Fields, R., 1990. The Meeting of the Buddha and the Goddess, in *Dharma Gaia: A Harvest of Essays on Buddhism and Ecology*, Badiner, A. H., ed.:3–7, Berkeley, CA: Parallax Press.

Fink, D. B., 2004. Judaism and Ecology: A Theology of Creation, downloaded from www.environment.harvard.edu/religion/religion/judaism/index.html, 2 Feb. 2004; referenced to *Earth Ethics* 10, no. 1 (Fall, 1998).

Fishbane, M., 2002. Toward a Jewish Theology of Nature, in *Judaism and Ecology: Created World and Revealed Word*. Tirosh-Samuelson, H., ed.:17–24, Cambridge, MA: Harvard University Press.

Foltz, R. C., 2002a. Islamic Environmentalism in Theory and Practice, in *Worldviews, Religion and the Environment: A Global Anthology*, Foltz, R. C., ed.:358–65, Belmont, CA: Thompson/Wadsworth.

Foltz, R. C., ed., 2002b. *Worldviews, Religion and the Environment: A Global Anthology*, Belmont, CA: Thompson/Wadsworth.

Foltz, R. C., 2003a. Introduction, in *Islam and Ecology: A Bestowed Trust*, Foltz, R. C., Denny, F. M., and Baharuddin, A., eds:xxxvii–xliii, Cambridge, MA: Harvard University Press.

Foltz, R. C., 2003b. Islamic Environmentalism: A Matter of Interpretation, in *Islam and Ecology: A Bestowed Trust*, Foltz, R. C., Denny, F. M., and Baharuddin, A., eds:249–80, Cambridge, MA: Harvard University Press.

Foltz, R. C., 2005a. Ecology and Religion: Ecology and Islam, in *The Encyclopedia of Religion*, Jones, L., ed.:2651–4, Farmington Hills, MI: Thomson Gale.

Foltz, R. C., 2005b. Islam, in *The Encyclopedia of Religion and Nature*, Taylor, B., and Kaplan, J., eds:858–62, London and New York: Thoemmes Continuum.

Foltz, R. C., 2005c. Islam, Animals, and Vegetarianism, in *The Encyclopedia of Religion and Nature*, Taylor, B., and Kaplan, J., eds:873–5, London and New York: Thoemmes Continuum.

Fox, P., 2001. God's Shattering Otherness: The Trinity and Earth's Healing, in *Earth Revealing, Earth Healing: Ecology and Christian Theology*, Edwards, D., ed.:85–104, Collegeville, MN: The Liturgical Press.

Fritsch, A. J., 1997. A Catholic Approach, in *The Greening of Faith: God, the Environment, and the Good Life*, Carroll, J. E., Brockelman, P., and Westfall, M., eds:125–36, Hanover and London: University Press of New England.

Gardner, G., 2002. *Invoking the Spirit: Religion and Spirituality in the Quest for a Sustainable World*, Worldwatch Paper 164, Washington, DC: Worldwatch Institute.

Gardner, G., 2006. *Inspiring Progress: Religion's Contributions to Sustainable Development*, New York and London: W. W. Norton and Company.

Gellman, J. Y., 2002. Early Hasidism and the Natural World, in *Judaism and Ecology: Created World and Revealed Word*, Tirosh-Samuelson, H., ed.:369–88, Cambridge, MA: Harvard University Press.

Gerstenfeld, M., 2005. Judaism and Sustainability, in *The Encyclopedia of Religion and Nature*, Taylor, B. R., and Kaplan, J., eds:937–8, London and New York: Thoemmes Continuum.

Girardot, N. J., Miller, J., and Xiaogan, L., 2001. Introduction, in *Daoism and Ecology: Ways within a Cosmic Landscape*, Girardot, N. J., Miller, J., and Xiaogan, L., eds:xxxvii–lxiii, Cambridge, MA: Harvard University Press.

Goodman, L. E., 2002. Respect for Nature in the Jewish Tradition, in *Judaism and Ecology: Created World and Revealed Word*, Tirosh-Samuelson, H., ed.:227–60, Cambridge, MA: Harvard University Press.

Gosling, D. L., 2001. *Religion and Ecology in India and Southeast Asia*, London and New York: Routledge.

Gottlieb, R. S., ed., 1996. *This Sacred Earth: Religion, Nature, Environment*, New York and London: Routledge.

Gottlieb, R. S., 2006a. *A Greener Faith: Religious Environmentalism and Our Planet's Future*, Oxford: Oxford University Press.

Gottlieb, R. S., 2006b. Introduction: Religion and Ecology – What is the Connection and Why Does it Matter? in *The Oxford Handbook of Religion and Ecology*, Gottlieb, R. S., ed.:3–21, Oxford: Oxford University Press.

Granberg-Michaelson, W., 2006. Covenant and Creation, downloaded from www.religion-online.org/showarticle.asp?title=2318, 11 Feb. 2006; referenced to *Liberating Life: Contemporary Approaches in Ecological Theology*, Birch, C., Eaken, W., and McDaniel, J. B., eds:27–53, Maryknoll, NY: Orbis books, 1990.

Green, A., 1996. Vegetarianism: A *Kashrut* for Our Age, in *This Sacred Earth: Religion, Nature, Environment*, Gottlieb, R. S., ed.:301–2, New York and London: Routledge.

Green, A., 2002. A Kabbalah for the Environment Age, in *Judaism and Ecology: Created World and Revealed Word*, Tirosh-Samuelson, H., ed.:3–16, Cambridge, MA: Harvard University Press.

Gross, R. M., 1997. Buddhist Resources for Issues of Population, Consumption, and the Environment, in *Buddhism and Ecology: The Interconnection of Dharma and Deeds*, Tucker, M. E., and Williams, D. R., eds:291–312, Cambridge, MA: Harvard University Press.

Gross, R. M., 2002. Toward a Buddhist Environmental Ethic, in *Worldviews, Religion and the Environment: A Global Anthology*, Foltz, R. C., ed.:163–70, Belmont, CA: Thompson/Wadsworth.

Gross, R. M., 2005. Buddhism – Tibetan, in *The Encyclopedia of Religion and Nature*, Taylor, B. R., and Kaplan, J., eds:244–6, London and New York: Thoemmes Continuum.

Guha, R., 2000. *Environmentalism: A Global History*, New York: Longman.

Haberman, D. L., 2000. River of Love in an Age of Pollution, in *Hinduism and Ecology: The Intersection of Earth, Sky, and Water*, Chapple, C. K., and Tucker, M. E., eds:339–54, Cambridge, MA: Harvard University Press.

Habito, R. L. F., 1997. Mountains and Rivers and the Great Earth: Zen and Ecology, in *Buddhism and Ecology: The Interconnection of Dharma and Deeds*, Tucker, M. E., and Williams, D. R., eds:165–75, Cambridge, MA: Harvard University Press.

Habito, R. L. F., 2005. Zen Buddhism, in *The Encyclopedia of Religion and Nature*, Taylor, B. R., and Kaplan, J., eds:1800–2, London and New York: Thoemmes Continuum.

Hahne, H., 2005. Jewish Intertestamental Literature, in *The Encyclopedia of Religion and Nature*, Taylor, B. R., and Kaplan, J., eds:913–18, London and New York: Thoemmes Continuum.

Halifax, J., 1990. The Third Body: Buddhism, Shamanism, & Deep Ecology, in *Dharma Gaia: A Harvest of Essays on Buddhism and Ecology*, Badiner, A. H., ed.:20–38, Berkeley, CA: Parallax Press.

Hall, D., 2001. From Reference to Deference: Daoism and the Natural World, in *Daoism and Ecology: Ways within a Cosmic Landscape*, Girardot, N. J., Miller, J., and Xiaogan, L., eds:245–64, Cambridge, MA: Harvard University Press.

Hamilton, M., 1995. *The Sociology of Religion: Theoretical and Comparative Perspectives*, London and New York: Routledge.

Harris, I., 1997. Buddhism and the Discourse of Environmental Concern: Some Methodological Problems Considered, in *Buddhism and Ecology: The Interconnection of Dharma and Deeds*, Tucker, M. E., and Williams, D. R., eds:377–402, Cambridge, MA: Harvard University Press.

Harris, I., 2002. Ecological Buddhism? in *Worldviews, Religion and the Environment: A Global Anthology*, Foltz, R. C., ed.:171–81, Belmont, CA: Thompson/Wadsworth.

Haught, J. F., 1996. Christianity and Ecology, in *This Sacred Earth: Religion, Nature, Environment*, Gottlieb, R., ed.:270–85, London and New York: Routledge.

Hayden, T., 1997. Forward, in *Earth's Insights: A Survey of Ecological Ethics from the Mediterranean Basin to the Australian Outback*, Callicott, J. B., ed.:xvii–xxiv, Berkeley, Los Angeles, London: University of California Press.

Haynes, J., 1998. *Religion in Global Politics*, London and New York: Longman.

Hervieu-Leger, D., 2000. *Religion as a Chain of Memory*, Cambridge: Polity Press.

Hessel, D. T., 2004. Christianity and Ecology: Wholeness, Respect, Justice, Sustainability, downloaded from www. environment.harvard.edu/religion/christianity/index.html, 2 Feb. 2004; referenced to *Earth Ethics* 10, no. 1 (Fall, 1998).

Hessel, D. T., and Ruether, R. R., 2000. Introduction: Current Thought on Christianity and Ecology, in *Christianity and Ecology: Seeking the Well-Being of Earth and Humans*, Hessel, D., and Ruether, R. R., eds:xxxiii–xlvii, Cambridge, MA: Harvard University Press.

Hiebert, T., 2000. The Human Vocation: Origins and Transformations in Christian Traditions, in *Christianity and Ecology: Seeking the Well-Being of Earth and Humans*, Hessel, D., and Reuther, R. R., eds:135–54, Cambridge, MA: Harvard University Press.

Ho, M., 1990. Animal Dharma, in *Dharma Gaia: A Harvest of Essays on Buddhism and Ecology*, Badiner, A. H., ed.:129–35, Berkeley, CA: Parallax Press.

Hobgood-Oster, L., 2005. Christianity – Feminist Theology, in *The Encyclopedia of Religion and Nature*, Taylor, B. R., and Kaplan, J., eds:360–2, London and New York: Thoemmes Continuum.

Hooper, P., and Palmer, M., 1992. St Francis and Ecology, in *Christianity and Ecology*, Breuilly, E., and Palmer, M., eds:76–85, London and New York: Cassell.

Hull, F., ed., 1993. *Earth & Spirit: The Spiritual Dimension of the Environmental Crisis*, New York: Continuum.

Hutterman, A., 2002. The Most Misunderstood Part of the Bible, in *Worldviews, Religion, and the Environment: A Global Anthology*, Foltz, R. C., ed.:280–9, Belmont, CA: Thomson/Wadsworth.

Ingram, P. O., 1997. The Jeweled Net of Nature, in *Buddhism and Ecology: The Interconnection of Dharma and Deeds*, Tucker, M. E., and Williams, D. R., eds:71–88, Cambridge, MA: Harvard University Press.

Izzi Deen, Mawil, Y., 1996. Islamic Environmental Ethics, Law, and Society, in *This Sacred Earth: Religion, Nature, Environment*, Gottlieb, R. S., ed.:164–73, New York and London: Routledge.

Izzi Dien, Mawil, 2003. Islam and the Environment: Theory and Practice, in *Islam and Ecology: A Bestowed Trust*, Foltz, R. C., Denny, F. M., and Baharuddin, A., eds:107–20, Cambridge, MA: Harvard University Press.

Izzi Dien, Mawil, Y., 1997. Islamic Ethics and the Environment, in *Islam and Ecology*, Khalid, F., and O'Brien, J., eds:25–36, London and Herndon, VA: Cassell.

Jacobs, M. X., 2002. Judaism and the Ecological Crisis, in *When Worlds Converge: What Science and Religion Tell Us about the Story of the Universe and Our Place in It*, Matthews, C. N., Tucker, M. E., and Hefner, P., eds:261–72, Chicago and La Salle: Open Court.

Jacobsen, K. A., 2005a. Ahimsa, in *The Encyclopedia of Religion and Nature*, Taylor, B. R., and Kaplan, J., eds:30–1, London and New York: Thoemmes Continuum.

Jacobsen, K. A., 2005b. Bhagavadgita, in *The Encyclopedia of Religion and Nature*, Taylor, B. R., and Kaplan, J., eds:172–3, London and New York: Thoemmes Continuum.

Jacobsen, K. A., 2005c. India, in *The Encyclopedia of Religion and Nature*, Taylor, B. R., and Kaplan, J., eds:823–7, London and New York: Thoemmes Continuum.

Jacobsen, K. A., 2005d. Jataka Tales, in *The Encyclopedia of Religion and Nature*, Taylor, B. R., and Kaplan, J., eds:903–5, London and New York: Thoemmes Continuum.

Jacobsen, K. A., 2005e. Prakriti, in *The Encyclopedia of Religion and Nature*, Taylor, B. R., and Kaplan, J., eds:1299–301, London and New York: Thoemmes Continuum.

Jain, B., 2002. Ecology and Spirituality in the Jain Tradition, in *Jainism and Ecology: Nonviolence in the Web of Life*, Chapple, C. K., ed.:169–80, Cambridge, MA: Harvard University Press.

James, G. A., 2000. Ethical and Religious Dimensions of Chipko Resistance, in *Hinduism and Ecology: The Intersection of Earth, Sky, and Water*, Chapple, C. K., and Tucker, M. E., eds:499–530, Cambridge, MA: Harvard University Press.

Jiyu, Z., 2001. A Declaration of the Chinese Daoist Association on Global Ecology, in *Daoism and Ecology: Ways within a Cosmic Landscape*, Girardot, N. J., Miller, J., and Xiaogan, L., eds:361–72, Cambridge, MA: Harvard University Press.

Jiyu, Z., and Yuanguo, L., 2001. 'Mutual Stealing among the Three Powers', in *Daoism and Ecology: Ways within a Cosmic Landscape*, Girardot, N. J., Miller, J., and Xiaogan, L., eds:113–24, Cambridge, MA: Harvard University Press.

Johnston, L., 2006. The 'Nature' of Buddhism: A Survey of Relevant Literature and Themes, *Worldviews: Environment, Culture, Religion* 10, 1:69–99.

Kalapurachal, K., Fr, 2003. Ecology and Religion: The Christian Perspective, in *Ecology and Religion: Ecological Concepts in Hinduism, Buddhism, Jainism, Islam, Christianity, and Sikhism*, Narayan, R., and Kumar, J., eds:101–25, New Delhi: Deep & Deep Publications (P) Ltd.

Kalland, A., 2005. The Religious Environmentalist Paradigm, in *The Encyclopedia of Religion and Nature*, Taylor, B., and Kaplan, J., eds:1367–71, London and New York: Thoemmes Continuum.

Kalton, M. C., 1998. Extending the Neo-Confucian Tradition: Questions and Re-conceptualization for the Twenty-First Century, in *Confucianism and Ecology: The Interrelation of Heaven, Earth and Humans*, Tucker, M. E., and Berthrong, J., eds:77–101, Cambridge, MA: Harvard University Press.

Kaplan, E. K., 2002. Reverence and Responsibility: Abraham Joshua Heschel on Nature and the Self, in *Judaism and Ecology: Created World and Revealed Word*, Tirosh-Samuelson, H., ed.:407–22, Cambridge, MA: Harvard University Press.

Kassmann, K., 1997. *Envisioning Ecotopia: The U.S. Green Movement and the Politics of Radical Social Change*, Westport, CT, London: Praeger.

Katz, E., 1994. Judaism and the Ecological Crisis, in *Worldviews and Ecology: Religion, Philosophy, and the Environment*, Tucker, M. E., and Grim, J. A., eds:55–70, Maryknoll, NY: Orbis Books.

Katz, E., 2001. Faith, God, and Nature: Judaism and Deep Ecology, in *Deep Ecology and World Religions: New Essays on Sacred Ground*, Barnhill, D. L., and Gottlieb, R. S., eds:153–67, New York: State University of New York Press.

Kaza, S., 1993. Planting Seeds of Joy, in *Earth & Spirit: The Spiritual Dimension of the Environmental Crisis*, Hull, F., ed.:137–48, New York: Continuum.

Kaza, S., 2001. The Gridlock of Domination: A Buddhist Response to Environmental Suffering, in *The Greening of Faith: God, The Environment and the Good Life*, Carrol, J. E., Brockelman, P., and Westfall, M., eds:141–57, Hanover and London: University Press of New England.

Kaza, S., 2002a. Green Buddhism, in *When Worlds Converge: What Science and Religion Tell Us about the Story of the Universe and our Place in It*, Matthews, C. N., Tucker, M. E., and Hefner, P., eds:293–309, Chicago and La Salle: Open Court.

Kaza, S., 2002b. To Save All Beings: Buddhist Environmental Activism, in *Worldviews, Religion and the Environment: A Global Anthology*, Foltz, R. C., ed.:193–207, Belmont, CA: Thompson/Wadsworth.

Kaza, S., 2005. Buddhism – North America, in *The Encyclopedia of Religion and Nature*, Taylor, B. R., and Kaplan, J., eds:242–4, London and New York: Thoemmes Continuum.

Khalid, F., 2005. Islamic Basis for Environmental Protection, in *The Encyclopedia of Religion and Nature*, Taylor, B., and Kaplan, J., eds:879–84, London and New York: Thoemmes Continuum.

Khanna, M., 2000. The Ritual Capsule of Durga Puja: An Ecological Perspective, in *Hinduism and Ecology: The Intersection of Earth, Sky, and Water*, Chapple, C. K., and Tucker, M. E., eds:469–98, Cambridge, MA: Harvard University Press.

Kinsley, D., 1994. *Ecology and Religion: Spirituality in Cross-Cultural Perspective*, Englewood Cliffs, NJ: Prentice Hall.

Kirkland, R., 2001. 'Responsible Non-Action' in a Natural World: Perspectives from the *Neiye, Zhuangzi*, and *Daode jing*, in *Daoism and Ecology: Ways within a Cosmic Landscape*, Girardot, N. J., Miller, J., and Xiaogan, L., eds:293–304, Cambridge, MA: Harvard University Press.

Kohn, L., 2001. Change Starts Small: Daoist Practice and the Ecology of Individual Lives, A Roundtable Discussion with Liu Ming, Rene Navarro, Linda Varone, Vincent Chu, Daniel Seitz, and Weidong Lu, in *Daoism and Ecology: Ways within a Cosmic Landscape*, Girardot, N. J., Miller, J., and Xiaogan, L., eds:373–90, Cambridge, MA: Harvard University Press.

Koller, J. M., 2002. Jain Ecological Perspectives, in *Jainism and Ecology: Nonviolence in the Web of Life*, Chapple, C. K., ed.:19–34, Cambridge, MA: Harvard University Press.

Kraemer, D., 2002. Jewish Death Practices: A Commentary in the Relationship of Humans to the Natural World, in *Judaism and Ecology: Created World and Revealed Word*, Tirosh-Samuelson, H., ed.:81–92, Cambridge, MA: Harvard University Press.

Kraft, K., 1996. The Greening of Buddhist Practice, in *This Sacred Earth: Religion, Nature, Environment*, Gottlieb, R. S., ed.:484–98, New York and London: Routledge.

Kraft, K., 1997. Nuclear Ecology and Engaged Buddhism, in *Buddhism and Ecology: The Interconnection of Dharma and Deeds*, Tucker, M. E., and Williams, D. R., eds:269–90, Cambridge, MA: Harvard University Press.

Kraft, K., 2005. Buddhism – Engaged, in *The Encyclopedia of Religion and Nature*, Taylor, B. R., and Kaplan, J., eds:239–41, London and New York: Thoemmes Continuum

Kumar, J., 2003. Islam and Ecology, in *Ecology and Religion: Ecological Concepts in Hinduism, Buddhism, Jainism, Islam, Christianity and Sikhism*, Narayan, R., and Kumar, J., eds:143–61, New Delhi: Deep & Deep Publications (P) Ltd.

Kumar, S., 2002a. Jain Ecology, in *Jainism and Ecology: Nonviolence in the Web of Life*, Chapple, C. K., ed.:181–90, Cambridge, MA: Harvard University Press.

Kumar, S., 2002b. Reverence for Life: A Jain Perspective, in *A Sacred Trust: Ecology and Spiritual Vision*, Cadman, D., and Carey, J., eds:57–67, London: The Temenos Academy and the Prince's Foundation.

Kuwako, T., 1998. The Philosophy of Environmental Correlation in Chu Hsi, in *Confucianism and Ecology: The Interrelation of Heaven, Earth and Humans*, Tucker, M. E., and Berthrong, J., eds:151–68, Cambridge, MA: Harvard University Press.

LaFargue, M., 2001. 'Nature' as Part of Human Culture in Daoism, in *Daoism and Ecology: Ways within a Cosmic Landscape*, Girardot, N. J., Miller, J., and Xiaogan, L., eds:45–60, Cambridge, MA: Harvard University Press.

LaFleur, W., 1990. Sattva – Enlightenment for Plants & Trees, in *Dharma Gaia: A Harvest of Essays on Buddhism and Ecology*, Badiner, A. H., ed.:136–44, Berkeley, CA: Parallax Press.

Lai, C., 2001. The Daoist Concept of Central Harmony in the *Scripture of Great Peace: Human Responsibility for the Maladies of Nature*, in *Daoism and Ecology: Ways within a Cosmic Landscape*, Girardot, N. J., Miller, J., and Xiaogan, L., eds:95–112, Cambridge, MA: Harvard University Press.

Lakoff, G., and Johnson, M., 1980. *Metaphors We Live By*, Chicago and London: University of Chicago Press.

Lal, V., 2005. Gandhi, Mohandas (1969–1948), in *The Encyclopedia of Religion and Nature*, Taylor, B. R., and Kaplan, J., eds:685–7, London and New York: Thoemmes Continuum.

Lancaster, L., 1997. Buddhism and Ecology: Collective Cultural Perceptions. *Buddhism and Ecology: The Interconnection of Dharma and Deeds*, Tucker, M. E., and Williams, D. R., eds:3–17, Cambridge, MA: Harvard University Press.

Larkin, L., 2001. The Relationship Quilt: Feminism and the Healing of Nature, in *Earth Revealing, Earth Healing: Ecology and Christian Theology*, Edwards, D., ed.:145–57, Collegeville, MN: Liturgical Press.

Laughlin, C. D., and Throop, C. J., 2001. Imagination and Reality: On the Relations between Myth, Consciousness, and the Quantum Sea, *Zygon*, vol. 36, issue 4 (December).

Lease, G., 1995. Introduction: Nature under Fire, in *Reinventing Nature? Responses to Postmodern Deconstruction*, Soule, M. E., and Lease, G., eds:3–16, Washington, DC, Covelo, CA: Island Press.

Lerner, B. D., 2005. Jewish Law and Environmental Protection, in *The Encyclopedia of Religion and Nature*, Taylor, B. R., and Kaplan, J., eds:921–3, London and New York: Thoemmes Continuum.

Levitas, R., 1990. *The Concept of Utopia*, New York: Syracuse University Press.

Levitas, R., 2000. Discourses of Risk and Utopia, in *The Risk Society and Beyond: Critical Issues for Social Theory*, Adam, B., Beck, U., and Van Loon, J., eds:198–210, London, Thousand Oaks, New Delhi: Sage Publications.

Lishka, D., 2005. Zhuangzi, in *The Encyclopedia of Religion and Nature*, Taylor, B., and Kaplan, J., eds:1802–6, London and New York: Thoemmes Continuum.

Llewellyn, O., 1992. Desert Reclamation and Conservation in Islamic Law, in *Islam and Ecology*, Khalid, F., and O'Brien, J., eds:87–97, London and Herndon, VA: Cassell.

Llewellyn, O. A., 2003. The Basis for a Discipline of Islamic Environmental Law, in *Islam and Ecology: A Bestowed Trust*, Foltz, R. C., Denny, F. M., Baharuddin, A., eds:187–247, Cambridge, MA: Harvard University Press.

Lodhal, M., 2005. Christianity – Methodism, in *The Encyclopedia of Religion and Nature*, Taylor, B. R., and Kaplan, J., eds:352–4, London and New York: Thoemmes Continuum.

Long, C. H., 2005. Cosmogony, in *The Encyclopedia of Religion*, Jones, L., ed.:1985–91, Farmington Hills, MI: Thomson Gale.

Loori, J. D., 1997. The Precepts and the Environment, in *Buddhism and Ecology: The Interconnection of Dharma and Deeds*, Tucker, M. E., and Williams, D. R., eds:177–84, Cambridge, MA: Harvard University Press.

Lovin, R. W., and Reynolds, F. E., 1985. In the Beginning, in *Cosmogony and Ethical Order: New Studies in Comparative Ethics*, Lovin, R. W., and Reynolds, F. E., eds:1–35, Chicago and London: The University of Chicago Press.

Lowdermilk, W. C., 2002. The Eleventh Commandment, in *Worldviews, Religion, and the Environment: A Global Anthology*, Foltz, R., ed.:12–16, Belmont, CA: Thompson/Wadsworth.

Loy, D. R., 2002. The Religion of the Market, in *Worldviews, Religion and the Environment: A Global Anthology*, Foltz, R. C., ed.:66–75, Belmont, CA: Thompson/Wadsworth.

McDaniel, J., 1994. The Garden of Eden, The Fall, and the Life of Christ, in *Worldviews and Ecology: Religion, Philosophy, and the Environment*, Tucker, M. E., and Grim, J. A., eds:71–82, Maryknoll, NY: Orbis Books.

McDaniel, J., 1997. The Sacred Whole: An Ecumenical Protestant Approach, in *The Greening of Faith: God, the Environment, and the Good Life*, Carroll, J. E., Brockelman, P., and Westfall, M., eds:105–25, Hanover and London: University Press of New England.

McDaniel, J., 2005. Christianity – Process Theology, in *The Encyclopedia of Religion and Nature*, Taylor, B. R., and Kaplan, J., eds:364–6, London and New York: Thoemmes Continuum.

McFague, S., 1987. *Models of God: Theology for an Ecological, Nuclear Age*, Philadelphia: Fortress Press.

McFague, S., 1996. The Scope of the Body: The Cosmic Christ, in *This Sacred Earth: Religion, Nature, Environment*, Gottlieb, R. S., ed.:286–96, London and New York: Routledge.

McFague, S., 2000. An Ecological Christology: Does Christianity Have It? in *Christianity and Ecology: Seeking the Well-Being of Earth and Humans*, Hessel, D., and Ruether, R. R., eds:29–46, Cambridge, MA: Harvard University Press.

McFague, S., 2001. New House Rules: Christianity, Economics, and Planetary Living, *Daedalus*, vol. 130, issue 4:125–40.

McFarland-Taylor, S., 2005. Christianity – Creation Spirituality, in *The Encyclopedia of Religion and Nature*, Taylor, B. R., and Kaplan, J., eds:363–4, London and New York: Thoemmes Continuum.

McGrath, A., 2003. *The Re-enchantment of Nature: The Denial of Religion and the Ecological Crisis*, New York, London, Toronto, Sydney, Auckland: Doubleday/Galilee.

McGuire, M., 1997. *Religion: The Social Context*, Belmont, CA: Wadsworth Publishing Company.

Maguire, D. C., 2000. *Sacred Energies: When the World's Religions Sit Down to Talk about the Future of Human Life and the Plight of the Planet*, Minneapolis: Fortress Press.

Makrides, V. N., 2005. Christianity – Greek Orthodox, in *The Encyclopedia of Religion and Nature*, Taylor, B. R., and Kaplan, J., eds:338–40, London and New York: Thoemmes Continuum.

Mander, J., 2002. In the Absence of the Sacred, in *Worldviews, Religion and the Environment: A Global Anthology*, Foltz, R. C., ed.:58–66, Belmont, CA: Thompson/Wadsworth.

Marshall, I. H., 2000. Commitment to Creation, in *The Care of Creation: Focusing Concern and Action*, Berry, R. J., ed.:94–8, Leicester: Inter-Varsity Press.

Martens, S., 2005. Chinese Environmentalism, in *The Encyclopedia of Religion and Nature*, Taylor, B., and Kaplan, J., eds:292–4, London and New York: Thoemmes Continuum.

Marty, M. E., 2003. 'But Even So, Look at That': An Ironic Perspective on Utopias, in *Visions of Utopia*, Rothstein, E., Muschamp, H., and Marty, M. E., eds:49–88, New York: Oxford University Press.

Masri, Al-Hafiz, B. A., 1997. Islam and Ecology, in *Islam and Ecology*, Khalid, F., and O'Brien, J., eds:1–24, London and Herndon, VA: Cassell.

Masuzawa, T., 2005. *The Invention of World Religions: Or, How European Universalism was Preserved in the Language of Pluralism*, Chicago and London: The University of Chicago Press.

Merchant, C., 2002. Dominion over Nature, in *Worldviews, Religion and the Environment: A Global Anthology*, Foltz, R. C., ed.:39–49, Belmont, CA: Thompson/Wadsworth.

Metzger, D., 1990. Four Meditations, in *Dharma Gaia: A Harvest of Essays on Buddhism and Ecology*, Badiner, A. H., ed.:209–12, Berkeley, CA: Parallax Press.

Metzner, R., 1994. The Emerging Cosmological Worldview, in *Worldviews and Ecology: Religion, Philosophy, and the Environment*, Tucker, M. E., and Grim, J. A., eds:163–72, Maryknoll, NY: Orbis Books.

Meyer, J. F., 2001. Salvation in the Garden: Daoism and Ecology, in *Daoism and Ecology: Ways within a Cosmic Landscape*, Girardot, N. J., Miller, J., and Xiaogan, L., eds:219–36, Cambridge, MA: Harvard University Press.

Midgley, M., 2005. *The Myths We Live By*, London and New York: Routledge.

Milani, F., 2003. Trees as Ancestors: Eco-Feminism and the Poetry of Forugh Farrokhzad, in *Islam and Ecology: A Bestowed Trust*, Foltz, R. C., Denny, F. M., and Baharuddin, A., eds:527–34, Cambridge, MA: Harvard University Press.

Miller, J., 2001. Envisioning the Daoist Body in the Economy of Cosmic Power, *Daedalus*, vol. 130, issue 4:265–82.

Miller, J., 2004. Daoism and Ecology, downloaded from www.environment.harvard.edu/religion/religion/Daoism/index.html, 2 Feb. 2004; referenced to *Earth Ethics* 10, no. 1 (Fall, 1998).

Miller, J., 2005a. Daoism, in *The Encyclopedia of Religion and Nature*, Taylor, B., and Kaplan, J., eds:447–50, London and New York: Thoemmes Continuum.

Miller, J., 2005b. Ecology and Religion: Ecology and Daoism, in *The Encyclopedia of Religion*, Jones, L., ed.:2635–8, Farmington Hills, MI: Thomson Gale.

Miller, J., Wang, R. G., and Davis, E., 2001. Sectional Discussion: What Ecological Themes are Found in Daoist Texts? in *Daoism and Ecology: Ways within a Cosmic Landscape*, Girardot, N. J., Miller, J., and Xiaogan, L., eds:149–53, Cambridge, MA: Harvard University Press.

Mische, P. M., 2000. The Integrity of Creation: Challenges and Opportunities, in *Christianity and Ecology: Seeking the Well-Being of Earth and Humans*, Hessel, D., and Ruether, R. R., eds:591–602, Cambridge, MA: Harvard University Press.

Moltmann, J., 2000. God's Covenant and Our Responsibility, in *The Care of Creation: Focusing Concern and Action*, Berry, R. J., ed.:107–13, Leicester: Inter-Varsity Press.

Nagarajan, V., 2000. Rituals of Embedded Ecologies: Drawing *Kolams*, Marrying Trees, and Generating Auspiciousness, in *Hinduism and Ecology: The Intersection of Earth, Sky, and Water,* Chapple, C. K., and Tucker, M. E., eds:453–548, Cambridge, MA: Harvard University Press.

Narayan, R., 2003. Ecological Crisis and Hindu Religious Thought, in *Ecology and Religion: Ecological Concepts in Hinduism, Buddhism, Jainism, Islam, Christianity, and Sikhism,* Narayan, R., and Kumar, J., eds:25–39, New Delhi: Deep & Deep Publications (P) Ltd.

Narayanan, V., 2001. Water, Wood, and Wisdom: Ecological Perspectives from the Hindu Traditions, *Daedalus,* vol. 103, issue 4:179–206.

Narayanan, V., 2005a. Dharma – Hindu, in *The Encyclopedia of Religion and Nature,* Taylor, B. R., and Kaplan, J., eds:479–81, London and New York: Thoemmes Continuum.

Narayanan, V., 2005b. Ecology and Religion: Ecology and Hinduism, in *The Encyclopedia of Religion,* Jones, L., ed.:2620–4, Farmington Hills, MI: Thomson Gale.

Narayanan, V., 2005c. Hinduism, in *The Encyclopedia of Religion and Nature,* Taylor, B. R., and Kaplan, J., eds:762–76, London and New York: Thoemmes Continuum.

Nash, J. A., 2005. Christianity – Christianity's Ecological Reformation, in *The Encyclopedia of Religion and Nature,* Taylor, B. R., and Kaplan, J., eds:372–5, London and New York: Thoemmes Continuum.

Nash, R., 1989. *The Rights of Nature: A History of Environmental Ethics,* Madison: University of Wisconsin Press.

Nasr, S. H., 1992. Islam and the Environmental Crisis, in *Spirit and Nature: Why the Environment is a Religious Issue,* Rockefeller, S. C., and Elder, J. C., eds:83–108, Boston: Beacon Press.

Nasr, S. H., 1996. *Religion and the Order of Nature,* New York, Oxford: Oxford University Press.

Nasr, S. H., 2002. The Spiritual and Religious Dimensions of the Environmental Crisis, in *A Sacred Trust: Ecology and Spiritual Vision,* Cadman, D., and Carey, J., eds:119–48, London: The Temenos Academy.

Nelson, L. E., 2000. Reading the *Bhagavadgita* from an Ecological Perspective, in *Hinduism and Ecology: The Intersection of Earth, Sky, and Water,* Chapple, C. K., and Tucker, M. E., eds:127–64, Cambridge, MA: Harvard University Press.

Nomanul Haq, S., 2001. Islam and Ecology: Toward Retrieval and Reconstruction, *Daedalus,* vol. 130, issue 4:141–78.

Norris, P., and Ingelhart, R., 2004. *Sacred and Secular: Religion and Politics Worldwide,* Cambridge: Cambridge University Press.

Northcott, M., 2000. The Spirit of Environmentalism, in *The Care of Creation: Focusing Concern and Action,* Berry, R. J., ed.:167–74, Leicester: Inter-Varsity Press.

Oelschlaeger, M., 1994. *Caring for Creation: An Ecumenical Approach to the Environmental Crisis,* New Haven and London: Yale University Press.

Ozdemir, I., 2003. Toward an Understanding of Environmental Ethics from a Qur'anic Perspective, in *Islam and Ecology: A Bestowed Trust,* Foltz, R. C., Denny, F. M., and Baharuddin, A., eds:3–38, Cambridge, MA: Harvard University Press.

Ozdemir, I., 2005. Muhammad, The Prophet of Islam (570–632), in *The Encyclopedia of Religion and Nature,* Taylor, B. R., and Kaplan, J., eds:1124–6, London and New York: Thoemmes Continuum.

Page, R., 1992. The Bible and the Natural World, in *Christianity and Ecology,* Breuilly, E., and Palmer, M., eds:20–34, London and New York: Cassell.

Palmer, M., and Finlay, V., 2003. *Faith in Conservation: New Approaches to Religions and the Environment*, Washington, DC: The World Bank.

Paper, J., 2001. Chinese Religion, 'Daoism', and Deep Ecology, in *Deep Ecology and World Religions: New Essays on Sacred Ground*, Barnhill, D. L., and Gottlieb, R. S., eds:107–26, Albany: State University of New York Press.

Paper, J., 2005. Chinese Traditional Concepts of Nature, in *The Encyclopedia of Religion and Nature*, Taylor, B., and Kaplan, J., eds:294–9, London and New York: Thoemmes Continuum.

Parks, S. D., 1993. Re-imagining the Role of the Human in the Earth Community, in *Earth & Spirit: The Spiritual Dimension of the Environmental Crisis*, Hull, F., ed.:85–93, New York: Continuum.

Parvaiz, M. A., 2005. Islam on Man and Nature, in *The Encyclopedia of Religion and Nature*, Taylor, B., and Kaplan, J., eds:875–9, London and New York: Thoemmes Continuum.

Pepper, D., 1996. *Modern Environmentalism: An Introduction*, London and New York: Routledge.

Peterson, A., 2002. Christian Theological Anthropology and Environmental Ethics, in *Worldviews, Religion, and the Environment: A Global Anthology*, Foltz, R. C., ed.:319–33, Toronto: Thomson Wadsworth.

Petruccioli, A., 2003. Nature in Islamic Urbanism: The Garden in Practice and in Metaphor, in *Islam and Ecology: A Bestowed Trust*, Foltz, R. C., Denny, F. M., and Baharuddin, A., eds:499–510, Cambridge, MA: Harvard University Press.

Pick, P. L., 1992. Tu Bi Shevat: A Happy New Year to All Trees, in *Judaism and Ecology*, Rose, A., ed.:67–9, London: Cassell.

Poceski, M., 2005a. Buddhahood of Grasses and Trees, in *The Encyclopedia of Religion and Nature*, Taylor, B. R., and Kaplan, J., eds:231–2, London and New York: Thoemmes Continuum.

Poceski, M., 2005b. Indra's Net, in *The Encyclopedia of Religion and Nature*, Taylor, B. R., and Kaplan, J., eds:847–8, London and New York: Thoemmes Continuum.

Prasad, R. M., 2003. Ecology and Buddhism, in *Ecology and Religion: Ecological Concepts in Hinduism, Buddhism, Jainism, Islam, Christianity, and Sikhism*, Narayan, R., and Kumar, J., eds:41–54, New Delhi: Deep & Deep Publications (P) Ltd.

Prime, R., 1996. *Hinduism and Ecology: Seeds of Truth*, London and New York: Cassell.

Rae, E., 2000. Response to Mark I. Wallace: Another View of the Spirit's Work, in *Christianity and Ecology: Seeking the Well-Being of Earth and Humans*, Hessel, D., and Ruether, R. R., eds:73–82, Cambridge, MA: Harvard University Press.

Rajotte, F., and Breuilly, E., 1992. Treatment for the Earth's Sickness – The Church's Role, in *Christianity and Ecology*, Breuilly, E., and Palmer, M., eds:98–118, London and New York: Cassell.

Rand, S., 2000. Love Your Neighbour as Yourself, in *The Care of Creation: Focusing Concern and Action*, Berry, R. J., ed.:140–6, Leicester: Inter-Varsity Press.

Randolph, R. O., 2005. Christianity and Animals, in *The Encyclopedia of Religion and Nature*, Taylor, B. R., and Kaplan, J., eds:375–7, London and New York: Thoemmes Continuum.

Raphals, K., 2001. Metic Intelligence or Responsible Non-Action? Further Reflections on the *Zhuangzi, Daode jing*, and *Neiye*, in *Daoism and Ecology: Ways within a Cosmic Landscape*, Girardot, N. J., Miller, J., and Xiaogan, L., eds:305–14, Cambridge, MA: Harvard University Press.

Rasmussen, L. L., 1994. Cosmology and Ethics, in *Worldviews and Ecology: Religion, Philosophy, and the Environment*, Tucker, M. E., and Grim, J. A., eds:173–80, Maryknoll, NY: Orbis Books.

Rasmussen, L. L., 2002. Global Eco-Justice: The Church's Mission in Urban Society, in *Worldviews, Religion and the Environment: A Global Anthology*, Foltz, R. C., ed.:582–90, Belmont, CA: Thompson/Wadsworth.

Regenstein, L. G., 1991. *Replenish the Earth: A History if Organized Religion's Treatment of Animals and Nature – Including the Bible's Message of Conservation and Kindness to Animals*, London: SCM Press.

Reid, D., 2001. Enfleshing the Human: An Earth Revealing, Earth Healing Christology, in *Earth Revealing, Earth Healing: Ecology and Christian Theology*, Edwards, D., ed.:69–84, Collegeville, MN: The Liturgical Press.

Riskin, S., 1992. Shemitta: A Sabbatical for the Land – 'The Land shall rest and the people shall grow', in *Judaism and Ecology*, Rose, A., ed.:70–3, London: Cassell.

Ro, Y., 1998. Ecological Implications of Yi Yulgok's Cosmology, in *Confucianism and Ecology: The Interrelation of Heaven, Earth and Humans*, Tucker, M. E., and Berthrong, J., eds:169–86, Cambridge, MA: Harvard University Press.

Rockefeller, S., 1992. Faith and Community in an Ecological Age, in *Spirit and Nature: Why the Environment is a Religious Issue*, Rockefeller, S., and Elder, J. C., eds:139–72, Boston: Beacon Press.

Rockefeller, S., 1997. The Wisdom of Reverence for Life, in *The Greening of Faith: God, the Environment, and the Good Life*, Carroll, J. E., Brockelman, P., and Westfall, M., eds:44–61, Hanover and London: University Press of New England.

Roeperstorff, A., and Bubandt, N., 2003. General Introduction: The Critique of Culture and the Plurality of Nature, in *Imagining Nature: Practices of Cosmology and Identity*, Roeperstorff, A., Bubandt, N., and Kull, K., eds:9–30, Aarhus: Aarhus University Press.

Rose, A., 1992a. The Environment; Israel's Remarkable Story, in *Judaism and Ecology*, Rose, A., ed.:82–90, London: Cassell.

Rose, A., 1992b. Introduction to the Jewish Faith, in *Judaism and Ecology*, Rose, A., ed.:9–18, London: Cassell.

Rose, A., 1992c. *Judaism and Ecology*, London and New York: Cassell.

Roskos, N., 2005. Christian Theology and the Fall, in *The Encyclopedia of Religion and Nature*, Taylor, B. R., and Kaplan, J., eds:312–14, London and New York: Thoemmes Continuum.

Rossing, B., 2000. River of Life in God's New Jerusalem: An Eschatological Vision for Earth's Future, in *Christianity and Ecology: Seeking the Well-Being of Earth and Humans*, Hessel, D., and Ruether, R. R., eds:205–24, Cambridge, MA: Harvard University Press.

Rothstein, E., 2003. Utopia and Its Discontents, in *Visions of Utopia*, Rothstein, E., Muschamp, H., and Marty, M. E., eds:1–28, New York: Oxford University Press.

Rukmani, T. S., 2000. Literary Foundations for an Ecological Aesthetic: *Dharma*, Ayurveda, the Arts, and *Abhijnanasakuntalam*, in *Hinduism and Ecology: The Intersection of Earth, Sky, and Water*, Chapple, C. K., and Tucker, M. E., eds:101–26, Cambridge, MA: Harvard University Press.

Rue, L., 2000. *Everybody's Story: Wising up to the Epic of Evolution*, Albany, NY: State University of New York Press.

Ruether, R. R., 1992. *Gaia and God: An Ecofeminist Theology of Earth Healing*, New York: HarperSanFancisco/HarperCollins.

Ruether, R. R., 2000a. Conclusion: Eco-Justice at the Center of the Church's Mission, in *Christianity and Ecology: Seeking the Well-Being of Earth and Humans*, Hessel, D., and Ruether, R. R., eds:603–13, Cambridge, MA: Harvard University Press.

Ruether, R. R., 2000b. Ecofeminism: The Challenge to Theology, in *Christianity and Ecology: Seeking the Well-Being of Earth and Humans*, Hessel, D., and Ruether, R. R., eds:97–112, Cambridge, MA: Harvard University Press.

Ruether, R. R., 2001. Deep Ecology, Ecofeminism, and the Bible, in *Deep Ecology and World Religions: New Essays on Sacred Ground*, Barnhill, D. L., and Gottlieb, R. S., eds:229–41, Albany: State University of New York Press.

Said, A. A., and Funk, N. C., 2003. Peace in Islam: An Ecology of the Spirit, in *Islam and Ecology: A Bestowed Trust*, Foltz, R. C., Denny, F. M., and Baharuddin, A., eds:155–84, Cambridge, MA: Harvard University Press.

Saritopak, Z., 2005. The Qur'an, in *The Encyclopedia of Religion and Nature*, Taylor, B. R., and Kaplan, J., eds:1321–5, London and New York: Thoemmes Continuum.

Scharper, S. B., 2002. Christianity and Ecological Awareness, in *When Worlds Converge: What Science and Religion Tell Us about the Story of the Universe and Our Place in It*, Matthews, C. N., Tucker, M. E., and Hefner, P., eds:273–82, Chicago and La Salle: Open Court.

Schmithausen, L., 2005. Buddhism, in *The Encyclopedia of Religion and Nature*, Taylor, B. R., and Kaplan, J., eds:232–6, London and New York: Thoemmes Continuum.

Schorsch, I., 1992. Learning to Live with Less: A Jewish Perspective, in *Spirit and Nature: Why the Environment is a Religious Issue*, Rockefeller, S. C., and Elder, J. C., eds:25–38, Boston: Beacon Press.

Schwartz, E., 2002. Response; Mastery, and Stewardship, Wonder and Connectedness: A Typology of Relations to Nature in Jewish Text and Tradition, in *Judaism and Ecology: Created World and Revealed Word*, Tirosh-Samuelson, H., ed.:93–106, Cambridge, MA: Harvard University Press.

Seidenberg, D., 2005. Jewish Environmentalism in North America, in *The Encyclopedia of Religion and Nature*, Taylor, B. R., and Kaplan, J., eds:909–13, London and New York: Thoemmes Continuum.

Seidenberg, D. M., 2005. Kabbalah and Eco-Theology, in *The Encyclopedia of Religion and Nature*, Taylor, B. R., and Kaplan, J., eds:945–50, London and New York: Thoemmes Continuum.

Seshagiri Rao, K. L., 2000. The Five Great Elements (*Pancamahabhuta*): An Ecological Perspective, in *Hinduism and Ecology: The Intersection of Earth, Sky, and Water*, Chapple, C. K., and Tucker, M. E., eds:23–38, Cambridge, MA: Harvard University Press.

Sheldrake, R., 1994. *The Rebirth of Nature: The Greening of Science and God*, Rochester, Vermont: Park Street Press.

Sherrard, P., 2002. For Every Thing That Lives is Holy, in *A Sacred Trust: Ecology and Spiritual Vision*, Cadman, D., and Carey, J., eds:1–32, London: The Temenos Academy.

Shilapi, S., 2002. The Environmental and Ecological Teachings of Tirthankara Mahavira, in *Jainism and Ecology: Nonviolence in the Web of Life*, Chapple, C. K., ed.:159–68, Cambridge, MA: Harvard University Press.

Shinn, L. D., 2000. The Inner Logic of Ghandian Ecology, in *Hinduism and Ecology: The Intersection of Earth, Sky, and Water*, Chapple, C. K., and Tucker, M. E., eds:213–41, Cambridge, MA: Harvard University Press.

Siddiq, M. Y., 2003. An Ecological Journey in Muslim Bengal, in *Islam and Ecology: A Bestowed Trust*, Foltz, R. C., Denny, F. M., and Baharuddin, A., eds:451–62, Cambridge, MA: Harvard University Press.

Sideris, J. H., 2006. Religion, Environmentalism, and the Meaning of Ecology, in *The Oxford Handbook of Religion and Ecology*, Gottlieb, R. S., ed.:446–64, Oxford: Oxford University Press.

Singhvi, L. M., 1990. *The Jain Declaration on Nature*, London: The Jain Sacred Literature Trust.

Sivaraksa, S., 1990. True Development, in *Dharma Gaia: A Harvest of Essays on Buddhism and Ecology*, Badiner, A. H., ed.:169–77, Berkeley, CA: Parallax Press.

Snyder, S., 2006. Chinese Traditions and Ecology: A Survey Article, *Worldviews: Environment, Culture, Religion*, 10, 1:100–34.

Solomon, N., 1992. Judaism and the Environment, in *Judaism and Ecology*, Rose, A., ed.:19–53, London and New York: Cassell.

Soorideva, S., 2003. Ecological Awareness in Jaina Culture, in *Ecology and Religion: Ecological Concepts in Hinduism, Buddhism, Jainism, Islam, Christianity, and Sikhism*, Narayan, R., and Kumar, J., eds:73–81, New Delhi: Deep & Deep Publications Ltd.

Sotitiu, E., 2005. Eastern Orthodox Monasticism, in *The Encyclopedia of Religion and Nature*, Taylor, B. R., and Kaplan, J., eds:334–5, London and New York: Thoemmes Continuum.

Soule, M. E., 1995. The Social Siege of Nature, in *Reinventing Nature? Responses to Postmodern Deconstruction*, Soule, M. E., and Lease, G., eds:137–70, Washington, DC, Covelo, CA: Island Press.

Sponberg, A., 1997. Green Buddhism and the Hierarchy of Compassion, in *Buddhism and Ecology: The Interconnection of Dharma and Deeds*, Tucker, M. E., and Williams, D. R., eds:351–76, Cambridge, MA: Harvard University Press.

Sponsel, L. E., and Sponsel, P. N., 1997. A Theoretical Analysis of the Potential Contribution of the Monastic Community in Promoting a Green Society in Thailand, in *Buddhism and Ecology: The Interconnection of Dharma and Deeds*, Tucker, M. E., and Williams, D. R., eds:45–68, Cambridge, MA: Harvard University Press.

Sproul, B. C., 1979. *Primal Myths: Creating the World*, San Francisco: Harper & Row Publishers.

Swartz, D., 1996. Jews, Jewish Texts, and Nature: A Brief History, in *This Sacred Earth: Religion, Nature, Environment*, Gottlieb, R. S., ed.:87–103, New York and London: Routledge.

Swearer, D. K., 1997. The Hermeneutics of Buddhist Ecology in Contemporary Thailand: Buddhadasa and Dhammapitaka, in *Buddhism and Ecology: The Interconnection of Dharma and Deeds*, Tucker, M. E., and Williams, D. R., eds:21–44, Cambridge, MA: Harvard University Press.

Swearer, D. K., 2001. Principles and Poetry, Places and Stories: The Resources of Buddhist Ecology, *Daedalus*, vol. 130, issue 4:225–42.

Swearer, D. K., 2004. Buddhism and Ecology: Challenge and Promise, downloaded from www.environment.harvard.edu/religion/religion/buddhism/index.html, 2 Feb. 2004; referenced to *Earth Ethics* 10, no. 1 (Fall, 1998).

Swearer, D. K., 2005. Ecology and Religion: Ecology and Buddhism, in *The Encyclopedia of Religion*, Jones, L., ed.:2627–31, Farmington Hills, MI: Thomson Gale.

Swearer, D. K., 2006. An Assessment of Buddhist Eco-Philosophy, *Harvard Theological Review*, April, 99:2:123–37.

Szerszynski, B., 2005. *Nature, Technology, and the Sacred*, Malden, MA, and Oxford: Blackwell Publishing.

Tatia, N., 2002. The Jain Worldview and Ecology, in *Jainism and Ecology: Nonviolence in the Web of Life*, Chapple, C. K., ed.:3–18, Cambridge, MA: Harvard University Press.

Taylor, B., 1996. Earth First!: From Primal Spirituality to Ecological Resistance, in *This Sacred Earth: Religion, Nature, Environment*, Gottlieb, R. S., ed.:545–57, New York and London: Routledge.

Taylor, B., 2001a. Earth and Nature-Based Spirituality (Part I): From Deep Ecology to Radical Environmentalism, *Religion*, 31:175–93.

Taylor, B., 2001b. Earth and Nature-Based Spirituality (Part II): From Earth First! And Bioregionalism to Scientific Paganism and the New Age, *Religion*, 31:225–45.

Taylor, B., 2004. A Green Future for Religion? *Futures* 36:991–1008.

Taylor, B., 2005a. Ecology and Religion: Nature Religions, in *The Encyclopedia of Religion*, Jones, L., ed.:2661–8, Farmington Hills, MI: Thomson Gale.

Taylor, B., 2005b. Radical Environmentalism, in *The Encyclopedia of Religion and Nature*, Taylor, B., and Kaplan, J., eds:1326–35, London and New York: Thoemmes Continuum.

Taylor, B., 2005c. Religious Studies and Environmental Concern, in *The Encyclopedia of Religion and Nature*, Taylor, B., and Kaplan, J., eds:1373–9, London and New York: Thoemmes Continuum.

Taylor, B., 2006. Religion and Environmentalism in America and Beyond, in *The Oxford Handbook of Religion and Ecology*, Gottlieb, R. S., ed.:588–612, Oxford: Oxford University Press.

Taylor, B., and Kaplan, J., eds, 2005. *The Encyclopaedia of Religion and Nature*, London and New York: Thoemmes Continuum.

Taylor, C., 2004. *Modern Social Imaginaries*, Durham and London: Duke University Press.

Taylor, R. L., 1998. Companionship with the World: Roots and Branches of a Confucian Ecology, in *Confucianism and Ecology: The Interrelation of Heaven, Earth and Humans*, Tucker, M. E., and Berthrong, J., eds:37–58, Cambridge, MA: Harvard University Press.

Thakur, V. K., 2003. Ecological Perceptions of Buddhism in India, in *Ecology and Religion: Ecological Concepts in Hinduism, Buddhism, Jainism, Islam, Christianity, and Sikhism,* Narayan, R., and Kumar, J., eds:55–69, New Delhi: Deep & Deep Publications (P) Ltd.

Thomas, S., 2000. Religious Resurgence, Postmodernism and World Politics, in *Religion and Global Order,* Esposito, J. L., and Watson, M., eds:38–65, Cardiff: University of Wales Press.

Thomas, S., 2005. *The Global Resurgence of Religion and the Transformation of International Relations,* New York: Palgrave Macmillan.

Timm, R. E., 1994. The Ecological Fallout of Islamic Creation Theology, in *Worldviews and Ecology: Religion, Philosophy, and the Environment,* Tucker, M. E., and Grim, J. A., eds:83–95, Maryknoll, NY: Orbis Books.

Tirosh-Samuelson, H., 2001. Nature and the Sources of Judaism, *Daedalus,* vol. 130, issue 4:99–124.

Tirosh-Samuelson, H., 2002a. Introduction: Judaism and the Natural World, in *Judaism and Ecology: Created World and Revealed Word,* Tirosh-Samuelson, H., ed.:xxxiii–lxii, Cambridge, MA: Harvard University Press.

Tirosh-Samuelson, H., 2002b. Response: The Textualization of Nature in Jewish Mysticism, in *Judaism and Ecology: Created World and Revealed Word,* Tirosh-Samuelson, H., ed.:389–404, Cambridge, MA: Harvard University Press.

Tirosh-Samuelson, H., 2005a. Ecology and Religion: Ecology and Judaism, in *The Encyclopedia of Religion,* Jones, L., ed.:2641–7, Farmington Hills, MI: Thomson Gale.

Tirosh-Samuelson, H., 2005b. Judaism, in *The Encyclopedia of Religion and Nature,* Taylor, B. R., and Kaplan, J., eds:925–37, London and New York: Thoemmes Continuum.

Tobias, M., 1994. Jainism and Ecology: Views of Nature, Nonviolence, and Vegetarianism, in *Worldviews and Ecology: Religion, Philosophy, and the Environment,* Tucker, M. E., and Grim, J. A., eds:138–49, Maryknoll, NY: Orbis Books.

Tucker, M. E., 1994. Ecological Themes in Taoism and Confucianism, in *Worldviews and Ecology: Religion, Philosophy, and the Environment,* Tucker, M. E., and Grim, J. A., eds:150–60, Maryknoll, NY: Orbis Books.

Tucker, M. E., 1998. The Philosophy of Ch'i as an Ecological Cosmology, in *Confucianism and Ecology: The Interrelation of Heaven, Earth and Humans,* Tucker, M. E., and Berthrong, J., eds:187–207, Cambridge, MA: Harvard University Press.

Tucker, M. E., 2001. Confucianism and Deep Ecology, in *Deep Ecology and World Religions: New Essays on Sacred Ground,* Barnhill, D. L., and Gottlieb, R. S., eds:127–52, Albany: State University of New York Press.

Tucker, M. E., 2002a. Confucian Ethics and the Ecocrisis, in *When Worlds Converge: What Science and Religion Tell Us about the Story of the Universe and Our Place in It,* Matthews, C. N., Tucker, M. E., and Hefner, P., eds:310–23, Chicago and La Salle: Open Court.

Tucker, M. E., 2002b. Religion and Ecology: The Interaction of Cosmology and Cultivation, in *The Good in Nature and Humanity: Connecting Science, Religion, and Spirituality with the Natural World,* Kellert, S. R., and Farnham, T. J., eds:65–89, Washington, Covelo, London: Island Press.

Tucker, M. E., 2003. *Worldly Wonder: Religions Enter Their Ecological Phase,* Chicago and La Salle, IL: Open Court Publishing Company.

Tucker, M. E., 2004. Confucianism and Ecology: Potential and Limits, downloaded from www.enivronment.harvard.edu/religion/confucianism/index.html, 2 Feb. 2004, referenced to *Earth Ethics* 10, no. 1 (Fall, 1998).

Tucker, M. E., 2005a. Confucianism, in *The Encyclopedia of Religion and Nature*, Taylor, B., and Kaplan, J., eds:407–11, London and New York: Thoemmes Continuum.

Tucker, M. E., 2005b. Confucianism and Environmental Ethics, in *The Encyclopedia of Religion and Nature*, Taylor, B., and Kaplan, J., eds:411–13, London and New York: Thoemmes Continuum.

Tucker, M. E., 2005c. Ecology and Religion: Ecology and Confucianism, in *The Encyclopedia of Religion*, Jones, L., ed.:2631–5, Farmington Hills, MI: Thomson Gale.

Tucker, M. E., 2006. Survey of the Field, in *The Oxford Handbook of Religion and Ecology*, Gottlieb, R. S., ed.:398–418, Oxford: Oxford University Press.

Tucker, M. E., and Berthrong, J., 1998. Introduction: Setting the Context, in *Confucianism and Ecology: The Interrelation of Heaven, Earth and Humans*, Tucker, M. E., and Berthrong, J., eds:xxxv–xlv, Cambridge, MA: Harvard University Press.

Tucker, M. E., and Grim, J. A., 1997. Series Forward, in *Buddhism and Ecology: The Interconnection of Dharma and Deeds*, Tucker, M. E., and Williams, D. R., eds:xv–xxxiii, Cambridge, MA: Harvard University Press.

Tucker, M. E., and Grim, J. A., 1998. Religions of the World and Ecology: Discovering Common ground, *Earth Ethics* 10, no.1 (Fall), downloaded from www. environment. harvard.edu/religion/religion/index.html

Tucker, M. E., and Grim, J. A., 2001. Introduction: The Emerging Alliance of World Religions and Ecology, *Daedalus*, vol. 130, issue 4:1–22.

Tucker, M. E., and Grim, J. A., 2005. Ecology and Religion: An Overview, in *The Encyclopedia of Religion*, Jones, L., ed.:2604–16, Farmington Hills, MI: Thomson Gale.

Tzu, L., 1996. From the Tao te Ching, in *This Sacred Earth: Religion, Nature, Environment*, Gottlieb, R. S., ed.:67–70, London and New York: Routledge.

Van Horn, G., 2006. Hindu Traditions and Nature: Survey Article, *Worldviews: Environment, Culture, Religion*, 10, 1:5–39.

Vogel, D., 2006. How Green is Judaism? Exploring Jewish Environmental Ethics, downloaded from www.findarticles.com/p/articles./mi_m0411/is_5_49/qi_73180737/pg_11; referenced to *Judaism*, Winter 2001, vol. 50, issue 1.

Waldau, P., 2005. Animals, in *The Encyclopedia of Religion and Nature*, Taylor, B. R., and Kaplan, J., eds:66–72, London and New York: Thoemmes Continuum.

Wallace, M. I., 2000. The Wounded Spirit as the Basis for Hope in an Age of Radical Ecology, in *Christianity and Ecology: Seeking the Well-Being of Earth and Humans*, Hessel, D., and Ruether, R. R., eds:51–72, Cambridge, MA: Harvard University Press.

Waskow, A., 1996. What is Eco-Kosher? in *This Sacred Earth: Religion, Nature, Environment*, Gottlieb, R. S., ed.:297–300, New York and London: Routledge.

Waskow, A., 2002. And the Earth is Filled with the Breath of Life, in *Worldviews, Religion, and the Environment: A Global Anthology*, Foltz, R. C., ed.:306–17, Belmont, CA: Thomson/Wadsworth.

Weiming, T., 1994. Beyond the Enlightenment Mentality, in *Worldviews and Ecology: Religion, Philosophy, and the Environment*, Tucker, M. E., and Grim, J. A., eds:19–29, Maryknoll, NY: Orbis Books.

Weiming, T., 1998. Beyond the Enlightenment Mentality, in *Confucianism and Ecology: The Interrelation of Heaven, Earth and Humans*, Tucker, M. E., and Berthong, J., eds:3–22, Cambridge, MA: Harvard University Press.

Weiming, T., 2001. The Ecological Turn in New Confucian Humanism: Implications for China and the World, *Daedalus*, vol. 130, issue 4:243–64.

Weiming, T., 2002. The Continuity of Being: Chinese Visions of Nature, in *Worldviews, Religion and the Environment: A Global Anthology*, Foltz, R. C., ed.:209–17, Belmont, CA: Thompson/Wadsworth.

Weller, R. P., and Bol, P. K., 1998. From Heaven-and-Earth to Nature: Chinese Conceptions of the Environment and Their Influence on Policy Implementation, in *Confucianism and Ecology: The Interrelation of Heaven, Earth and Humans*, Tucker, M. E., and Berthong, J., eds:313–41, Cambridge, MA: Harvard University Press.

Wensveen, L., van, 2000. Christian Ecological Virtue Ethics, in *Christianity and Ecology: Seeking the Well-Being of Earth and Humans*, Hessel, D., and Ruether, R. R., eds:155–71, Cambridge, MA: Harvard University Press.

Wensveen, L., van, 2005. Christianity – Theology and Ecology (Contemporary Introduction), in *The Encyclopedia of Religion and Nature*, Taylor, B. R., and Kaplan, J., eds:354–5, London and New York: Thoemmes Continuum.

Wescoat, J. L., Jr, 2003. From the Gardens of the Qur'an to the 'Gardens' of Lahore, in *Islam and Ecology: A Bestowed Trust*, Foltz, R. C., Denny, F. M., Baharuddin, A., eds:511–26, Cambridge, MA: Harvard University Press.

Wescoat, J. L., Jr, 2005a. Gardens in Islam, in *The Encyclopedia of Religion and Nature*, Taylor, B., and Kaplan, J., eds:688–9, London and New York: Thoemmes Continuum.

Wescoat, J. L., Jr, 2005b. Islam and Environmental Ethics, in *The Encyclopedia of Religion and Nature*, Taylor, B., and Kaplan, J., eds:866–8, London and New York: Thoemmes Continuum.

White, L., Jr, 1967. The Historical Roots of Our Ecological Crisis, *Science* 155 (10 March):1203–7.

Whitney, E., 2005. White, Lynn (1907–1987) – Thesis of, in *The Encyclopedia of Religion and Nature*, Taylor, B., and Kaplan, J., eds:1735–7, London and New York: Thoemmes Continuum.

Wielenga, B., 2003. Christianity and Ecology, in *Ecology and Religion: Ecological Concepts in Hinduism, Buddhism, Jainism, Islam, Christianity, and Sikhism*, Narayan, R., and Kumar, J., eds:125–40, New Delhi: Deep & Deep Publications Ltd.

Wiley, K. L., 2002. The Nature of Nature: Jain Perspectives on the Natural World, in *Jainism and Ecology: Nonviolence in the Web of Life*, Chapple, C. K., ed.:35–59, Cambridge, MA: Harvard University Press.

Williams, D. R., 1997. Introduction, in *Buddhism and Ecology: The Interconnection of Dharma and Deeds*, Tucker, M. E., and Williams, D. R., eds:xxxv–xlii, Cambridge, MA: Harvard University Press.

Woodhead, L., and Heelas, P., 2000. *Religion in Modern Times*, Oxford: Blackwell.

WWF (World Wildlife Fund), 1986. *The Assisi Declarations: Messages on Man & Nature from Buddhism, Christianity, Hinduism, Islam, & Judaism*, Gland, Switzerland: World Wildlife Fund.

Xiaogan, L., 2001. Non-Action and the Environment Today: A Conceptual and Applied Study of Laozi's Philosophy, in *Daoism and Ecology: Ways within a Cosmic Landscape*, Girardot, N. J., Miller, J., and Xiaogan, L., eds:315–40, Cambridge, MA: Harvard University Press.

Index